The LANDSCAPE MODEL of Learning

DESIGNING STUDENT-CENTERED EXPERIENCES FOR COGNITIVE AND CULTURAL INCLUSION

Jennifer D. Klein   Kapono Ciotti

Foreword By Ron Berger

Solution Tree | Press

Copyright © 2022 by Solution Tree Press

Materials appearing here are copyrighted. With one exception, all rights are reserved. Readers may reproduce only those pages marked "Reproducible." Otherwise, no part of this book may be reproduced or transmitted in any form or by any means (electronic, photocopying, recording, or otherwise) without prior written permission of the publisher.

555 North Morton Street
Bloomington, IN 47404
800.733.6786 (toll free) / 812.336.7700
FAX: 812.336.7790

email: info@SolutionTree.com
SolutionTree.com

Visit **go.SolutionTree.com/diversityandequity** to download the free reproducibles in this book.

Printed in the United States of America

Library of Congress Cataloging-in-Publication Data

Names: Klein, Jennifer D., author. | Ciotti, Kapono, author.
Title: The landscape model of learning : designing student-centered experiences for cognitive and cultural inclusion / Jennifer D. Klein, Kapono Ciotti.
Description: Bloomington, IN : Solution Tree Press, 2022. | Includes bibliographical references and index.
Identifiers: LCCN 2021055357 (print) | LCCN 2021055358 (ebook) | ISBN 9781952812958 (paperback) | ISBN 9781952812965 (ebook)
Subjects: LCSH: Student-centered learning. | Learning, Psychology of. | Inclusive education. | Multicultural education.
Classification: LCC LB1027.23 .K54 2022 (print) | LCC LB1027.23 (ebook) | DDC 371.39/4--dc23/eng/20220419
LC record available at https://lccn.loc.gov/2021055357
LC ebook record available at https://lccn.loc.gov/2021055358

Solution Tree
Jeffrey C. Jones, CEO
Edmund M. Ackerman, President

Solution Tree Press
President and Publisher: Douglas M. Rife
Associate Publisher: Sarah Payne-Mills
Managing Production Editor: Kendra Slayton
Editorial Director: Todd Brakke
Art Director: Rian Anderson
Copy Chief: Jessi Finn
Senior Production Editor: Tonya Maddox Cupp
Content Development Specialist: Amy Rubenstein
Acquisitions Editor: Sarah Jubar
Proofreader: Evie Madsen
Text and Cover Designer: Laura Cox
Associate Editor: Sarah Ludwig
Editorial Assistants: Charlotte Jones, Elijah Oates

*To all our students, past, present, and future,
who go on to make the world a better place.*

Acknowledgments

The authors would both like to thank the educational thought leaders who agreed to be interviewed and involved in this book, including Jill Ackers-Clayton, Amy Anderson, Chad Carlson, Roberto d'Erizans, Rohit Kumar, Susannah Johnson, Michael Lipset, Shabbi Luthra, Tara O'Neill, Kristen Pelletier, Page Valentine Regan, Tony Simmons, Herb Lee, Rod Todorovich, and the NAIS DLI team. We are particularly grateful to Ron Berger for writing our foreword, and to Jan Iwase, Sandra Chapman, and Dwayne Priester for sharing their stories.

We would also like to thank our peer reviewers and editors for helping refine our work. We are forever grateful to Solution Tree for sharing our vision with the world.

—Jennifer D. Klein and Kapono Ciotti

I would like to acknowledge the incredible value my coauthor Kapono Ciotti brought to this project as a thought partner and friend; you teach me something new with every story, and I feel lucky to be on this path with you. I also want to recognize the influence of a few mentors who have inspired my educational thinking, including Arnie Langberg, Judith Baenen, and Silvia Rosenthal Tolisano. Losing Silvia Rosenthal Tolisano (aka @LangWitches) in early 2021 was a huge blow to the future of education, and I am grateful to have known Silvia as a thought partner, travel partner, and friend for the years we walked together. May her memory be for a blessing in countless classrooms around the world.

I would also like to recognize Jessica Portillo Limones, who at ten years old began to show me the world of education through her eyes. I still ask myself what she might say when facing an equity challenge or a cultural difference. She's changed my practice and my heart; I'm grateful for all she's taught me and am proud to be grandma to her beautiful daughter Isabella.

Finally, thank you to family and friends for supporting my creative life and often radical decisions. My sister Heather, and her daughters, Alex and Ella, live in my heart wherever I go. I am grateful to my parents, Edward A. Klein and Sally V. Klein, for stepping beyond the traditional when it came to our education. From them, I developed a deep appreciation for the kind of education that honors and challenges every child appropriately, and for the positive role that parents can play in a school community. Finally, I would like to dedicate this book to my mother, whose death in the fall of 2019 brought me back to my original purpose, drawing me back to Denver and to prioritizing home, family, and the writer's life.

Just as it takes a village to raise a child, it takes a broad, diverse, and empowered community to build a world of inclusive prosperity. I am grateful to every member of my #EdTribe.

—Jennifer D. Klein

My coauthor, Jennifer D. Klein, brought her knowledge, wisdom, and experience as a writer and editor to this project. Her clarity of thought and willingness to explore pedagogy and practice added tremendously to my own thinking. I know this is just the start of a long and powerful journey on *our landscape* of education.

I would like to acknowledge my family. They each supported me to my *horizon* in different ways. My wife, Ndeye, for her patience, support, and kind heart. My two sons, Bira and Fallou, for teaching me and growing me as a father. My parents, Joe and Kili, who are both lifelong educators and the primary influence on me becoming a teacher. And my two brothers, Nainoa and Makana, who have been steadfast friends.

I also want to recognize several mentors who have shaped my thinking and grounded me along this path. Dr. Robert G. Peters has been my kindergarten principal, my mentor, and my friend. His clarity of thought and inquisitive spirit guided me in progressive education. Auntie VerlieAnn Melina-Write, EdD, brought me to the mission of serving Indigenous learners. Mr. Walid Abushakra believed in me and gave me an opportunity of a lifetime in Cairo. E.D.B.E.L.K.: We lived collaboration and it made us all stronger. And to all my education leader friends: thank you.

—Kapono Ciotti

Solution Tree Press would like to thank the following reviewers:

Charlcy Carpenter
Mathematics Teacher
Burns Middle School
Lawndale, North Carolina

Kelly Hilliard
Mathematics Teacher
McQueen High School
Reno, Nevada

John D. Ewald
Education Consultant
Former Superintendent, Principal, Teacher
Frederick, Maryland

Visit **go.SolutionTree.com/diversityandequity** to download the free reproducibles in this book.

Table of Contents

Reproducible pages are in italics.

Acknowledgments	v
Table of Contents	ix
About the Authors	xiii
Foreword	xvii
Introduction: Why Are We Here?	1
The Traditional Way of Teaching Versus the Landscape Model	6
Important Terms	10
How This Book Is Organized	15
Our Hopes for This Book	18
Reflective Questions	19
Takeaways	20

Part 1: Understanding the Landscape Model 21

Chapter 1: The Landscape Model's Three Elements	23
The Ecosystem	24
The Horizon	31
The Pathway	35
Reflective Questions	43
Takeaways	44

Chapter 2: Eight Guiding Principles 45
It Is False to Set Up Education Like a Racetrack Because Students Vary
in Their Gifts and Needs 46
The Zone of Proximal Development Serves All Students 47
Inclusive Prosperity Requires a Shift Toward Asset-Based Thinking and
Relationship Building 48
Student-Centered Educational Practices Are Key 50
Critical Pedagogy Asks Us to Challenge the Dominant Theory and Exist in
a Reality That Accepts Multiple Lenses 51
When Learning Is Purposeful and Vigorous, Students Enjoy Their
Education and Learn More Deeply 53
It Is Possible to Personalize Learning and Still Ensure Success on More
Traditional Measures 56
Educators Need to Believe in Every Student, Build and Maintain a Sense
of Hope and Optimism, and Have the Courage to Make It Happen 57
Reflective Questions 59
Takeaways 60
Synthesis Tool, Part 1 . . . . *61*

Part 2: Implementing the Landscape Model 63

Chapter 3: The Ecosystem 65
Holding Space for Identity Development 67
Strategies for Holding Space for Identity Development 70
Integrating Students' Contexts Into the Classroom 79
Strategies for Integrating Students' Contexts Into the Classroom 80
Developing Inquiry to Understand Where Students Are in the Learning
Ecosystem 85
Strategies for Developing Inquiry to Understand Where Students Are
in the Learning Ecosystem 86
Reflective Questions 92
Takeaways 92

Chapter 4: The Horizon 93
Goal Setting to Support Defining the Horizon 95
Strategies for Identifying Aspirations to Support Defining the Horizon . . . 97
Strategies for Goal Setting to Support Defining the Horizon 100
Defining the Horizon for Academic Excellence 108

Strategies for Defining the Horizon for Academic Excellence 111
Reflective Questions 115
Takeaways 116

Chapter 5: The Pathway 117

Leveraging Asset-Based Mindsets and Communication 118
Leveraging Assets Along the Pathway 121
Strategies for Leveraging Assets Along the Pathway 122
Supporting Student Growth in Discipline-Specific Skills 130
Strategies for Supporting Student Growth in Discipline-Specific Skills at a
 Personal Level 132
Planning Units That Put Students at the Center of Their Educational Journey . . .136
Strategies for Planning Units That Put Students at the Center of Their
 Educational Journey 136
Reexamining What the Outcomes of Good Education Should Be 142
Strategies for Shifting Educational Outcomes on the Pathway 147
Reflective Questions 150
Takeaways 150
Synthesis Tool, Part 2 . . . . *151*

Part 3: Leading the Landscape Model 153

Chapter 6: Student Growth Assessment on the Landscape . . 155

Problems With Traditional Grading 156
Student Protagonism in Evaluation on the Landscape 164
Formative Evaluation and the Power of Feedback-Revision Cycles 165
Co-Constructed Rubrics With Student Protagonists 172
Reflective Questions 176
Takeaways 176

Chapter 7: Challenges of Implementation 177

The Challenges in Private and Public School Settings 177
The Challenges of Understanding and Discussing Identity 179
The Challenges of Educational Management Technologies 181
The Challenges of Buy-In and Accountability 182
The Challenges in Traditional and Progressive Contexts 184
The Challenges in International School Settings 187
The Challenges and Opportunities of Parents and Other Caregivers 188
The Challenge of Policies and Politics 190

Reflective Questions 193
Takeaways 193

Chapter 8: Landscape Model Implementation for Long-Term Success 195

Educator Profiles and Recruitment 196
A Shared Vision of What's Possible 201
Strategies for Tapping Into the Community 206
Transformative Professional Learning 211
Curriculum Adjustment 215
Student and Course Reorganization 218
Student Protagonism in Building School Culture 221
Three-Year Plan Development 225
Impact Evaluation of the Landscape Model 228
Reflective Questions 230
Takeaways 231
Reflection and Discussion Tool for Teachers on the Landscape *232*
Reflection and Discussion Tool for School Leaders on the Landscape *233*

Chapter 9: Opportunities for the Future 235

Education Evolution to Follow Human Development 236
The Next Frontier for Education .239
What Education Could Be 247
Reflective Questions 251
Takeaways 252
Synthesis Tool, Part 3 . . . .*253*

Epilogue: Why This Work Matters 257

Appendix 261

References and Resources 265

Index 281

About the Authors

Jennifer D. Klein is a product of experiential project-based education herself, and she lives and breathes the student-centered pedagogies used to educate her. She became a teacher during graduate school in 1990, quickly finding the intersection between her love of writing and her fascination with educational transformation and its potential impact on social change. She spent nineteen years in the classroom, including several years in Costa Rica and eleven in all-girls education, before leaving the classroom to support educators' professional learning in public, private, and international schools. Motivated by her belief that all children deserve a meaningful, relevant education like the one she experienced herself, and that giving them such an education will catalyze positive change in their communities and beyond, Jennifer strives to inspire educators to shift their practices in schools worldwide.

Jennifer has a broad background in global education and global partnership development, student-centered curricular strategies, diversity and inclusivity work, authentic assessment, and experiential, inquiry-driven learning. She has facilitated workshops in English and Spanish on four continents, providing the strategies for high-quality, globally connected project-based learning in all cultural and socioeconomic contexts, with an emphasis on amplifying student voice and shifting school culture to support such practices. She is committed to intersecting global student-centered learning with culturally responsive and anti-racist teaching practices, and her experience includes deep work with schools seeking to address equity, take on brave conversations, build healthier community, and improve identity politics on campus.

Jennifer has worked with organizations such as the Buck Institute for Education, the Center for Global Education at the Asia Society, The Institute of International Education, Fulbright Japan, What School Could Be, the Centre for Global Education (Edmonton), TakingITGlobal, and the World Leadership School, to name a few. Most recently, she served as head of school at Gimnasio Los Caobos (Bogotá, Colombia) for three years, where she was able to put her educational thinking into practice with profound impact on the quality of students' learning and their growth as agents of change.

Jennifer's first book, *The Global Education Guidebook: Humanizing K–12 Classrooms Worldwide Through Equitable Partnerships*, was published by Solution Tree Press in 2017. She holds a bachelor of arts from Bard College in Annandale-on-Hudson, New York, and a master of arts from the University of Colorado Boulder, both in literature and creative writing. Additionally, Jennifer completed her principal licensing studies at the University of Denver. She currently lives in Denver, Colorado.

To learn more about Jennifer's work, visit Principled Learning Strategies (https://principledlearning.org), and follow her at @jdeborahklein on Twitter.

Kapono Ciotti, PhD, attributes his educational philosophy to his own schooling experience in a progressive, social-constructivist school during his early years in Honolulu, Hawai'i. He taught in Honolulu, Hawai'i, and Dakar, Senegal, for over a decade before moving into school leadership. Kapono has led schools in the United States and internationally, where he put into practice the philosophy of "students making the world a better place," shifting school culture to impact-based education practice. His strong belief in education being an act of social justice drives his work.

Kapono has worked internationally in educational change organizations, leading the work of deeper learning and place- and culture-based pedagogy. In these roles, he has trained teachers in over one hundred schools and school districts on four continents, impacting hundreds of thousands of students. In addition, Kapono spent fifteen years as national faculty for the National Association of Independent Schools in diversity, equity, and justice, facilitating national and international learning experiences. As a curriculum writer, he has authored multiple curricula for federal and nonprofit programs. His work has significantly contributed to the organizations What School Could Be, the Buck Institute for Education, EdLeader21, the Pacific American Foundation, and many others.

Kapono holds a PhD in international education leadership from Northcentral University in San Diego, California, a master's degree in social change and development from the University of Newcastle, Australia, in Callaghan, and a bachelor's degree in language and culture from The Evergreen State College in Olympia, Washington. He lives between Hawai'i; Cairo, Egypt; and Dakar, Senegal.

To learn more about Kapono's work, visit KaponoCiotti (https://kaponociotti.wordpress.com) or follow him at @kaponoc on Twitter.

To book Jennifer D. Klein or Kapono Ciotti for professional development, contact pd@SolutionTree.com.

Foreword

By Ron Berger

For all of our differences and arguments regarding what "good" education looks like, there is one dimension of this debate for which almost all Americans and citizens around the world show remarkable agreement. Almost all parents from all walks of life, backgrounds, and cultures have similar hopes for the schools our children attend. We hope our children will be known and cared for; valued and respected across all their identities; given meaningful, purposeful, and challenging academic work; afforded rich opportunities in arts and athletics; nurtured to become respectful, responsible, kind, and courageous people; and supported and inspired to achieve more than they think possible and to build a successful life.

What would it look like if these shared and beautiful hopes were at the center of the schooling experience—for all children? How would school be different? This is the question that Jennifer D. Klein and Kapono Ciotti, bringing decades of deep experience leading and improving schools around the world, center in this book. The authors bring an asset-based perspective to the potential of all students from all backgrounds and advocate for schools that unleash the potential in every student.

The framework they offer for education, built on metaphors from the natural world, makes good sense to me. The nonprofit education organization where I work, EL Education, was born from a collaboration between Harvard Graduate School of Education and Outward Bound—a marriage of commitment to academic excellence to a focus on character, courage, and collaboration. When students in an Outward Bound wilderness course stand together at the bottom of an intimidating mountain, their mission is not to race to the top but rather to work together to make sure they all succeed and stand on the summit together.

At the beginning of EL Education (then called Expeditionary Learning) we asked, "What if school were that way?"

That is exactly the notion of this book. In Klein and Ciotti's language, school can be a positive ecosystem (a culture that recognizes the best in all); with a clear horizon (a shared vision of the mountain top); and pathways set by student protagonism (student agency and leadership). They promote a vision of inclusive prosperity (working together to ensure all students reach the summit) and rightful presence (elevating the voices of everyone in the community—especially those who have been marginalized).

But this book is much more than a critique of educational systems and an alternate aspirational framework. The authors mine their personal experiences and the broad field of student-centered learning to offer a wealth of concrete practices that schools can use for transformation. The metaphors of ecosystem, horizon, and pathway are fleshed out with a curated set of structures and strategies that schools and systems can implement right away.

In addition to understanding the framework, readers will benefit from taking time to dig into the concrete guidance. My suggestion is to look carefully at the practices and protocols the authors describe in these pages and focus on a few strategic ones to implement or deepen in your journey of school improvement. Most of us in education are not building schools from scratch with unlimited resources and the grace to experiment. We are working in existing schools and systems. Change is hard and slow. But the practices that the authors describe—things like project-based learning, portfolios, home visits, student-led conferences, student shadowing, affinity groups, portraits of a graduate, critique protocols, Socratic seminars—are all powerful practices in their own right.

Any one of these practices can become an engine for positive change that can catalyze improvement across a school. I have shadowed high school students and I am always humbled and enlightened by how much educators do not understand about what students actually experience in a day and how much stronger learning could be if we restructure parts of the school experience. I have seen schools implement student-led family conferences and watched everything about those schools improve: students are empowered to take responsibility for their work and learning; teachers are compelled to deepen their instruction to prepare students more effectively; families are welcomed and honored by the school as partners in the work and are proud of their children's ability to guide and reflect on their learning.

What resonates most for me in this book's vision is the assumption that we underestimate the potential of students to do great things. Students want to achieve things that make them proud and that make their families, friends, and communities proud. If we build school cultures where all students feel safe and valued, and we connect student learning to a virtuous purpose—students getting smart to do good for the world—we can inspire students to reach higher and work harder together. This belief in students does not just live in this book's ideals. It is at the heart of the powerful educational practices this book describes for us.

After almost fifty years working in education and many published books, the thing I am known for by most educators is a six-minute video: Austin's Butterfly (EL Education, 2016). The story of Austin as a first-grade student improving his scientific illustration of a butterfly through multiple drafts with critique from peers is an inspiring model. But what one cannot see in those six minutes is the culture and pedagogy—the ecosystem—that supported Austin and his classmates to succeed.

Austin was not just drawing a butterfly. He was creating a note card that would be sold across the state of Idaho in the U.S., raising funds for pollinator habitats. He had a noble mission and a purpose for working hard. His peers were nested in a culture of reflection, critique, and revision; they kept portfolios, led their own family conferences, and regularly presented evidence of their learning to the broader community. The practices described in The Landscape Model were present in Austin's school, and this is what shepherded his success. Read this book carefully and bring its wisdom into your own setting—there is much to learn.

INTRODUCTION

Why Are We Here?

*When a flower doesn't bloom, you fix the
environment in которую it grows, not the flower.*

—Alexander Den Heijer

We, the authors of this book, share many common traits and perspectives, but perhaps most important is our shared experience of truly nurturing, student-centered, happy educational experiences in our childhoods. We are both very much the product of those experiences; they have made us who we are as educators and leaders, people who believe that students must be protagonists in their own learning journeys. We both exude joy and passion when we speak of our childhoods, of the educators and learning experiences that honored who we were and brought out the best in us, because we were happy at schools that formed us as lifelong learners, problem solvers, and independent thinkers.

We also share frustration over how often schools and educational organizations focus on ensuring *access* for all students instead of working toward the highest level of *success* possible for each student. We first came together around this topic in 2016, both of us disappointed because access was such a low standard to strive toward, and this book is the result of that disappointment and our inherent desire to fix a problem with equity at its core. Why couldn't education work toward something bigger than just getting every student into the room? Much like the United Nations' (2000) Millennium Development Goal of "equal access to all levels of education," it feels like an important first step, but not an appropriate end goal (p. 5). It feels like everyone is shooting too low—which the United Nations' 2015(b) Sustainable Development Goals addresses by adjusting the goal to ensure "*quality* education . . . for all" (p. 14). Access is necessary before quality is even possible, but our language matters, and a focus on *access* keeps us from serving all students well.

As educators, we have built such an industrialized system in education that we don't even seem to notice when we use words like *access*; it has become commonplace to assume our work will only function on a very basic level for some learners. As long as they don't fall off the assembly line, we can call ourselves successful, right? It feels wrong to us as authors, and we know it feels wrong to many educators working those assembly lines. What might it look like, we asked ourselves, to leave the industrial model behind and strive for the best outcomes possible for every student?

What happened for us as children is what we both believe should happen for every student around the world: an education that recognizes the potential of every individual, recognizes the whole student in all his or her messy human complexity, and helps students strengthen areas needing growth while also fostering talents and passions. It is an education that engages learners in real problem solving, connects them to the world and their own communities, awakens their conscience, and motivates them toward engagement as agents of change (Robinson, 2016). This sort of education was the vision of John Dewey (1938) a century ago, central to the pedagogies espoused by Paolo Freire (2000), Sir Ken Robinson (2016), Yong Zhao (2012, 2021), and many other educational thought leaders. It is an education that strives to foster the essential skills—and honor the essential humanity—of all students. It is an education students can *enjoy*, one that centers on vigor and the joy of learning; ensures all students thrive, feel safe, and know they belong; and are seen for all they are and might become. It is an education that supports and never limits, that honors and never diminishes, and that nurtures while building autonomy—an education where student agency and voice reign supreme, as we explain later in this introduction.

If we, as educators, do it right, we can retire the inadequate goal of *access* and move education toward the higher and more urgent, more equitable goal of helping all students reach their highest possible level of individual *success*.

We recognize that many communities are still grappling with access in very real ways, particularly since the beginning of the COVID-19 pandemic. In parts of the world with minimal technological infrastructure, for example, basic access to school has been seriously compromised, with UNESCO (2022) data finding that COVID school closures and technological access challenges affected over 37 million learners around the world. Even in more developed countries, we see significant drops in the educational outcome of students without technology or parents who can support their learning. Clearly, access is pivotal; without it, there can be no achieving higher levels of success. But when we let access become the highest goal, we dehumanize students and build educational systems that fail to elevate all students to their highest potential.

We believe that an education that strives for the highest levels of success for each student is possible anywhere, and that it is desirable everywhere. It is possible across cultures, across political systems, languages, and socioeconomic differences, including the divide between private school and public school. It is an education we believe can happen in large classrooms and schools as much as in smaller learning communities, although packed classrooms and gigantic schools are a byproduct of designing education using an industrial model—a byproduct educators should avoid wherever possible. It is an education that doesn't require brick-and-mortar learning environments or fancy technological tools to be successful, though both might enrich its impact if designed with learners in mind. In the end, it is an education that requires only the will to think differently about how to work with students and what they need from their education.

In this book, we ground our work in metaphors that come from nature for a reason: we believe that educating students is a growth process that mirrors the growth of plants and the movement of species and water and wind across landscapes, *not* a factory production line. Educationalist Sir Ken Robinson (2008) spoke often of educators as gardeners who don't force growth but instead create the conditions for growth to occur. Traditional education was built on goals developed during the industrial revolution, with students educated in age-group batches, with the same starting and ending point for all (Matus, n.d.). Colonialism exported that form of education across the planet, with colonizing nations like Britain, Spain, and France bringing European educational ideologies to bear on the educational systems of colonized nations across Africa, Asia, and the Americas (Southard, 2017).

But students aren't assembled on a factory production line, nor are they trained like animals; students grow like plants, and they flower and amaze us when the conditions are right. As a result, we believe that education can and should occur on a landscape, a true ecosystem of learning, and *The Landscape Model of Learning* attempts to provide the thinking and tools that will allow any educator to make our vision a reality in their classrooms, schoolhouses, districts, and countries. The landscape model is based on three elements of the metaphor.

1. **The ecosystem:** In this element, educators strive to understand students deeply in terms of their previous learning and current needs, but also in terms of their life experiences. The goal is to understand the experiences, academic abilities, and identities students bring into the

learning ecosystem when they enter our classrooms. Understanding a student's identity and broader context allows educators to understand where students are positioned on the landscape, with a focus on leveraging strengths and avoiding assumptions based on culture or other factors of identity.

2. **The horizon:** In this element, educators work with students to define the horizon they are working toward. The goal is to understand students' goals—and the aspirations of their families—in ways that leverage students' interests and talents but also help them grow in areas of weakness. The horizon is about collaboratively identifying what success looks like for each student, without allowing educators' assumptions to limit students' potential.

3. **The pathway:** In this element, educators work with students to plan out their pathway toward that horizon. Using waypoints such as curricular scope and sequence, specific standards, and their professional judgment, educators work with students to chart their course across the landscape. Recognizing that students may not be headed toward the same horizon, the work at this point focuses on co-constructing personalized pathways through pedagogical structures that position students as protagonists.

Not every student starts with the same level of performance, the same background knowledge, or the same *anything* for that matter. We feel that educators are often asked to spend too much time getting students who struggle unstuck, while letting those at the head of the pack just cruise along. And if it is true that some students start the year significantly ahead or behind in foundational grade-level skills, and one student makes up months and months of learning in a year, while another who started ahead barely moves forward—how do educators honor and measure growth when grade-level curricula assume fixed starting and ending points?

The constraints of the factory model are as complex as the landscape model is simplistic. Students truly do not start in the same place; assuming they do creates dissonance at best and behavioral issues at worst. Providing rigid boundaries to learning makes for easier planning but also puts a higher demand on educators to engage students by entertaining or disciplining them, rather than lighting in them their own fire to journey forward. While standardization and rigidity might make schooling more manageable, schools grounded in fixed ideas about students' potential, particularly those that haven't done enough to deconstruct implicit biases and the inequitable systems that create them, have done a great deal of damage to the potential of young people. While explicit biases are just as destructive, they tend to be easier to identify and address, whereas implicit biases are, by their nature, more unrecognized, often based on stereotypes and assumptions that the individual and collective community don't even realize they're making. As a result, many educators see bias as something *other* teachers have, but have difficulty recognizing it in their own practices. This makes implicit bias particularly difficult to deconstruct, while its impact is just as negative for students as more explicit bias.

We see these impacts in many forms, several of which will be explored more deeply later in this book. Research finds that negative stereotypes, such as the behavioral and cultural assumptions that lead to disproportionally higher rates of suspension for African American boys in U.S. schools, can be incredibly damaging, with Black boys perceived as "violent" in cases where White boys are viewed as "having a bad day" for the same behavior (Mills College, 2020). Even positive stereotypes, such as the assumption that Asian Americans are academically high achieving, can cause undue pressure on Asian students of all ages, ignoring students' unique needs and selves. Research also finds that implicit biases connected to gender negatively affect girls, particularly in mathematics outcomes, and that Black girls are disproportionally penalized for being assertive in the classroom as compared to their White counterparts (Chemaly, 2015). As Mills College (2020) asserts, "Whatever the stereotype, viewing students as a group instead of as individuals leaves them at risk for not getting the support they need to learn." Whether because of students' cognitive challenges, exceptional giftedness, cultural identity, race, gender identity, sexual orientation, or socioeconomic background, educators' implicit biases, however unintentional, often limit students' goals and, in doing so, cut short potential careers and futures.

Certainly, we have examples of students who thrived despite such experiences with educator bias, like Mae Jemison's insistence that she *would* become a scientist when told by her White kindergarten teacher that she should strive to become a nurse instead (as cited in Changing the Face of Medicine, n.d.). We know from her work that Dr. Jemison went on to become not just a doctor but the first female African American astronaut in history (Changing the Face of Medicine, n.d.). Sadly, the stories we never hear are of the countless students who give up along the way, who believe the limited perspective of the adults who educate them, the stories of students who never strive for more because they've been told it's impossible, or because some element of their circumstances suggests such aspirations are unrealistic. This is where the landscape model of learning comes in.

This work will require the deep commitment and inclusive vision of school leaders. At the end of the day, leaders will need a high tolerance for challenge, a natural tendency to listen to, trust, and validate the ideas of students, and a solutions-oriented mindset that keeps their communities focused on the goal, however challenging or distant that horizon may feel some days. We generally see the most success where school leaders ensure their team spans a diversity of talents, skills, and world views, whatever the initiative undertaken. In the case of the landscape model, the leadership and instructional coaching team needs to include individuals who share the students' background, as well as individuals with specific skill sets like the ability to train and coach others in the use of brave spaces, project-based learning, and asset- and strengths-based teaching and learning. It will also be important to have members of the leadership team who are trained in strategies for understanding and deconstructing implicit bias. While this is a long wish list, such a team might be built over several years, and it can be complemented by teachers who have those skills and want to devote some of their time to helping lead the initiative.

The most common qualification of educators suited to this work, whether they teach on the landscape or lead the effort, is their ability to understand what the current educational system feels like for students who aren't well served by it. We as authors find ourselves touching back on our stories again and again in this book, both stories of students who succeeded and stories of students failed by the systems we've worked in. We let those failures guide our work toward something better, keeping students in our hearts in all we do. We are guided by elements of our culture and community, too, by our sense of planetary interdependence, and by the urgency we feel to create an educational system that prepares students for the challenges of *today and tomorrow*, not twenty years ago (and definitely not one hundred years ago). Everyone we interviewed for this book had this same quality in common: they spoke of students' needs more than of educators' needs; they addressed broader systemic challenges with students in mind first, and they told warm, moving stories that captured how and why they work toward the highest level of success possible for every single child. We encourage any reader of this book to do the same, particularly those who will lead this work and will need to inspire others to chart a different course forward in education.

The Traditional Way of Teaching Versus the Landscape Model

Education, as educators know it, has existed since only the 19th century. Grade levels and subject matters, classrooms, and the shuffling of students through hallways at the command of bells, is the invention of a small group of university academics in response to U.S. education reformer Horace Mann's visit to Prussia in 1843 (Rose, 2012). This trip exposed Mann to the solution the Prussians proposed to meet the challenges of supplying their military with soldiers of a similar and minimal level of education. On return to the United States, Mann and a group of university academics used this model to support, rather than the military system, the U.S. industrial complex, with the goal of supplying its industry with workers of a similar and minimal level of education.

Since that time, schooling has seen varying degrees of success and failure. As a global society, we have tried to address these challenges and failures through centralized solutions, like the United States' federal No Child Left Behind Act and Race to the Top (U.S. Department of Education, 2009), and the U.K.'s Education Reform Act (1988), to name a few. Centralized solutions like these have focused on creating manuals for educators to follow, so to speak. They place administrators in supervisory positions, overseeing the implementation of schooling that looks like checking tasks off a list. As Sir Ken Robinson (2016) writes, the standards movement was meant to make educational systems "more efficient and accountable. The problem is that these systems are inherently unsuited to the wholly different circumstances of the 21st century" (p. xxi). Society has also addressed this through decentralized solutions, like giving districts and individual schools the freedom to pursue innovative models and individualized programs like Advancement Via Individual Determination (AVID, n.d.), the magnet school movement (Kitchens & Brodnax, 2021), and one-to-one technology programs (Herold, 2016) to name just a few. These initiatives have supported some progress, but results have been mixed.

Other educational reformers have been finding their way back to older practices from a time long gone. The inquiry-based style of Socrates, the lessons of Indigenous place-based learning (a style of teaching and learning grounded in the context of place, providing learners contextualized opportunities), and the interpersonal connection and personalization of the one-room schoolhouse have all come back into vogue (Getting Smart, eduInnovation, & Teton Science School, 2017). These practices are positive, inherently student centered, and have, in many cases, been helpful when it comes to ensuring culturally responsive, relevant educational experiences for students. Furthermore, they align well with the landscape model of learning.

Senior learning designer and author Jill Ackers-Clayton, who reimagines learning spaces with Fielding International as much as what happens inside of them, describes most traditional schools as prison-like, with "double-loaded corridors and doors that close," siloing subject areas and isolating students' experiences (personal communication, May 12, 2021). Many educators, she points out, own 90 percent of the creativity and decision making in each of those contained spaces, controlling their domains tightly and offering little room for true student agency. Maybe they pepper in some tightly controlled student choice, with popsicle-stick draws or limited-choice menus, but ultimately, it's a system designed for control and compliance more than agency. In these systems, what happens to students who don't fit the pacing guide, students like Ackers-Clayton herself, who escaped her boring classes by crawling through her school's air conditioning vents to listen to the best educators in the building? When asked what she envisions for the future, Ackers-Clayton is unapologetic about suggesting that we stop making small changes, be unwilling to just prune the forest as it stands, and instead collectively "burn the forest down" to reimagine education from scratch (personal communication, May 12, 2021).

While we know that reimagining education from scratch is a monumental proposition in most contexts, this book proposes changing the paradigm from a factory to a landscape. It is time for a model that supports educators in their quest to grow students and to do so in a way that provides usable strategies like those contained in this book. When using the landscape model, we acknowledge that students bring prior knowledge and experiences to their learning journey. We acknowledge that some students may start squarely on the landscape, while others may begin the year over a metaphorical river and stuck in a bog. Students' journeys are all slightly different, as is their end point on the school year's conclusion, but they all move forward toward an endless, ever-advancing finish line of endless growth. The educator becomes more of a shepherd than a lecturer—more of a guide than an assembly line monitor.

Amy Anderson, executive director of RESCHOOL Colorado, notes that traditional schools are *institutionally* centered instead of *learner* centered, prioritizing efficiency and designed for the middle, rather than striving to meet the needs of individual learners:

> There are great people that work in the system, that care and would love to do it differently. But the system's not designed to do it differently, and there's no incentive nor the time and space. Even when you're in charge of "innovation," you get sucked into running the existing system because that's what you do. (personal communication, April 2, 2021)

Anderson believes that much more is possible, particularly when education leverages all elements of students' lives the way social services strive to, from the deeper involvement of parents and guardians, to advisors who grew up in the same neighborhoods, to opportunities for students to pursue meaningful, passion-based experiences both inside the schoolhouse and beyond its walls (personal communication, April 2, 2021). The authors agree and believe that the landscape model leverages exactly what Anderson indicates, whether by rebuilding the whole educational system, as we address in the last chapter (page 235), or by making reasonable modifications to the existing system, as we address throughout this book.

The landscape metaphor is by no means an easier path, but it is more effective and is so because of the three elements that form the foundation of teaching and learning in the landscape model.

1. **Ecosystem:** The ecosystem is a metaphor for the learning environment, where each student is a unique organism at a distinct point on the landscape because of the contexts and identities students bring with them into the classroom. Rather than seeing learning as starting and ending at fixed points for all students, this element invites us to consider students as beginning their learning from many different points on the landscape, and it asks educators to understand who students are as deeply as possible. Understanding a child's culture, race, upbringing, socioeconomic advantages or disadvantages, previous learning, learning challenges, and more allows us to work toward the most appropriate goals (horizon) for each child, to support them in the most appropriate ways, and to co-construct the best pathway to the highest level of success possible.

2. **Horizon:** The horizon is a metaphor for the goals we work toward with students, that "end" point on the landscape that we might call *mastery* or *success*. While we recognize that schooling sets a common end point for all students in most parts of the world, in the form of standards and national exams, we are also keenly aware that those goals make some students feel stuck all the time, and make others feel limited. The horizon is not a fixed point—it is a lifelong learning journey. But in practical terms, this element is about working with students to define what success and mastery look like for *them*, given what each brings to the ecosystem and where they are positioned on the landscape.

3. **Pathway:** The pathway is a metaphor for how we get from where students are (on the landscape) to where they can go (horizon). On any landscape, we have pathways, some more traveled and some lightly etched by wind, water, or animals. This element asks us to work with students to design the best pathways through learning, the pathways that best suit the needs of students as individuals or groups of individuals. Rather than envisioning the learning process as identical

for all students, this element asks educators to recognize that there are many ways to reach the horizon.

This metaphor may sound exciting to some and terrifying to others. How does one shepherd a class of thirty students? It is far easier and more organized to keep the herd tightly packed together. How might one navigate the demands of an administrator conducting a walkthrough to see the exact standard for the day's lesson on the top right-hand corner of the whiteboard and every student able to recite the learning objective? It is easier to be "on page 53," for example, because it's Thursday, rather than have each of your thirty students working on a different page or skill. But educating this way ignores the messiness of what students bring into the classroom with them, of the lives they lead and the families they come from, and doing so dehumanizes every one of them. We believe that a more humanizing, individually appropriate education is possible, and that such an education will result in excellence from more students, demonstrated in more varied ways that leverage their strengths and full selves. While the landscape requires something *different* from educators, we don't believe it will amount to extra work, particularly as teachers learn to harness pedagogies with student agency at their core.

Important Terms

The authors have been investigating three terms we believe help capture our vision for education in general and the landscape model in particular: (1) student protagonism, (2) inclusive prosperity, and (3) rightful presence. The landscape model hinges on each of these terms, and the broader concepts they address, because they move education beyond the factory line toward something much more authentic, inclusive, and student centered, which will improve learning experiences and outcomes for all students.

Student Protagonism

Sadly, the English language rarely uses the word *protagonism*, only the word *protagonist*. Even *protagonist* is a word we rarely hear in reference to education in the English-speaking world, more commonly used to describe main characters in literature. When Jennifer was working as a head of school outside of Bogotá, Colombia, she found that *protagonismo* was a fairly common educational term in Spanish for active student participation in learning experiences, for a sort of ownership over the learning journey, albeit limited by the goals of the educator and broader curriculum. As a student of literature and writing, Jennifer was immediately compelled to adopt the word *protagonismo* in her daily work, to help teachers and parents expand their thinking about just how much student agency might be achievable.

Student protagonism is crucial to any form of student-centered learning. In its simplest form, student choice, such as that seen in pedagogical approaches like project-based learning, problem-based learning, inquiry-based learning, and design thinking, motivates students by tying learning to their interests, which in turn improves learning outcomes (Taub et al., 2020). In its highest form, such as the level of student agency we envision for the landscape, protagonism requires constant critical thinking and metacognition, as students learn to understand their own learning needs (ecosystem), set goals for their own growth (horizon), and identify steps to achieve that growth (pathway). When students participate in these processes, instead of having the teacher define and control their pathway, their motivation to meet those goals increases significantly (Taub et al., 2020). And in a practical sense, student protagonism will lower the pressure on teachers to manage all aspects of learning—moving more of the tracking, monitoring, and managing to the students themselves and freeing up educators' time for scaffolding, guiding, and supporting students' growth.

Protagonism suggests that students lead the way, not that they follow passively; it suggests that they construct meaning, not just consume information; and it suggests that they act from center stage, not from the audience, because this play is *theirs*. The idea of students as creators of knowledge is not a new one, born in the earliest forms of constructivist education such as Montessori, Waldorf, and Reggio Emilia, and tied to the highest levels of Bloom's (1956) taxonomy. Students as creators lives at the heart of modern student-centered learning, an essential element of pedagogies like project-based learning, design thinking, "maker" education, STEM education, and deeper learning. The emergence of educational technologies makes the shift more urgent, in our opinion, as students need to use technologies in creative and constructive ways that set them up to thrive in an increasingly digital present and future (Oddone, 2016). If all we do is ask students to recall, summarize, or passively consume technology, we are missing an opportunity to foster the skills our students need for our times and our uncertain future.

While what Jennifer has seen in many Latin American schools may fall short of student agency in its highest form, the authors agree that the word *protagonism* provides the language to describe what's possible: that students can and should become the main characters of their own learning stories. And this leads us to our next term, as the landscape model asks us to ensure that such protagonism, and all the learning journey entails, be inclusive in its design and implementation, equally powerful and meaningful for all students, regardless of where they are on the landscape.

Inclusive Prosperity

Because we want to remove limits and personalize possibilities, we find terms like *diversity* and *inclusion* inadequate in this context. Diversity suggests that we have a broad mix of people at the table but offers little guidance once we have that mix. Inclusion, though a reasonable improvement over diversity, still suggests that educators have the power to include or not, and it therefore negates the unique right of protagonism we believe every student should have, always. This distinction is particularly important when we consider the negative impact that implicit bias can have on educators' sense of what students are capable of; if teachers hold the power to include or not, their assumptions become more dangerous. In fact, according to professors Angela Calabrese Barton and Edna Tan (2020), "Reform efforts focused on inclusion do little to disrupt systemic inequities in classroom practice" (p. 434).

We came across the term *inclusive prosperity* early in our investigations, originally an economic concept calling for policy changes that shift profit distribution systems. Applied to education by Roberto d'Erizans (2018), head of school at the Millennium School in San Francisco, in a letter to his faculty at the Graded School, the term:

> signals both unity and an inclusive view of success. Not just success in traditional terms, but a desire to jointly work for the betterment of each other's lives. It signifies joining together, not leaving anyone behind, as we work in unison to meet our goals.

The concept of inclusive prosperity resonates for the authors as an intentional orientation for this deeper work: we are not just making sure all kinds of students are *at* the table (diversity), nor that traditional power structures are allowing them a certain, albeit limited power (inclusion), as we see in schools with limited and highly controlled forms of student choice—or none at all. Instead, inclusive prosperity suggests that everyone in educational communities has a role in ensuring all students receive acceptance and support and that stakeholders view students as the little humans they are, recognizing the experiences, gifts, and challenges each brings into the classroom. It suggests all students can *thrive*, not just survive their schooling. It suggests not just the protagonism of every individual but, by extension, the prosperous power of the whole classroom or learning community. Inclusive prosperity might even guide educators toward a better understanding of the classroom and broader community culture they need to build to support the success of every individual. As d'Erizans puts it, "Collective action leads to collective responsibility; inclusive action leads to inclusive communities" (personal communication, June 1, 2021).

Inclusive prosperity is the heart of the landscape model, as an education built on the goal of all students reaching their highest level of prosperity, or success, has the potential to erase many educational inequities we find in schools and the broader social inequities that a limited education creates. Further, such prosperity can only happen when educators recognize every student's essential humanity and potential and his, her, or their essential right to a voice in his, her, or their own education.

Rightful Presence

During our investigations, the term *rightful presence* emerged, a term that comes originally from critical justice studies of the potentials and limitations of sanctuary cities (Squire & Darling, 2013). These studies sought to look critically, through an equity lens, at how well historical and modern social systems have been designed to support and protect the rights of immigrants and refugees in cities across the United States. Schools are built on similar systems, and critical justice orientations in the classroom, more often referred to as *critical pedagogy*, seek to identify and deconstruct systemic injustices that harm students. Addressing the inadequacies of terms like *inclusion*, Barton and Tan (2020) apply the concept of rightful presence to education, establishing it as a critical justice effort that moves educators beyond common conceptions of equity and asking us to design schools and classrooms in ways that ensure the essential, inalienable rights of all students:

> What *rightful presence* offers teaching and learning exceeds the limits of equity. Rightful presence, as a justice-oriented political project, focuses on the processes of reauthoring rights towards *making present* the lives of those made missing by the systemic injustices inherent in schooling. (pp. 435-436)

"Making present the lives of those made missing" (Barton & Tan, 2020, p. 436) captures beautifully the idea of the schoolhouse as a place where one can and should deconstruct the injustices of the broader society—and of education itself—allowing educators to rebuild something better and ensure the highest levels of achievement possible for every student (another concept worthy of deconstruction). Rightful presence suggests that such presence is a right, not a gift those in power bestow, which Paulo Freire (2000), liberation theologist, author, and the grandfather of the critical pedagogy movement, insists is essential if the goal is to avoid perpetuating oppressive and dehumanizing systems. Such presence is—or should be—a natural, rightful state afforded to every student in every circumstance. Ultimately, rightful presence also suggests student protagonism; it requires that students aren't just *in* the classroom but are *active members of* a learning community, members who consistently see themselves as owners of their own education and who feel valued for their own voices and experiences. As Barton and Tan (2020) assert:

> When allies, such as teachers, help students to challenge and transform what participation in the disciplines entails or what meaningful representations of learning look like . . . they shape opportunities for humanizing participation by valuing students as cultural and whole people, whose knowledge/wisdom, experiences, and fraught histories are integral to disciplinary learning. (p. 436)

And what *do* we mean by achievement, then? We believe that educational policymakers around the world have simplified this term to make it more easily assessed: the ability to accurately recall content knowledge or demonstrate academic skills, on demand, usually on a multiple-choice exam. Bloom's (1956) taxonomy has long established that pure recall is a low-level thinking skill, yet even many project-based classrooms depend on summative products that simply summarize the content learned, albeit in a unique or creative form. We believe students from all backgrounds and cognitive abilities are capable of taking on real challenges, of doing real problem solving, and of doing real thinking. But this can only happen if educators reframe the concept of success to focus more on the individual's movement across the landscape: their application and articulation of learning, their willingness to challenge themselves, and their progress toward mastery.

Is achievement the same for every student? Of course not. Toddlers walk at different points in their development, and they are no less children based on this. It's when students enter formal schooling that we, as educators and parents, start expecting a similar starting and ending point for all students of a given age each year. The systems of school are easier to manage when we have concrete, uniform ways of determining what students are learning, but standardizing achievement requires standardizing how we view students, which we believe is dangerous. Achievement should be as personalized as the pathway to get there, and honoring the complexity of each student's multiple identities, gifts, and challenges will inevitably lead to higher-quality, transferable, and deeply purposeful learning for all, even if specific outcomes vary from student to student.

While we believe that education is a political act, at its best and worst, political perceptions or partisan divisions should not impede improving educational systems. On a certain level, we all want the same things from education, particularly when it comes to our own children: that it be meaningful, that it be useful now and later, that it be enjoyable and appropriately challenging. We can use the landscape model across socioeconomic differences, for example, because other than professional development, there are no real costs involved in making the shift. Educators can use it with all age groups, across all academic disciplines, and in rural and urban settings. They can use it in private schools, in public schools, and in charter schools, although there may be challenges to overcome in more traditional contexts, particularly in regions where schools and educators have less autonomy to respond to the needs of their communities. And educators can use it in small and large schools and classrooms, though we recognize that tracking and managing this kind of learning may be easier in smaller classrooms, at least in the first year or two of implementation as educators build out their strategies and toolboxes.

We also believe that both inclusive prosperity and rightful presence are meant to apply to absolutely every student who enters our schools, and that it's our job to fit the education we offer to the communities we serve more than it is our students' responsibility to fit themselves into our schools. When we say "every student," we mean that we have designed this model with intentionality around all aspects of identity, including the cognitive needs and strengths of each, the socioeconomic situation they've been raised in, the cultural and racial orientations of the family, and the sexual and gender orientation of each student. Students each deserve to experience appropriate challenge—not based on a limited or stereotype-laden view of what their identity suggests they're capable of, but based on an expansive, inclusive conception of their potential as whole human beings and their inherent right to be seen and treated as such.

How This Book Is Organized

This book offers a practical road map to inclusive prosperity for classroom teachers, curriculum designers, instructional coaches, and educational leaders. It not only provides theory, classroom stories, and broader case studies, but also the specific strategies that teachers and leaders need to put the landscape model into practice. We want this book to change how readers approach their work next Monday morning—not in some distant future—so supporting implementation has been a key goal throughout our writing process. Because of the model's reliance on student-centered practices, the strategies offered connect to many of the trends in student-centered learning, including personalized learning, project-based learning (PBL), design thinking, authentic assessment, deeper learning, and learning for mastery, among others. We rely on the ideas and research of key thought leaders in education, including a few emerging voices, as well as on the practical experiences of teachers and school leaders in our global networks. We both believe strongly that educational practitioners need to lead the way to educational transformation more than policymakers or theorists. Everyone we've interviewed has real practice in common, including our foreword author, Ron Berger. We have relied most on their experiences to support our model because they were working toward inclusive prosperity and student protagonism long before we designed our landscape model, and they know what works for kids. Just as we want educators to really listen to and understand the experiences and perspectives of students, we believe that educational progress requires that policymakers really listen to and understand the experiences and perspectives of our best educators.

Part 1 (page 21) provides the foundations for this work, including our purpose, vision, and central principles. In chapter 1 (page 23), we provide an overview of the landscape model that allows readers to gain a holistic sense of our vision, as well as an initial understanding of each element and its interplay with the others. Chapter 2 (page 45) establishes eight foundational principles on which the model is built, a set of principles we believe are essential building blocks or through lines at the heart of our thinking—and the model's successful implementation.

In part 2 (page 63), we explore the implementation of the three elements of the landscape model, providing educators with the theory and practical tools needed to be successful with each. Chapter 3 (page 65) looks at the element of the ecosystem, in which we invite educators to understand, deeply and with a strengths-based lens, the context each student comes from and what they bring into the learning environment, which allows us to define their starting point on the landscape. Chapter 4 (page 93) looks at the element of the horizon, in which educators work with students and their families to determine the short- and long-term goals appropriate for each learner (each student's horizon). The chapter includes a look at issues like implicit bias, which can impact the goal-setting process. Finally, chapter 5 (page 117) explores the element of the pathway, in which educators work with students to co-create a personal (and personalized) learning journey that leverages each student's full self and potential.

See table I.1 (page 17) for the strategies included in this book for each element, and table A.1 (page 262) in the appendix for a thorough look at what each offers.

In part 3 (page 153), we look toward broader potential use of the landscape model and to the future of education. Chapter 6 (page 155) looks at the complexities of assessment with the landscape model, providing tools and strategies for documenting and tracking student growth. Recognizing that all assessment should be authentic and personalized, we also address strategies for the model's

Table I.1: Strategies Included for Each Landscape Model of Learning Element

The Ecosystem	
• Journaling • Iceberg Model of Culture • Cross the Line • Affinity Groups • Brave Space • Empathy Interviews	• Place-Based Learning—Concentric Circles • Virtual Home Visits • Know-Wonder-Learn (KWL) and RAN charting • Question Formulation Technique • Socratic Seminars
The Horizon	
• A Letter to Myself • The Headline of My Year • Storyboards and Vision Boards • WOOP • ANCHOR	• Student-Led Conferences • Portrait of a Graduate • SOAR Model Analysis • Capstone Projects
The Pathway	
• Passion Projects • Affinity Mapping • Design Thinking as a PBL Structure • Student Portfolios • Workshop Model for Skill-Based Disciplines • Student Shadowing	• Student-Centered Iterative Unit Planning • Zone of Proximal Development • Collaborative Protocol for Defining Outcomes • Wise Criticism

use in larger classroom settings. Chapter 7 (page 177) addresses some of the core challenges of implementation in different geographic and cultural contexts, from its use in more traditional academic contexts to its use in economically disenfranchised schools and districts. The chapter's goal is to prepare readers for these challenges and to provide strategies for addressing them. Chapter 8 (page 195) looks at leading long-term school and district transformation, giving school leaders the resources needed to chart their own course toward inclusive prosperity. It includes guiding principles for designing and implementing a professional development plan to equip all educators with the tools and skills needed to manage the landscape approach, including three-year plan development guidance. Chapter 9 (page 235) looks at opportunities for the future of educational transformation, exploring new movements and schools already leading educators toward new—and occasionally ancient—ways of thinking about our common goals and approaches. In the epilogue (page 257), we offer a few last thoughts about why the work of educational transformation is so urgent. Finally, the appendix (page 261) offers a table listing each strategy in part 2.

Our Hopes for This Book

We know that we are educating in a time of standardized expectations in education, and we recognize the challenges that climate creates. This book includes our most radical hopes for the future of education, but it is also grounded in and realistic about what it means to use the landscape model while simultaneously fulfilling broad academic expectations and preparing students for standardized exams, particularly those which serve as gatekeepers to higher education and other high-impact opportunities. It would be irresponsible to create an educational model that ignores the very real demands of university entrance, for example. But we also see pedagogical shifts beginning in the best universities around the world, and we believe that something more personalized is possible and desirable across the K–12 and postsecondary spectrum spectrum. Ivy league universities such as Stanford, Harvard, and the Massachusetts Institute of Technology (MIT) were among the first to start using student-centered strategies such as design thinking, while community colleges and trade schools have long been focused on practical skill building with an apprentice system that looks a lot like student protagonism. Even the temporary elimination of Standardized Achievement Tests (SATs) as a requirement for university entrance during the COVID-19 pandemic, and their replacement with more authentic forms of achievement articulation like student portfolios, is a good sign. Around the world, educators are calling for a new normal post-pandemic, not just a return to the factory line, and we hope the landscape model offers a way to envision what that new normal might include.

We wish to recognize the impact that the COVID-19 pandemic has had on education around the world. We have had many discussions about the way COVID has reshaped educational thinking, including the good (educators and students learning to navigate digital learning more nimbly), the bad (a predominant return to teacher-centered, less collaborative approaches in online learning), and the ugly (the exodus of excellent teachers and the increased disenfranchisement of millions of young people unable to participate in deep learning because of the digital, political, and socioeconomic divide). We both fear the "race to catch up" mindset we see emerging among those facing the worst levels of disenfranchisement, the constant mentions of "learning loss" in the news, and we know the pressure this can cause for students and educators. After all, if almost everyone in the world is behind, are *any* of us really behind?

We both loved the story shared by a middle school teacher in New Mexico, of a Pueblo Indian mother from Kewa Pueblo who chose to pull her two sons out of school completely in March of 2020, at the beginning of the pandemic (G. Tafoya, personal communication, January 7, 2021). She told school leaders that she would be glad to have her sons repeat a year if needed after the pandemic, but that the situation provided a perfect opportunity for her family to focus on the traditions of their culture and ancestry. Instead of trying to push academic content in the middle of the scariest thing many of us have experienced and forcing her children to sit online for hours a day, she helped her sons improve their language skills in Keres and taught them to weave, to farm, to harvest, and to cook—and by doing so, to look to their own culture for the answers they need when life gets hard. For many Indigenous cultures and marginalized communities around the world, such local, place-based learning experiences ensure students see traditional skills and the historical knowledge and experiences of their families as valuable—even more valuable than the kinds of knowledge the SATs prioritize (Getting Smart, eduInnovation, & Teton Science School, 2017). In many communities, such work, more often done in the home than in the schoolhouse, amounts to a decolonization of values that honors the unique goals of specific populations, rather than measuring success against those of the dominant culture.

The authors would love to believe that the COVID-19 pandemic could end up being a chance to get off the hamster wheel and focus education on what matters, as this mother chose to do for her sons. It's impossible for us to predict where education will be by the time this book is published, honestly. But we know that any tragedy can be turned into an opportunity for growth and that our calling as educators is to prepare students for whatever that future might be. If we provide young people with an education based on their strengths, which never limits their possibilities, an education that positions them as protagonists and honors all facets of who they are as learners and people, students will be prepared to thrive in an uncertain and complex world. They might even turn out to be those key protagonists who reshape our collective future for the better.

Reflective Questions

Respond to the following questions alone or with your school team.

- How well do you feel your educational context is addressing the learning needs of students as individuals? If you asked your students how supported and heard they feel, what do you think they might say, and how varied might their answers be?

- How well do you feel your educational context encourages engaged, student-centered practices? To what extent do you use pedagogical strategies that encourage student voice and choice, and where do you see opportunities to increase student agency in your community?

- How inclusive were your own educational experiences? As part of the minority or majority culture, with whatever learning needs or talents you might have had, did you ever experience implicit bias from educators? If so, how did it impact your learning, sense of self, or both?

Takeaways

The following summarizes key ideas from the chapter.

- The landscape model is possible anywhere, and desirable everywhere.
- Inclusive prosperity is about ensuring that every student reaches their highest level of success possible.
- Student protagonism is the heart of equitable and inclusive education.
- Every student has the inherent right to be seen as a full human and treated as such.

Part 1

Understanding the Landscape Model

CHAPTER 1

The Landscape Model's Three Elements

I like to think of the landscape not as a fixed place but as a path that is unwinding before my eyes, under my feet. To see and know a place is a contemplative act. It means emptying our minds and letting what is there, in all its multiplicity and endless variety, come in.

—Gretel Ehrlich

The old model that many of us received as a guide in colleges of education and practical experiences, implicitly or explicitly, has always felt like a racetrack even more than it feels like a factory line, though the factory line has become a more common metaphor because of Ken Robinson's (2016) work. Students line up on a starting line at the start of the school year, engines humming, excited to hit the gas. The school year starts, and the race begins. Nine months later, some race cars are broken on the side of the track and others are stuck in pit row, being fixed by the pit crew. Our hope as teachers is that most have crossed the finish line, able to be promoted to the next race, or rather, grade. This model has always felt lacking for the authors. Firstly, we have never taught a class where every student starts with the same level of performance, the same background knowledge, the same *anything* for that matter. We always felt that we spent more time as teachers with students "in the pit," getting them unstuck, and letting those at the front of the pack move along with minimal support. And if it is true that some students start the year significantly ahead or behind the metaphorical starting line in whatever subject it might be—and one student makes up months and months of learning in a year, while another who started ahead barely moves—how do we honor and measure growth when our starting and ending points are so fixed?

Many educators already recognize that the paradigm of education does not serve students or educators as well as it should. Whether we are in the classroom or the boardroom, we know that children are unique and, as such, shouldn't be treated like race horses. Most educators can tell when the conditions are right for learning just by walking into a classroom space and watching the teacher-student dynamics and learning flow at play. So can most parents and guardians. But for some reason, most educational systems prioritize test results and academic standards over culture and community, over building the kinds of conditions that don't just *allow* for growth, but *spark* it.

The landscape model of learning is our vision of how schools and districts might shift their thinking away from the racetrack model and toward a student-centered design, which leverages student protagonism to ensure inclusive prosperity for all students. We believe that the model offers a different way of thinking about how students move through their learning and how educators might best support success for each of them. In this chapter, we will explore each of the three elements, debunking various myths about education and offering each element as a more inclusive response that addresses and unpacks that myth. See figure 1.1 for a visual of the landscape model.

The Ecosystem

The goal of understanding students' broader context and what they bring into the learning ecosystem is not about judging students by their background or assuming educators know what students are capable of based on, for example, their gender or race. In fact, the goals of this element focus on combating the implicit biases we are often blind to, and learning to see students fully, across multiple facets of their lives: their families, their homes, the values they've grown up with, the way they see themselves, and their aspirations for the future. It's about developing a deep understanding of who students are and what they bring to the classroom, across the spectrum of their experiences and identities, so that we are educating whole human beings, not empty vessels.

The Myth of the Empty Vessel

When we begin to address context, we need to debunk one core myth first: students are not a blank slate, a *tabula rasa* (Locke, 1690/1997) that education serves to fill. In fact, students' prior learning, their family backgrounds, and other aspects of their identity enter the classroom in myriad ways, inevitably impacting each student's learning potential and needs in unique ways. Ultimately, students'

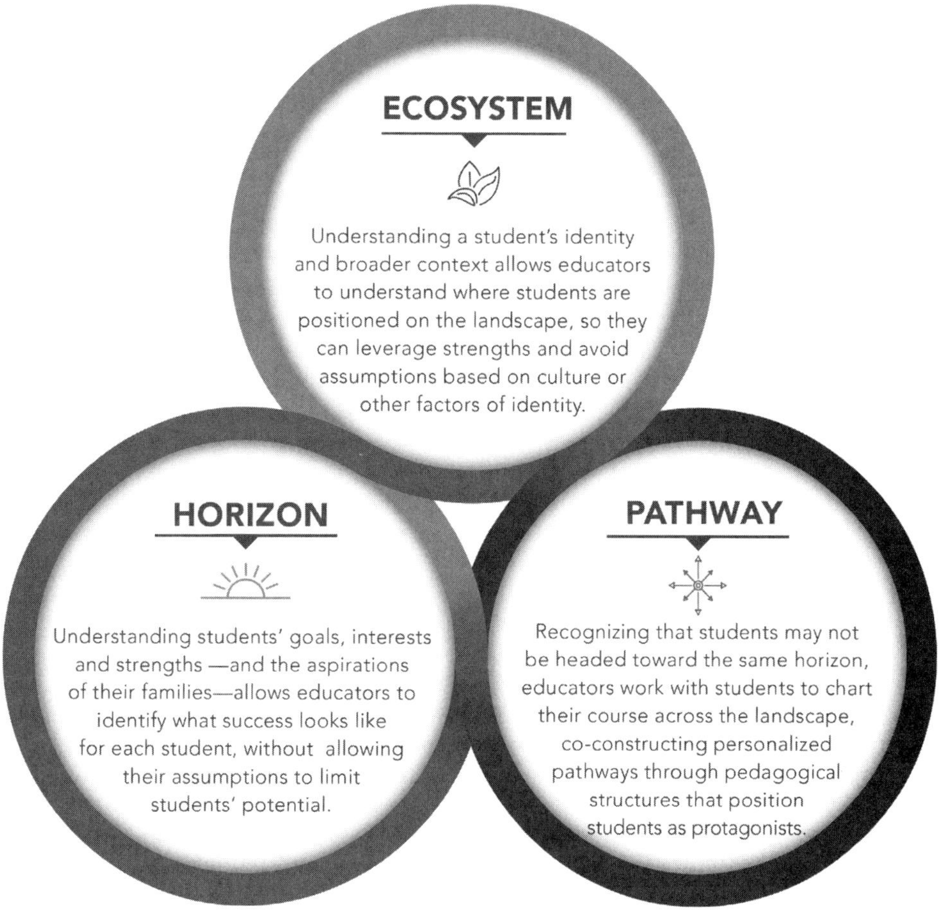

ECOSYSTEM

Understanding a student's identity and broader context allows educators to understand where students are positioned on the landscape, so they can leverage strengths and avoid assumptions based on culture or other factors of identity.

HORIZON

Understanding students' goals, interests and strengths —and the aspirations of their families—allows educators to identify what success looks like for each student, without allowing their assumptions to limit students' potential.

PATHWAY

Recognizing that students may not be headed toward the same horizon, educators work with students to chart their course across the landscape, co-constructing personalized pathways through pedagogical structures that position students as protagonists.

Figure 1.1: Visual of the landscape model of learning.

race, family cultures, religious orientations, languages spoken at home, gender identity, sexual orientations, and socioeconomic class will influence their learning, often as much as their cognitive strengths and challenges (Ibe et al., 2018). Whether those influences are positive or negative is not the point. Because students don't leave their identities at the door when they enter our classrooms, it behooves us to do all we can to understand students' contexts, so we can understand where they are starting on the landscape.

What It Means to Understand the Broader Context Students Bring to the Ecosystem

Given that students are not a tabula rasa, *understanding the broader context students bring to the learning ecosystem* means understanding what each student brings into the schoolhouse, knowing each student as a person, and knowing the individuality and the context he, she, or they bring from groups the student belongs to or identifies with (family, race, ethnicity, religion, and so on).

The following sections explore culture, socioeconomic status, and sex and gender, but these are just starting points of identity and those experiences that create a context for students on the landscape. In the Hawaiian language, this idea is articulated as *makawalu*. This word, which literally means *eight eyes*, captures the concept that all situations must be explored through multiple lenses and dimensions, and it extends this concept to explore the interconnectedness of all life. When practicing *makawalu*, one must engage in the critique of assumptions. Questions one asks include: Does someone else see this same situation differently? And what is an observation of fact and what are the inferences I am making? Most importantly, *makawalu* asks us to engage in the platinum rule. If the *golden rule* is to do to others what *you* would want done to you, the *platinum rule* is to do to others what *they* would want done to them (Alessandra & O'Connor, 1996).

The platinum rule and *makawalu* ask us to think about the context that others bring into a situation and to consider it as we make decisions. They capture the essence of the element of understanding the broader context students bring to the ecosystem. As shepherds of learning, educators must understand the many dimensions of their students' contexts and understand how those dimensions connect, interact, and shape them as learners on the landscape.

PERSPECTIVES ON INCLUSIVE VALUES
The Platinum Rule

At Gimnasio Los Caobos, just outside of Bogotá, Colombia, Jennifer was able to shift school culture significantly through use of the platinum rule, particularly when it came to all community members understanding each other's lives and identities more fully and accurately. On first presenting the concept to the faculty, Jennifer found that teachers were confused about how to implement it, particularly the religion teachers who had been teaching the golden rule their entire careers. In fact, several immediately objected to the shift, asking how they would ever know enough about students to know how each student wished to be treated.

Jennifer's enthusiastic response, "You'll have to ask them," elicited an epiphany for most educators in the room, and the faculty ended up in a powerful conversation about increasing their dialogue with students, parents, and each other, in order to understand each other more fully. This led to additional work around asking good questions and building safe classrooms where students would be comfortable answering. Over the course of the first year of implementation, Caobos saw far more of this kind of understanding-context dialogue, including attempts at courageous conversations in many classrooms. In particular, the religion

> teachers developed a whole new curriculum to teach the new concept. A 360° diagnostic evaluation of student life the following year, which surveyed all stakeholder groups with questions about all aspects of the school, indicated that the majority of students felt their teachers understood and supported them.

Culture

Culture is a significant lens through which all people experience the world. Our personal lens is our reality, but it's often not the same reality those around us share, says Tara O'Neill, director of the STEMS² Masters in the College of Education at the University of Hawai'i at Mānoa (personal communication, November 11, 2021). This dissonance causes misunderstandings of intention that can lead to ineffective (or wrong) educational choices. For example, ignoring the student with the pose and look of the farmer in the portrait in the following story ignores an opportunity to check in on a student's social-emotional well-being and make a genuine connection. These intercultural differences are a central challenge for any international educator working with students of different nationalities, and often working outside of their own culture themselves, given that their success with students and parents depends on accurately reading cultural cues—and responding accordingly. But these differences can be just as acute in any classroom where the educator doesn't share the culture or experiences of his, her, or their students. Researchers such as Gloria Ladson-Billings (1994, 2014) show how culture can impact not just how students see themselves, but also the degree to which they achieve in school. Culturally responsive teaching has been studied in multiple settings, showing conclusively that addressing culture explicitly, be it the culture of the student or the culture of the place, does support learning success (Ladson-Billings, 1994, 2014).

PERSPECTIVES ON CULTURE
The Power of Multiple Lenses

Hanging behind Kapono's desk in Cairo, Egypt, at the American International School in Egypt, is a painting of an Egyptian farmer, his head cocked slightly to the left, held gently in his hand. It is a gaze of longing and fondness, it seems, until Kapono shared this assumption with an Egyptian colleague. "No," replied the colleague, "This man is not looking at something longingly. He has the weight of the world on his shoulders. He is waiting for someone to ask, 'What's wrong?'" A simple pose shares a message in one culture that is significantly different than

> one might assume in another. What lenses are we seeing our students through? What lenses are our students seeing schooling through? How does culture color their expectations and experiences, and how might our cultural lens shape our facilitation and delivery of learning? The strategies embedded in the landscape model will help readers address these important questions.

Educators can understand and address intercultural differences through the lenses of *culturally responsive teaching*, a pedagogy Ladson-Billings (1994) pioneered and Geneva Gay (2018) championed. Culturally responsive teaching, the practice of explicitly leveraging culture in teaching and learning experiences, recognizes the importance of including a student's cultural reference points and experiences in their schooling, and as such is a powerful lens to understand and leverage culture to positively impact student success.

Culturally responsive teaching includes seven key elements (Ladson-Billings, 1994, 2021). The two most important tenets to building an understanding of students' broader context on the landscape are learning within the context of culture and culturally mediated instruction.

Learning within the context of culture is most important when a student's culture does not correspond to the prevailing cultural norms of the school. Students who come from many Indigenous and non-Western cultures, for example, may enter a typical North American classroom and find the individual work style foreign and isolating. Culturally responsive teaching asks us to learn about the culture of all students present and ensure that different learning styles are available. When styles clash, the norms of the classroom culture are made explicit, allowing students to know the rules of the learning game, so to speak.

Instruction that is culturally mediated means incorporating and integrating diverse ways of knowing and understanding into learning experiences. Different from learning in the context of a culture, this tenet asks educators to expose all learners to diverse ways of knowing. For example, a culturally mediated second-grade science classroom studying interdependence would naturally incorporate content from the prescribed curriculum. However, it could *also* include an exploration of interdependence from the perspective of Indigenous people in the area, whether or not Indigenous students are present. Similarly, the learning might also include the voices and perspectives of modern Korean environmental activists, whether or not there are Korean students in the classroom.

Socioeconomic Status

Culture is just one aspect of the broader context students bring into the learning ecosystem with them. Socioeconomic status is another. It is not hyperbole to say that the income level of a student's parents can help us accurately predict their SAT scores—one of many reasons high-stakes standardized tests are a detriment to the educational process. In fact, studies show that over 21 percent of a student's SAT score can be attributed to their socioeconomic status (Meyer & Benavot, 2013; Sackett et al., 2012).

Students from low socioeconomic status are up to twice as likely to display learning-related behavior problems (Islam & Khan, 2017). While in some cases these can be attributed to a learning disability, in many cases these learning-related behaviors are not hardwired into the brain or predetermined at birth but are an addressable product of the availability of resources. Research by Tuba Seçgin and Semra Sungur (2020) and Paul Tough (2014) clearly attributes lower phonological awareness to low socioeconomic status experiences from birth through lower elementary, and research shows these gaps exist before children enter school. These studies show that the phonological gap is real but caused by economic status rather than an innate ability (or inability). Research also shows long-lasting effects of low socioeconomic status on students, with low socioeconomic status linked to problems with memory and social-emotional processing that in turn lead to lower income and poor health in adulthood (Seçgin & Sungur, 2020; Tough, 2014). On a basic level, socioeconomic status differences signal differences in the availability of resources and, as such, suggest that not all students will be able to turn in "pretty" work unless equitable resources are provided in the classroom. It is clear that students' socioeconomic dimension plays a major role in where they start on the landscape—but in a just world, it should play no role in where they arrive.

Sex and Gender

Sex and gender are other major contextual pieces to explore. Each student's sex and gender come with them to the landscape, impacting the student's starting place and ability to move through learning experiences. PhD candidate Page Regan explains it this way:

> Simplified, sex and gender are different components of human identity and experience. Sex refers to a medical assignment at birth based on anatomy and chromosomes including male, female or intersex. Gender is an inner, cognitive sense of being a man, woman, or other gender. Gender is expressed or communicated to others through mannerisms, clothing, demeanor, behavior, and the adoption of social roles often

> characterized as masculine or feminine. While gender is socially considered to be binary—either man or woman, masculine or feminine—the interrelationship between sex, gender, and expression is expansive and manifests differently across culture, place, and individual experience. Common terms to refer to gender include cisgender, transgender, and nonbinary; however, terminology is consistently changing and evolving. (personal communication, April 19, 2022)

In fact, sex and gender are our primary filter as students enter school. We try to ensure a balance of boys and girls in a classroom, we often line up students to go to recess with boys or girls first, and we reinforce gender norms through assigning colors such as pink to girls and blue to boys (Nduagbo, 2020).

These gender assignments, and the assumptions that come with them, pose significant dangers in an educational setting. Girls, for example, continue to be underrepresented in science and mathematics education, which in turn exaggerates their underrepresentation in the labor market (Breda & Napp, 2019). How might this underrepresentation impact a girl on the learning landscape? Sex, gender, and gender expectations also interact with cultural expectations and create stereotypes that create an important context for students on the landscape. *Stereotype threat*, the self-worry of confirming negative stereotypes about a group one belongs to (Steele & Aronson, 1995), impacts girls, for example, by an average of sixty-two points on the SAT. When researchers ask students their sex prior to taking the SAT, girls perform measurably lower than when they are asked to report their sex after taking the test (Breda & Napp, 2019). Stereotype threat, and the doubt and anxiety it creates in the brain, impacts performance.

We can also see this play out in experiments where researchers ask lower elementary students of all genders to draw a picture of a scientist. Almost exclusively, students draw older White men. However, as Herb Lee of the Pacific American Foundation, a nonprofit grounded in Native Hawaiian practice, asserts, when students receive exposure to gender, age, and racially balanced role models—as well as the opportunity to *do* science themselves, rather than just learn *about* science—the same students, when asked to draw a scientist, overwhelmingly draw the scientist looking like themselves (personal communication, August 30, 2014). Teachers in science classrooms around the world use this intervention to bias and stereotype threat with success, and it's an easy intervention to test out yourself.

Understanding students' identities when it comes to gender identity and sexual orientation is much more about creating space for students' own development than it is knowing what a given student's identity *is*. It's not the educator's job to try to figure out what students are still trying to figure out for themselves.

Young people need to choose for themselves when and how they wish to share their orientations with the adults and peers around them, and even well-intentioned attempts to define for or figure out kids' orientations can end in significant harm for LGBTQ+ youth. Whether students come out on their own or are accidentally (or intentionally) "outed" by peers or adults trying to figure out their identity for them, LGBTQ+ youth are among the most vulnerable populations in K–12 education, more likely than their peers to experience increased discrimination, bullying, self-harm, homelessness, and violence (Centers for Disease Control and Prevention, n.d.). Educators using the landscape model use strategies to hold space for students to question and explore their own identities, safely and privately, and work to establish the kinds of relationships that make all students—LGBTQ+ or otherwise—feel safe enough to be themselves without threat.

In the worst cases, schools function, as Regan puts it, "to perpetuate inequalities and an understanding of 'normal,' as opposed to educating" (personal communication, May 4, 2021). As a transgender person who is studying education foundations, policy, and practice, and who is looking to rewrite the norms of education to better support queer youth, Regan finds that too often education doesn't just fail to teach to the students in the room but also may even intentionally try to determine the kinds of people they become—with too little regard for who the child already *is* and might *want* to be (personal communication, May 4, 2021). Espousing an education focused more on creating space for identity development and an understanding of self and others, and grounded in the ideas of critical pedagogues like Paulo Freire and bell hooks, Regan is interested in creating space in education for deep, meaningful reflection and self-awareness, not just academic achievement. The authors believe that the landscape model will help educators understand how to do this across the curriculum.

The Horizon

On better understanding the identities and experiences students bring to their learning, we can define the horizon, or outcomes of education, in a much more personal way. When we define goals *with* and *for* each student as an individual, educators must let go, at least to some degree, of the belief that all students should learn exactly the same content and skills. While we recognize that current educational systems across the world function on the opposite premise and that most countries have developed extensive standards for education as well as myriad standardized exams to validate this form of student achievement, we believe that the system is built on a powerful fallacy: the well-rounded student.

The Myth of the Well-Rounded Student

It is true that schools should expose students to a well-rounded curriculum and a variety of experiences. How does a student know that he, she, or they could become an astronaut if not exposed to aerospace education? Certainly, art class inspires some students to become artists and others to appreciate beauty more, and physical education creates healthy bodies and allows students exposure to sports, games, and theories they would otherwise never be exposed to. But a well-rounded curriculum is not the same as a well-rounded person. Students are not carbon copies of each other. They come varied in their talents and aspirations—as they should.

The well-rounded student doesn't go to Harvard Law or Juilliard, nor to vocational school to become a top mechanic or a successful farmer, turning soil and sun into food. So, is there a value in specialization? Should we have schools that specialize in performing arts like Juilliard, or schools that specialize in engineering like Massachusetts Institute of Technology? We think most people would say, "Of course, how would we educate the next generations of artists, farmers, educators, and doctors?" The authors would say that yes, there is always a value to specialized schools, and that in fact *all* schools should create space for specialization at *all* ages, for students to make choices that allow them to leverage their passions and talents. This doesn't mean ignoring what our systems insist all students need to know and the guiding curricular documents we've created to achieve that learning, nor does it mean avoiding the way exposure to new experiences can help students discover new interests, but it does mean recognizing that the budding artist may not need all the same mathematics skills as the future engineer.

As the academic, author, speaker, professor of education, and self-proclaimed educational antagonist Yong Zhao (2021) calls it, students have *jagged profiles* in that they have multitudes of experiences and diverse qualities, which offer a way to leverage strengths, interests, passions, and innate talents. If it is true that not all of us will make it to the NBA, then it is certainly true we all have a different *horizon*. But the jagged profile is not just for the high school senior. It is as much for the toddler, the middle schooler, and the adult learner. Zhao (2021) tells his story of failing to live up to the goal of his education in his childhood in China. Judged by his ability to farm rice, Zhao was considered a failure. His success only came into focus when he was able to change his own horizon, becoming a celebrated educational thinker and author many times over. The profile of a successful rice farmer, a valued and needed profession, is different from that of a successful author and educator. The profile of a happy kindergartener who can't sit still, who needs to move as part of the learning process, is different from that of a classmate who may be enthralled by sitting and drawing for hours on end. Both students deserve a well-rounded curriculum and exposure to many experiences. But both students also deserve to be happy, fulfilled, and successful, be it as a rice farmer, author, mechanic, lawyer, artist, or athlete.

Ultimately, the landscape model makes it possible to set goals and design learning experiences that *do* still meet the expectations of the systems educators currently live and work in, wherever we may be. As technology changes the face of education, however, it's no longer clear whether all students must take algebra, to name just one example, given that computers can manage complex equations more accurately and quickly than humans ever will. Whatever your answer when it comes to algebra or any discipline impacted by automation, we hope you will make more time for the personalized educational profile, the jagged profile that honors each student's context and builds toward their highest potential.

What It Means to Define the Horizon

We chose to use the word *horizon* to represent each student's potential and how that potential growth is mapped in a strengths-based way that is culturally and cognitively responsive but never limiting. At the core, this image comes from the work of Sarah Lewis (2014), who looks across the history of great artists, writers, and thinkers, as well as following the Vassar College women's archery team and other groups that practice tirelessly toward excellence, to understand the nature of the search for mastery. Using the metaphor of Utah's Salt Flats, Lewis (2014) describes absolute mastery not as perfection, but as a limitless horizon people strive toward their whole lives:

> Mastery requires endurance . . . Mastery is . . . not the same as success—an event-based victory based on a peak point, a punctuated moment in time. Mastery is not merely a commitment to a goal, but to a curved-line, constant pursuit. (pp. 7–8)

When we write of defining a student's horizon, we hope that educators envision a landscape that evokes the "curved-line, constant pursuit" Lewis (2014) references: any flat, open space where the horizon is visually limitless and beyond definition, even appearing to recede farther into the distance as we approach. While this image can elicit frustration, suggesting that mastery is basically unattainable, anyone who has learned to play an instrument or speak a new language from scratch knows the importance of progress across a lifetime of practice. The point is not to make the horizon feel eternally unreachable, but to recognize that our students' horizons should be as *limitless* as possible. This element is all about how we might build systems and strategies that support students' aspirations for growth.

When it comes to classroom practices, there are many strategies that can help make students' horizons less limited, less restricted by educators' often incomplete perceptions of what students are capable of. The first and most important step for educators is to unpack their own implicit biases about students' capacities; as they do so, they are better able to adjust systems in their instruction and classroom management that might be excluding particular individuals or groups. Becki Cohn-Vargas and Dorothy M. Steele (2015) make this point clear, outlining the importance of identity-safe classrooms, and stressing the importance of cultivating a sense of belonging in schools. Through an identity-safe classroom we are able to remove these perceived limits, extending the horizon for all students. We trust that the majority of educators don't want to believe they're working from within systemic inequities that have created biases that direct their choices. We trust that most educators believe all students are capable of their own unique form of greatness. But we also know that many educators are far from unpacking their understanding of bias and that all teachers and their students are better for it when they learn to do so. Markus Appel and Nicole Kronberger (2012) make a clear argument for this, asserting that anxiety stemming from ignored implicit bias impacts student performance in testing, and certainly compounds over time.

Individual Horizons and Peaks

Jennifer remembers an eye-opening moment she had while running a mock interview with a colleague for a school she was designing while studying to become a principal. Jennifer had written a vision statement about an inner-city learning community that recognized and lifted every student, a school that erased the social injustices and limitations of the society around it. But when asked what kinds of writing she might teach in her lower-income, inner-city high school classroom, the mock interviewee answered that these students would need to learn to write job applications. She was a perfectly well-intentioned, high-quality teacher, and her private school students loved her in part because she challenged them. But she set the bar so low for these lower-income, inner-city students that she would only have limited students in that context, never teaching them the kind of high-level writing and thinking required for a college education or a professional future. We believe that the horizon is about each student's limitless potential, and that defining goals needs to start with students' own aspirations, not teachers' assumptions. Here, student protagonism helps us ensure that our work toward students' individual horizons is designed in ways that leverage what we know about them from understanding what they bring into the learning ecosystem.

From Kapono's background, the Native Hawaiian saying *kulia i ka nu'u*, meaning to strive for the highest peak, captures another way to explore the horizon. The current educational paradigm is to set outcomes for all students that are the same, while *kulia i ka nu'u* means to challenge oneself to the highest personal peak of excellence. This then demands that we set goals that are relevant, attainable, and challenging for each student. Is that fair? Does this mean lowering standards? To understand this saying and all it implies, it's important to consider the educator who takes pride in the number of students who fail. Many of us have been that teacher at one point in our career, or have at least worked with that teacher, who boasts about how rigorous their class is, bragging that "half of my students don't make it out with a passing grade!" It wasn't until Kapono was exposed to the work of the Perception Institute that he truly grasped the potential damage of rigor-as-outcome and how measuring success as progress toward the horizon and toward personal peaks can powerfully transform education.

Whether the image is one of a salt flat or the jagged peak of a mountain, the idea is that each person has not only his, her, or their own *path* but also his, her, or their own *destination*. Defining our horizon does not mean lowering standards. It does mean providing both high challenges and high support. It is both the limitless potential of the curved horizon and the striving for the highest peak at the same time. It is allowing for different students to strive for different peaks, and to make room for a jagged profile of our graduates.

The Pathway

There are many paths to success. We know this in our own lives: some of us find success on the sports field, others as musicians or artists, while others navigate the traditional classroom with ease. Educators and philosophers of different generations have made this point, that learners don't all follow the same path; they move through learning in a myriad of ways. Some have written about different types of intelligences. Others have advocated for differentiated degree programs, splitting vocational education from a university pathway, for example. When we standardize education, we force all students toward the same goals regardless of the broader context they bring into the learning ecosystem. Instead, the pathway refers to how the student makes their way toward the horizon; it is the personalized path that allows them to succeed on the landscape.

The Myth of Standardization

Standardization of education was sparked by movements such as the United States' federal No Child Left Behind Act (2002) and Race to the Top (USDE,

2009), and the U.K.'s Education Reform Act (1988), in an effort to ensure consistency in educational outcomes across a given district, state or province, or country. As the movement gained traction inside the United States, its influence rippled across the world, bolstered by international accountability systems such as the Programme for International Student Assessment (PISA), which collects data from eighty-eight countries as of 2022 and offers achievement comparisons across countries. Sir Ken Robinson (2016) points out that social and personal factors motivated standardization, but that most efforts to standardize have hurt education more than they've helped. Ironically, the standards movement was intended to improve educational equality by ensuring all students received the same learning and reached their potential, but its impact has been to further highlight the inequities caused by shoving all students of a given age onto the same racetrack.

Unfortunately, the more standardized the curriculum, the less it fits the needs of students as individuals. Even the *Race to the Top* title elicits the imagery of the racetrack, the very model the authors are trying to deconstruct. While the authors understand the urge to standardize, and the increased efficiency it can create, we do not believe it is a good thing for students as varied, complex human beings with myriad experiences, strengths, and challenges. In fact, we see standardization as dehumanizing. As Robinson (2016) puts it, ". . . people don't come in standard versions," and only some areas of education lend themselves to standardization (p. 160). In fact, "Many of the most important developments that schools should be encouraging do not [lend themselves to standardization]" (Robinson, 2016, p. 160). Furthermore, he describes the standards movement as favoring direct instruction and multiple-choice assessment, and as skeptical of portfolios, open-book tests, and other, more authentic demonstrations of learning.

What does it look like for educators and institutions to plan with the landscape in mind, seeking whatever highest level of success is possible with each student? The foundation of our answer lies in the belief that simplifying our planning down to a narrow, standardized pathway is rarely good for students. Yes, it can take more time and work to chart the pathway in a deeply personalized way, and yes, we may need to organize teachers' time and priorities differently in order to accomplish it, particularly in larger classrooms. But the reality is that educators around the world are already combating the myth of standardization every time they step outside the government curriculum to provide a student with what he, she, or they need as an individual. We can standardize the goals to some degree, but when and how each student reaches said goals and communicates their learning best is anything but standard.

We believe that the key factor for success is to position students as protagonists in their own learning journey. Deep student protagonism is more than students talking for a minute or two about their learning during traditional conferences, or occasionally having teacher-controlled, limited choice; it's about involving students as central actors in all we do in schools, so that their motivation is intrinsic and their learning is personalized. When we explore the pathway from where students are in the ecosystem to the horizon they're working toward, student protagonism—and the pedagogies to support it—will be key.

What It Means to Chart the Pathway

How do we plan for students to be the protagonists of their learning so that motivation is intrinsic and learning is personalized? Planning with this in mind allows us to acknowledge reality and for a personal learning journey to take shape, even in the context of a traditional school unit, which allows all students to reach their own highest levels of success. While educators will be centrally involved at every step, and will need to establish personal milestones and checkpoints with students at regular intervals throughout the year, positioning students as protagonists in their own learning means letting them lead their own growth on the pathway from where they are to the horizon they aspire to reach.

Some terms educators should explore here are *student choice*, *voice*, and *agency*. *Student choice* refers to providing students with some say in their education, allowing the educator to hear from them, and for the students to make key choices in their learning, in many cases like an old-fashioned "choose your own adventure" book. The book is written, the chapters are set, but readers can choose path A or B, determining their own outcome. This metaphor may be a bit simplistic, but it captures the typical implementation of *choice*, which is generally limited and teacher controlled. *Voice* is another, slightly more elevated form of student protagonism in which students have a voice in the workings of their classroom and school—but it is still a lesser form of protagonism than agency, as there are far too many examples of tokenistic voice. It is only minimally impactful for a student government, for example, to be allowed to voice their opinion in selecting the theme of prom (albeit important to most teenagers), but for the administrators to ignore them when it comes to more pressing issues of school governance. The following section addresses what we really mean by student agency, which we use intentionally as a synonym for protagonism at its highest form. We will also explore personalized learning and culturally responsive teaching as they apply to students' pathways across the landscape.

Student Agency

The best implementation of choice and voice looks like genuine *student agency*, and as such is a core element of the landscape model, what we mean when we use the term *student protagonism*. When it comes to school culture, true *student agency* looks more like students as part of a focus group, rewriting a school mission statement. In the classroom, *student agency* refers to the student acting on the learning with a significant degree of autonomy from the teacher (Taub et al., 2020). Well implemented, strong *student agency* means units are planned, but the outcome of the unit is not set. The student may emerge from the unit with outcomes that were unexpected in the planning stages, and schools that value student agency would deem this a desirable outcome (horizon)—while schools entrenched in standards-based thinking might consider it a "wrong answer" because it's not in the textbook.

One excellent example of student agency comes from Jennifer's experiences as head of school in Colombia. The Gimnasio Los Caobos preparatory school requires students to enroll in two interdisciplinary entrepreneurship projects in high school, in addition to several smaller versions of entrepreneurship projects in elementary and middle school. At each grade level, a slightly different focus is in place: create an enterprise that's environmentally conscientious or even helps reverse the impacts of climate change; create an enterprise that supports human rights, and so on. While students work within teacher-constructed structures to guide their work and all students experience some of the same learning, such as business economics, graphic design, and purpose orientation activities, the businesses they develop are entirely their own. The student who loves coding creates an app; the student who believes in servant leadership creates a nonprofit; the student who wants to provide safety and dignity for displaced people creates temporary housing. In this way, students consistently go beyond the kind of limited voice and choice described earlier, where the end point—and all pathways to it—are teacher prescribed.

An example of powerful student agency happens at Wai'alae School, where Kapono served as head of school and chief education officer. Each year, the Wai'alae fifth-grade class participates in a unit where students pitch a product for production, use that pitch to secure an investment of twenty dollars from friends or family, and then produce and sell their product. That's not the agency part yet, though. After the sales event, and after profits and losses are calculated, students spend the next unit researching nonprofits in their region that they feel are making the most difference, and students (not adults) choose where half of the profits go. But the agency continues. Students invest the other half of the profits annually into a microloan platform where each fifth-grade class manages an ever-growing portfolio of thousands of real dollars that the class then decides how to allocate in microloans in the developing world. The learning happens when the loans are repaid, and even more learning happens when they do not. In this example, student agency—also known as protagonism—is not an afterthought but takes center stage in the learning process.

Ensuring students are protagonists in their own education is about much more than strategies for limited choice; it's about real student agency, and building students' skills as problem finders and solvers, for their lives inside school and beyond. If educators own 90 percent of the creativity and control in a more traditional classroom, as author and learning designer Ackers-Clayton suggests, a school guided by student agency has a culture students own and maintain (personal communication, May 12, 2021). Rohit Kumar is the CEO of the Apni Shala Foundation in India, an organization dedicated to better preparing public schools and educators for the work of deep inclusion by improving social-emotional learning approaches. He consistently takes student agency a step further, focusing not just on skills and strategies but on preparing students by actively involving them in changing the broader systems that create inequities to begin with. In the schools the Apni Shala Foundation works with, making the systems themselves increasingly inclusive, safe, and compassionate is a consistent focus (R. Kumar, personal communication, May 4, 2021). Using the example of girls being bullied by boys outside the restroom on one campus, Kumar describes how students identified the problem not just as the boys' behavior but also the restroom's location. Once the school moved the restroom to a more visible position on campus, the bullying stopped. According to Kumar, most of his teachers come from homes as impoverished as the students, so their work is a collective process of unlearning and re-envisioning what's possible, with student agency at the core. He insists that there are no villains in any given scenario—the problem is the problem, and the goal should be preparing students to change the underlying systems that cause it.

Personalized Learning

The term *personalized learning* may be the closest to capturing the concept of how students move through learning on the pathway. Personalization means starting from the student, knowing what they can do, their strengths and their interests, and facilitating their growth toward their next stage of learning. One mistake people make using this term is interchanging it with the idea of differentiation.

Without legalistic definitions readily available, there is significant disagreement about what these terms mean. Carol Ann Tomlinson (2008, 2017), professor and chair at University of Virginia's Curry School of Education, gives us the most commonly accepted definition of differentiation. She explains it as the modification of five classroom elements: content, process, products, affect, and the learning environment (Tomlinson, 2008, 2017). This differs from how many settings use the term, but for the sake of clarity, we will use Tomlinson's definition in this book. Differentiation starts with the content and skills the curriculum prescribes, and modifies the experience for the student by providing supports or modifications. It is curriculum centered and student friendly. Differentiation is by no means negative, but it is not personalization—and not what we aspire to on the horizon.

As author Tim Kubik (2018) puts it, "Treating learning as a question of personal relationships still tends to assume that teaching is something that adult learners must do for, or manage for, their young learners" (p. 96). Personal learning, on the other hand, as Kubik (2018) describes, is about student agency; it's about students making well-informed decisions, with the support of their teachers, about their pathways and goals. It's about students building a deep sense of personal purpose and managing more of their own learning. While the authors believe that personal learning is what the landscape is best built on, we also recognize that allowing for different ends for different students may feel impossible in many school contexts. As a result, we are choosing to use the term *personalized*. We agree with Kubik (2018) that educators' goal should be to ensure as *personal* a learning experience as possible, albeit with the need to *personalize* toward prescribed curricular ends in many contexts.

Personalized learning starts with the child and asks what their next stage of development is. No educator would say it is efficient to teach to the middle if there was only one child in the middle. Yet the question lingers as to what a teacher teaches and how the teacher determines this. As Zhao (2012, 2021) proposes, the best learning is built from the ground up by students, with teachers, in an evolving role of coworker in learning. Educational coach Susannah Johnson, an emerging voice in individualized learning, asserts that "When we empower learners to own the learning, and we do have to actively ensure they understand that it is their learning journey, we are moving into human development, not just education" (personal communication, January 18, 2022).

For the sake of clarity, the authors will use the term *personalized learning* here to capture this realistic yet aspirational goal: learning should start from what the student *can* do, and the best path forward should involve the student in codesigning the pathway of learning. At this point, educators will likely ask, "Are you telling me that I need to create a lesson for each student in my class? I have twenty-eight of them, and they are all in different places and like different things. How can I personalize for twenty-eight kids?" The answer is in the landscape. Personalization does not mean creating one unit for John, another for Juanita, and another for Ibrahim. The landscape model of learning asks educators to use their professional judgment and guiding documents such as standards (like Common Core State Standards [CCSS], Next Generation Science Standards [NGSS], and the like) to define the boundaries of the landscape.

For example, a unit created for fifth graders to examine how interdependence occurs among plants, animals, and decomposers in the environment is important for all students to engage in (NGSS, n.d.). Educators, scientists, and policymakers agree that interdependence is a key concept. That unit becomes the edges of the landscape. How students navigate through this landscape and explore interdependence is their personalized pathway. Some students may come to the landscape understanding how a garden works. For example, a rural school in Hawai'i serves a demographic of students who are primarily the children of farmers. Leveraging their prior knowledge would be magical for them because farming is such a central part of their lives, an element of identity and previous learning students already bring into the learning ecosystem. Yet, not everyone at the school has grown a plant. Where does the student who has grown up on a farm start on the landscape? Should everyone start from *zero*, assuming no knowledge of how plants grow and their interaction with animals and decomposers? Should we assume knowledge from *all* students? The answer is clearly no to both. This is because we already know that the landscape is the true reality rather than the factory. Mariëtte H. van Loon and colleagues' (2013) research backs up this claim, by highlighting the power of prior knowledge. These researchers show that prior knowledge has a significant impact on learning achievement, further showing that inaccurate prior knowledge is a significant barrier to future learning (van Loon et al., 2013). It is certainly important to take into consideration a student's context of prior knowledge to be successful.

When we start from what students already know and are good at, and understand how far we can take them, charting the pathway ultimately takes student agency to a whole other level. As author and educational philosopher Alfie Kohn (2021) explains, "What matters isn't how well a teacher holds students' attention; it's whether a teacher knows enough about how learning happens to stop being the center of attention." Protagonism is the ultimate evolution of student agency, where the student becomes the main character of their own educational journey.

Student-as-protagonist is not a teacher-free environment. On the contrary. It takes a lot of skill, knowledge, and finesse to guide, nurture, and shepherd learning, as opposed to controlling it. Students-as-protagonists recognize their own agency, and rather than choosing between teacher-presented options A and B, they identify the problem to solve and the potential solution. The protagonist students-as-designers receive training from educators in the tools necessary to ask the right questions, make the right observations, then interpret and infer before framing the right problem, which they then solve. This approach works as well for our earliest learners as for our oldest, with varying degrees of student autonomy according to their age and experience. Whether it is the kindergartener manifesting their own learning journey in student-led conferences, as we discuss in chapter 4 (page 104), or a high school classroom where students are working on a variety of solutions to a core local challenge, pedagogies such as project-based learning and design thinking provide the structures and strategies to allow teachers to scaffold standardized skills and knowledge while still allowing students to walk along different pathways.

Kapono has had the privilege of facilitating in schools embracing design thinking (Hasso Plattner Institute of Design at Stanford University, n.d.) as a core strategy for the student-as-protagonist. *Design thinking* is an iterative problem-solving and solution-creating process that begins with developing empathy, and then leverages a rapid prototyping process to solve complex problems. Stanford University School of Engineering made it popular, and several groups including Lime Design (https://limedesign.ca) and HI FusionED adapted it for education.

At one particular school, a computer science class was learning about 3-D printing and the computer code needed to power the process. Rather than the educator teaching coding or starting by asking all students to print a 3-D bust of their favorite celebrity, the teacher asked students to start with a design-thinking strategy: empathy interviews (Nelsestuen & Smith, 2020). They went out into their school community and talked to people about challenges they faced in their daily lives. Upon returning to the classroom, the students then analyzed these data from the interviews and identified a solvable challenge: one particular staff member had problems getting certain plumbing parts sent to the campus. Delays and backlogs were both financially costly and cost the school time without essential services. The students identified the challenge and went about designing a solution, 3-D printing the parts that the maintenance engineer needed. Students were the drivers, the protagonists of their learning. They still learned the code, they still used the printer, but they did so from a position of intrinsic motivation and heightened agency—and were able to provide a real solution to a real challenge in their community.

Culturally Responsive Teaching

Culturally responsive teaching also provides a lens on how we chart the course. The sixth principle of culturally responsive teaching is reshaping the curriculum (Ladson-Billings, 1994, 2021). The imperative of curricular work is well articulated by professor emerita of language, literacy, and culture Sonia Nieto (1996), who asserts that educators must:

> Take a serious look at their curriculum, pedagogy, retention and tracking policies, testing, hiring practices, and all the other policies and practices that create a school climate that is either empowering or disempowering for those who work and learn there.

Nieto (1996) proposes that educators must look critically at their curriculum to ensure that all students *see themselves* in it and that it supports every student, expanding how they make meaning, build understanding, and develop as learners. On the landscape, this looks like paying attention to the cultures that students bring with them, how those cultures interact, and how they may provide context for learning. A specific example is the idea of seasons as taught in the Common Core standards. Winter, spring, summer, and fall are important concepts that simply don't exist as presented in the standards in certain places close to the equator, and therefore the concepts don't exist in certain cultures (NGSS, n.d.). A culturally responsive version of this standard might look like exploring what role latitude plays in the Hawaiian language having one word for a hot dry season, and another word for a cool wet season, and using this as a starting point to explore seasons in science.

These three elements make up the landscape model. Together, they provide a framework from which we can explore and share strategies that are concrete, tangible, and effective. The authors believe that this deceptively simple reimagining of education, from the racetrack to the landscape, will allow educators to think very differently about education, to see students more fully as individuals, and to see learning as a journey from where students are to where their talents, passions, and real experiences might take them, toward a horizon they've been involved in defining, on a pathway they own as the central protagonists of their learning journeys.

Reflective Questions

Respond to the following questions alone or with your school team.

- How are you already finding ways to get to know your students' broader contexts and understand what they bring into the learning ecosystem with them? What strategies have worked, and how might you learn more about your students' strengths, interests, values, identities, and previous learning experiences?

- How are you already defining learning goals with or for your students? How might you involve students more in that process, and how will you make sure your perceptions don't interfere with establishing a limitless horizon in collaboration with them?
- How are you already personalizing the pathways and supporting your students' need to succeed? How might you involve students more in establishing the pathway through their learning journeys, to make sure each student gets the right supports and challenges along the way?
- How much of your own education resembled what we describe here? How much of it didn't? How did your educational experiences impact your sense of what was possible for you in life?

Takeaways

The following summarizes key ideas from the chapter.

- The landscape model of learning includes three elements that help educators ensure the highest levels of success possible for all students.
- The element of the ecosystem allows educators to understand all of the experiences and identities students bring into the learning ecosystem in order to honor and leverage their whole selves in the learning process.
- The element of the horizon asks educators to co-create goals with students in order to avoid limiting their potential with our own assumptions.
- The element of the pathway asks educators to work with students to establish personal (and personalized) pathways in order to ensure that the learning journey challenges them appropriately.

CHAPTER 2

Eight Guiding Principles

*You cannot teach a man anything;
you can only help him to find it within himself.*

—Galileo Galilei

The landscape model is, in its essence, a set of student-centered strategies that allow educators to build equity and opportunity for all students in ways that meet them where they are. As we authors developed the model, we found ourselves relying on a great deal of shared educational thinking that feels inherent to us but may not be obvious for—or shared by—all readers. At the heart of the model live the following eight guiding principles or through lines, which come from our shared experiences and research, and which we feel are essential to the most effective application of the model.

1. It is false to set up education like a racetrack because students vary in their gifts and needs.

2. The Zone of Proximal Development (Vygotsky Learning Conference, n.d.) serves all students.

3. Inclusive prosperity requires a shift toward consistent asset-based thinking and relationships.

4. Student-centered educational practices are key to guaranteeing student protagonism and multiple pathways for learners.

5. Critical pedagogy asks us to examine and challenge the dominant theory and exist in a reality that accepts multiple lenses.

6. When learning is purposeful and vigorous, students enjoy their education and learn more deeply.

7. It is possible to personalize learning and still ensure success on more traditional measures of that learning.

8. Educators need to believe in every single student, build and maintain a deep, enduring sense of hope and optimism for what's possible, and have the courage to make it happen.

Each principle argues for a pedagogical approach, educational philosophy, or educator mindset that we believe is essential to putting students at the center of their own learning journeys, and ensuring the levels of equity required to establish *inclusive prosperity*. While schools that do not actively pursue all of these educational goals can implement the model with some success, they are key building blocks for equity and protagonism in learning, philosophical and pedagogical through lines we will build on throughout our exploration of implementation in part 2 (page 63). We encourage schools without these tendencies to consider their implementation alongside the landscape model. Refer to the reproducible "Synthesis Tool, Part 1" (page 61) for help planning, and to our exploration of how to develop a three-year plan in chapter 8 (page 225) to see how educators may work several of these principles into their school's long-term strategic planning.

It Is False to Set Up Education Like a Racetrack Because Students Vary in Their Gifts and Needs

While some degree of standardization may be necessary to ensure consistency, over-standardizing your conception of the learning journey hurts all students in some way—and educators feel the fallacy every day in their work.

If you've ever done the famous *cross the line* activity with the questions social justice educator and violence prevention expert Paul Kivel (2002) developed, you'll know that something as nuanced as having more than fifty books in your house growing up will influence your starting place as a learner, as will something more significant like having access to preschool (see more on this protocol in chapter 4, page 93). The absence of such factors has impacts well into adolescence and adulthood, creating skill gaps and, because of them, opportunity gaps as well. Family history, particularly systemic traumas or limitations, also play a major role in academic success, from the Black student whose family has been denied opportunities across generations to the Latina who will be the first in her family to graduate from high school, to the Japanese American who grew up with grandparents who were forced into internment camps, to the closeted transgender student still trying to figure out who they are (Li & Qiu, 2018). Bottom line, we are all different because humans are the sum of our experiences, and what we carry into the classroom will be different as well.

Clearly, we would love to see all students receive the same advantages and opportunities—but recognizing that this is not the case, why do we continue to assume that every student should have the same starting point? And why do we so often make students from disadvantaged backgrounds *feel* their disadvantages the whole way through the race toward that fixed finish line? As educators, when we shift our thinking from racetrack to landscape, it becomes less about who had what or where students *should* be, and more about where each student *is*. In this way, an education built on the landscape model has the potential to recognize and address gaps (if it's even appropriate to use the term *gaps* on the landscape), to foster specific gifts, and to flex to the learning needs of each student—and can do so without making students feel they are perpetually losing a race they were never set up to win.

The Zone of Proximal Development Serves All Students

The *Zone of Proximal Development* (ZPD) is a term the Russian philosopher Lev S. Vygotsky (1978), who proposed that learning happens best in the zone between what a student can do alone, with no assistance, and what a student can do with adult assistance, made popular. In other words, the zone in which learning challenges students (not too easy), but they are still able to do the work themselves with minimal coaching (not too hard). Vygotsky (1978) asserts that this zone is based on the individual student's level, and can be known by the educator through techniques such as conferring and formative assessments that demonstrate progress toward learning objectives, where the educator discovers what the student can currently do and then gleans the student's next stage of development.

While the ZPD is often associated with special education in particular, the authors believe that it serves all students and should be a central through line for educators using the landscape model. We all learn differently because we are different human beings with different minds, and educating on the landscape is all about recognizing where students are and might go next. The ZPD is an overarching theory that helps us do exactly that on the landscape, offering a lens that's useful in all three elements of the model but particularly helpful if we use it to guide planning, as we will explore in chapter 5 (page 117).

- In trying to determine what students bring into the learning ecosystem, the ZPD helps educators understand what students can do without adult support, and what they can do with support.

- In trying to determine the best horizon with students, the ZPD helps educators define a challenging horizon that will create productive struggle but which will not make students feel defeated (Blackburn, 2018).

- In planning and charting out the pathway through learning, the ZPD helps educators make developmentally appropriate choices throughout the learning journey.

By recognizing what students can do now and what they are developmentally ready to do next, educators can work with students to chart a pathway that meets their individual needs, whatever those might be. This approach is just as valuable for the gifted child as for the child struggling with a skill, as it honors where they are and where we might take them next, just as the landscape model is designed to do.

Inclusive Prosperity Requires a Shift Toward Asset-Based Thinking and Relationship Building

Certainly, education needs to include many opportunities for students to fail, struggle, and work toward mastery, and addressing students' weaknesses will always have its place as educators help students learn and grow. But our ability to hook into students' passions and unique qualities is and will always be key to motivating that harder growth. Early educational thought leader Grace Rotzel (1971), who founded The School in Rose Valley in 1929, referred to strengths-based, whole-child education as "developing all of the native capacities of each child, instead of just teaching him to read, write, and gather facts" (p. 3). When educators focus on leveraging students' "native capacities," as Rotzel suggests, we can avoid limiting what's possible for each student in the classroom and can build better relationships with students. Zhao (2021) describes what he calls "deficiency-driven education" in much of his work, in which educators determine learning outcomes, create standardized tests to assess them, and then judge students based on their *deficits* in each, with the focus on "making up for" each deficit. As Zhao (2021) puts it, "There is very little respect for what the student wants, what the student *can* do, or what the student might be good at." As Jennifer (Klein, 2017) explores in *The Global Education Guidebook: Humanizing K–12 Classrooms Worldwide Through Equitable Partnerships*, interactions loaded with deficit-based assumptions only widen the gap between individuals and groups, whereas a focus on finding and understanding assets leads us toward equitable relationships and trust, toward "seeing the essential humanity in others by acknowledging that every person has his or her own complex set of gifts, needs, and hopes" (p. 1).

When educational relationships are grounded in asset thinking instead of deficit thinking, in the *native capacities* Rotzel (1971) describes and other research backs (New York University Steinhardt, 2021), they are more likely to foster positive outcomes for students; conversely, educational systems grounded in deficit thinking are far less likely to do so. Early movements in public education in the United States, such as the alternative schools that emerged in the 1970s and 1980s, struggled against a predominant deficit stereotype that students of color from the inner city needed more structure and almost militarized systems of rules that, according to deficit-based thinking, were not present at home, and most of which were not conducive to personal or academic growth (Langberg, 1993; Mader, 2022). These stereotypes persist for marginalized populations across the United States; a multiyear study of just under three thousand students in Tennessee finds that preschool programs with inflexible, deficit-based approaches to working with poor children significantly reduces the learning benefits of offering a preK experience at all (Mader, 2022).

Early U.S. alternative schools show that students from the inner city who were protagonists, able to rewrite the rules of society inside their schoolhouses, were more successful academically (Langberg, 1993). Arnold Langberg (1993), one of the most important thought leaders in alternative education in the United States, and founder of the second alternative school in the country, consistently found that students from inner-city and socioeconomically disadvantaged backgrounds thrived more in flexible school cultures that fostered trust, autonomy, and relationships, though he recognized that it took time for educators and students to unlearn their previous experiences. Sadly, we still model many intervention-based schools in U.S. neighborhoods of color around the same concepts of control and dominance because of the incorrect and broadly held belief that marginalized students need more structure. A central tenet in project-based learning and expeditionary learning is that "when teachers step back, students step up" (Klein, n.d.), and PBL schools have demonstrated this truth across socioeconomics and geography. But if educators never trust students enough to step back, they will never see what their students are capable of.

Additionally, research clearly supports the connection between relationships and learning (Sparks, 2019; Waterford.org, 2019). Students who feel the adults at school believe in them—and who are able to build healthy, constructive, and honest relationships with those adults—will always be more successful. A 2019 analysis of forty-six studies confirms that strong teacher-student relationships have a direct correlation with short- and long-term improvements in nearly every area that matters, from student academic engagement to grades, even after controlling for differences in students' backgrounds (Sparks, 2019). Further, students will generally be more prone to work hard, more resilient when they face challenges or setbacks, and more likely to take risks in their learning if the teachers who educate them see, understand, and honor their full selves.

There are different types of relationships, however, and not all directly benefit students' learning processes. Victoria Theisen-Homer's (2018) research finds a tendency for *instrumentally focused relationships* among educators in low-income schools, in which teachers hold a position of power over students and expect compliance, and a propensity for *reciprocally focused relationships* among educators in high-income, predominantly White institutions, in which students and educators share power and work together (Theisen-Homer, 2018). The former offers only a one-way relationship, which Theisen-Homer (2018) describes as "structured as a controlled means to a particular end: student compliance," while students in reciprocally focused relationships with their teachers "not only learned to think for themselves, but also had adults who affirmed and responded to their thoughts and experiences" (as cited in Sparks, 2019).

As educators, we have all taught students who push our buttons or challenge our patience, but on a basic level, the landscape model requires that we build reciprocal relationships with every student, and that our work with them be grounded in all they do well and are capable of doing better.

Student-Centered Educational Practices Are Key

A growing body of research suggests that student-centered educational practices significantly increase student engagement and motivation through authentic learning experiences, which in turn improve student outcomes. Two aggregated studies that Terada (2021) cites on the effectiveness of project-based learning, which involved over six thousand students in over one hundred U.S. schools, half of whom came from lower-income households, found that "project-based learning is an effective strategy for all students, outperforming traditional curricula not only for high-achieving students, but across grade levels and racial and socioeconomic groups." These results were consistent in both the study of PBL-style Advanced Placement courses in high school, which found that students from low-income backgrounds performed as well as their wealthier peers; and in a study of science education in the elementary years, which found that elementary students in PBL classrooms consistently outperformed their counterparts in traditional science classrooms, regardless of their reading skills, race, and socioeconomic class (as cited in Terada, 2021).

Where protagonism is the goal, strategies such as PBL and design thinking allow educators to build structures for student voice and choice, real-world roles, problem solving, and other elements that ensure personalization and student agency during the learning process. These approaches address core content standards through multiple pathways, and we achieve both individual and group mastery through strategies that ensure motivation and engagement through the relevance, authenticity, and complexity of the real-world challenges each project addresses. Pedagogical structures such as project-based learning and design thinking make it easier, with practice, for educators from preK through higher education to personalize learning according to passions and strengths while still meeting standards and working on areas of challenge, and for students to be protagonists in their own growth and learning.

Student-centered approaches also offer educators specific ways to manage personalized learning down multiple pathways in larger classrooms. Besides the obvious impact, that engaged students of all ages are generally easier to teach, student-centered educators find that students develop autonomy and self-management skills when they take on significant challenges and feel empowered as learners, particularly as they unlearn the more compliance-based systems they may have experienced previously (Taub et al., 2020). While these approaches can require more initial planning from educators, in order to ensure alignment to standards, the development of skills, and the use of processes that support high-quality work, managing student-centered learning is certainly easier than trying to keep a large class of any age engaged in a teacher-centered lecture—and is much more effective at building deep, transferable, *lasting* skills and knowledge in a personalized way.

Critical Pedagogy Asks Us to Challenge the Dominant Theory and Exist in a Reality That Accepts Multiple Lenses

Also playing a key role in the landscape model is *critical pedagogy* (Freire, 1968/2000; see also Aksakalli, 2018), the lens through which we challenge the existing and predominant educational models that were designed with a one-size-fits-all approach that does *not* fit all members of the human family in any context. Critical pedagogy invites us as a society to understand how the dominant views of *reality* in a given context impact how we build our systems, in this case our educational systems. In that sense, educators need to ensure that they are well versed in using multiple lenses when they seek to understand students' broader contexts, lives, and daily realities. Just as important, educators who know how to employ critical pedagogy can teach students to understand reality from a multitude of perspectives.

Critical pedagogy requires educators to understand and dismantle systems of education built by the dominant group when those systems actively work against the success of all students. Critical pedagogues ask us to recognize the very different nature of reality each human experiences, inviting the intentional transformation of learning experiences to ensure those differences are understood (Aksakalli, 2018). Freire (1968/2000) notes throughout his work that most education is designed like a bank, with educators depositing knowledge in their students' minds with little critical thinking or dialogue, a practice which maintains the status quo and avoids any need to recognize the essential humanity and varied experiences of the students. In his groundbreaking *Pedagogy of the Oppressed*, Freire (1968/2000) insists that only an education founded in dialogue, reflection, and "problem-posing" can avoid perpetuating oppressive systems and is therefore essential to the liberation of any person being oppressed or dehumanized by elements of their reality:

> In problem-posing education, people develop their power to perceive critically *the way they exist* in the world *with which* and *in which* they find themselves; they come to see the world not as a static reality, but as a reality in process, in transformation. (p. 64)

Freire (1968/2000) calls the result of such an education the development of *conscientização*, meaning that students learn to "perceive social, political, and economic contradictions, and to take action against the oppressive elements of reality" (p. 17). The authors believe that the use of critical pedagogy is central for educators and students, both in marginalized communities and those with more wealth and opportunity. On the landscape, critical pedagogy helps educators understand what students carry into the learning ecosystem with them, and being able to view reality from their students' eyes will help educators work with them to define appropriate horizons and pathways with less bias. Part of the goal of student protagonism is the development of such consciousness in students as well, so that they can be part of rebuilding systems that limit them and their communities.

The *engaged pedagogy* espoused by bell hooks (1994), which she describes as "education as the practice of freedom" (p. 13), focuses on socioeconomic class and its impact on values, attitudes, and biases. Inspired by Freire's (1968/2000) and Thích Nhất Hạnh's (1994) work, hooks (1994) encourages educators to teach from the heart as much as the mind (as cited in Specia & Osman, 2015). She writes, "To teach in a manner that respects and cares for the souls of our students is essential if we are to provide the necessary conditions where learning can most deeply and intimately begin" (hooks, 1994, p. 13). Such recognition of the need to care for and cultivate students' *souls* is a deeply humanizing way of interpreting critical pedagogy, one which requires entering the reality of students and honoring their actual lived experience and full selves. Not only is this practice essential to students' growth toward freedom but it's also key to providing learning experiences that serve *all* students' needs and to creating the conditions for deep and meaningful learning.

Educating through a lens of critical pedagogy also requires us to deconstruct the savior mindset of many educators. While the urge to "save" comes from a very real place of compassion and love, it also suggests that the students they're saving cannot decide for themselves how to solve their own challenges, which is deeply dehumanizing. For example, when teachers from privileged backgrounds work in marginalized communities, which happens with thousands of young college graduates every year, many believe their goal is to prepare students to *leave* their communities, to get out of their contexts to something these teachers perceive as better. But as author and learning designer Jill Ackers-Clayton points out, leaving the neighborhood *isn't* necessarily the student's or family's goal, who call that neighborhood home and want to see it improve and thrive (personal communication, May 12, 2021). As Jennifer (Klein, 2017) suggests in *The Global Education Guidebook*, being educated by someone who thinks you need saving turns students into "empty vessels who can only survive with the outsiders' solutions, not whole people with multifaceted lives and their own ideas about how to improve their communities" (p. 6). The authors believe that better things happen for students when educators really understand and value the communities young people come from, and empower students to actively solve the problems their communities face, rather than seeing themselves as saviors whose goal is to rescue students from their contexts.

When Learning Is Purposeful and Vigorous, Students Enjoy Their Education and Learn More Deeply

Too often, educators try to convince students that the purpose of their learning will be clear to them later, after college; or, they motivate students by leaning on the claim that students will need good grades to get into college. Any of us who grew up as "escape artists," personalities who cleverly avoid what they don't find immediately engaging and relevant, rather than using our intelligence to do the task at hand, know how little motivation these approaches offer. It is hard—if not impossible—to motivate a disengaged third grader through the threat of college entrance exams, for example. Ultimately, students and educators need to know *why* they're learning what they're learning, to know why it *matters*—to them, to their classroom, to their school, and to their broader local and global communities in the moment (Belet, 2017). That only happens when students have chances to challenge themselves in meaningful ways and apply what they're learning authentically and purposefully. And teachers can only develop relevant, meaningful challenges and establish appropriate horizons if they understand their students' broader contexts.

Furthermore, education around the world claims a correlation between education and suffering; we often fear there is a lack of academic *rigor* when we don't see the *drill and kill* of more traditional learning environments (Klein, 2016, 2018). This is not to say that education should never include hard work or frustration; in fact, student-centered learning will probably invite *more* challenge and therefore more frustration than traditional models, as it's designed to do so. Struggle can be productive. As education professors Tesha Sengupta-Irving and Priyanka Agarwal (2017) explore, finding the right amount of struggle, in the student's Zone of Proximal Development, truly accelerates learning. And *productive struggle*, which lies between scaffolding and support, provides additional ideas about how we might challenge each student in constructive ways (Blackburn, 2018). Perhaps even more importantly, if educators approach learning as a *vigorous* experience rather than a *rigorous* one, an education founded in energy and vitality more than stiffness and inflexibility, they can create an education all students enjoy and one in which students invest deep effort in their own growth.

PERSPECTIVES ON WORD CHOICE
Vigor Versus Rigor

There is a persistent use of the word *rigor* to describe educational practices that support high levels of challenge and achievement. We talk about rigorous learning constantly, perhaps without even realizing how problematic this word really is. *Rigor*, derived from Latin, is rigidity, firmness, or severity in the treatment and fulfillment of norms, and translates as *stiffness, inflexibility,* or *rigidity*. When we envision a rigorous education using the word's actual meaning, it's not such a great image for students. In the authors' opinion, an education that's stiff and inflexible is exactly what creates the need for extrinsic motivators and complex systems of compliance and discipline to curb behavioral issues (Klein, 2020). This is not to say that consequences should never exist, but that a rigorous education sounds unappealing and may not motivate all students to love and invest energy in their own learning process.

Jennifer writes often about why educators need to replace the word *rigor* with the word *vigor* when we talk about school. *Vigor*, also from Latin,

> describes the internal force or energy of a living thing, as well as effort, energy, or enthusiasm; it translates as *being full of life* or *lively*. A lively, energetic education that engages our internal forces as humans sounds much more like one students would invest time and energy into—and one educators would probably enjoy more, too. A vigorous education reaches just as high as *rigor* in terms of achievement, if not higher, because the motivation for excellence that *vigor* suggests comes from students' own internal energy and enthusiasm. It is the kind of education that might even make kids leap out of bed in the morning, excited about the journey, and that they might talk about at the kitchen table over dinner. And instead of expecting every student to fit into an inflexible system, *vigor* evokes the landscape, where we always strive for success but with a recognition of who students really are, where they hope to go in life, and how we might go there together. As Jennifer (Klein, 2020) writes on the topic, "Rigor may lead to episodic successes . . . but mastery is a lifelong pursuit, one pursued with vigor and enthusiasm and passion by those who are committed to their own growth."

Author and inspirational speaker Simon Sinek (2009, 2018) uses corporations to explain how poorly—and briefly—extrinsic rewards like salary play in job performance or company loyalty. He describes his now famous "golden circle" analogy, pointing out that most corporations focus on the outer circles of *what* they do and *how* they do it, but that only the innermost circle inspires loyalty and intrinsic motivation—*why* they do it:

> Knowing your WHY is not the only way to be successful, but is the only way to maintain a lasting success and have a greater blend of innovation and flexibility. When a WHY goes fuzzy, it becomes much more difficult to maintain the growth, loyalty and inspiration that helped drive the original success. By difficult, I mean that manipulation rather than inspiration fast becomes the strategy of choice to motivate behavior. This is effective in the short term but comes with a high cost in the long term. (Sinek, 2009, p. 50)

When we apply this logic to schooling, most traditional education does exactly the same: we focus on *what* students need to learn, and *how* we need to teach it, but we rarely address *why* beyond that cursory "you'll need it later" logic. Without the *why*, education becomes about short-term compliance, not deep, long-term engagement with ideas and growth; in education, this is the "high cost in the long term" that Sinek (2009) identifies. Just like employees will work for the money when there is no *why* they connect to, students will do their work for the grade and adult approval (extrinsic motivation), not their own learning. If you ask your children why they're doing what their homework includes, and the answer is "because the teacher told us to," it's a sign your children have little or no sense of the purpose behind that learning—which also suggests they will be unlikely to remember it for long or transfer that learning to other contexts.

A purposeful education is one that ties learning experiences to the world beyond the schoolhouse, which asks why about *everything*, and which fosters student motivation through authenticity, complexity, and relevance. Purpose isn't antithetical to joy, either; if anything, students who understand the *why* behind their learning tend to see themselves as protagonists and work from an intrinsic sense of self-motivation—which in itself is a more joyful orientation. Ultimately, an engaging, enjoyable education where all students thrive is not mutually exclusive to deep learning; in fact, the authors believe they are mutually dependent.

It Is Possible to Personalize Learning and Still Ensure Success on More Traditional Measures

We encourage use of the landscape model with full recognition of the current educational climate and the challenges more traditional systems pose, particularly when it comes to the gatekeepers of opportunity and higher education. Traditional gatekeepers include the designers at the College Board who determine educational priorities through the SATs; educational ministries that develop national exams, often administered across multiple grade levels, in nearly every country in the world; the Programme for International Student Assessment (PISA), which seeks to aggregate educational data globally; and any university admissions team offering access to higher education through merit-based scholarships that rely only on traditional demonstrations of learning and success. Given this, we consistently address how more traditional expectations can be met through the landscape model, including but not limited to the role of standards, benchmarks, disciplinary frameworks, and the essential skills our times require.

Much of the perceived battle between content and skills begins with the use of the term *soft skills* to describe what are really the *essential* skills of our times. Yes, it's more difficult to standardize the measurement of a student's soft skills in collaboration, creativity, or critical thinking, but only in the sense that educators have to think differently, beyond the "right or wrong answer" mentality many have grown to trust too much (Wagner, 2009; Wagner & Dintersmith 2016). When we explore what university and business leaders are looking for, we can see how essential these skills really are (Bauer-Wolf, 2019; Wagner & Dintersmith, 2016). In fact, given that students can find just about any piece of information online, critical thinking and the ability to distinguish lies from facts—and the urge to dig deeper into a given "truth" in order to understand it from a variety of perspectives—has become even more important than the content itself. We believe these are *survival* skills, and that a given learning experience can and should include skills alongside content, even if standardized tests do little to measure such skills.

We also want students to be as well equipped as possible to articulate their learning in many forms and contexts, whether that's on the authentic assessments we create inside the schoolhouse or on the standardized exams that will get them that scholarship, internship, or next opportunity. But we also want them to be able to *live* and *use* their learning, and that requires equipping them with the skills that set them up for a lifetime of inclusive prosperity. This means that educators need to find a middle path that allows them to take small steps toward the landscape now, a middle path where students still learn content alongside essential skills, and where students are educated in authentic, skill-based ways while they also learn to articulate their learning on more standardized assessments. We can't wait for these broader systems to change before we do what's best for our students. While we authors work to change the broader systems, we remain committed to helping educators personalize learning and increase student protagonism while still meeting the more traditional academic expectations of the moment.

Educators Need to Believe in Every Student, Build and Maintain a Sense of Hope and Optimism, and Have the Courage to Make It Happen

The conversations we've had with educational thought leaders brought us to several core conclusions, the most important of which have more to do with our hearts than our academic goals. Educators who transform students' lives "believe that our work is not merely to share information but to share in the intellectual and spiritual growth of our students" (hooks, 1994, p. 13). It is a very specific teacher profile, really, if hard to demonstrate clearly in an interview, and anyone who calls education their calling has at least some of it. It's an orientation toward hope, optimism, and courage, with an implicit belief in the ability of every student to grow when we create the right conditions in our classrooms and schools.

As authors Debbie Silver, Jack C. Berckemeyer, and Judith Baenen (2015) frame it, "When individuals decide to become teachers, they enter an unbreakable pact with the future. They promise to do the best they can with what they have and with what they know in order to mold successfully the next generation" (p. 5). That very act of deciding to become an educator, they insist, is in itself an act of optimism and hope. Kumar of the Apni Shala Foundation also believes that the best educators have an intense belief in the potential of children, and they use all the resources available, as creatively as they need to, in order to ensure the results that they want to see. He says this of board members and administrators as much as classroom teachers, citing genuine, deep commitment as the most important quality of inclusive communities (personal communication, May 4, 2021).

Regan, whose studies focus on critical pedagogy through the lens of LGBTQ+ students, believes that hope is another essential ingredient. Many studies find that hope—or lack thereof—has a direct impact on academic achievement (Yoon et al., 2015). Regan states:

> It's critical that I have hope for humans as loving, and thinking, and communal, and capable, and intellectual, and brilliant. . . . That hope is critical, or I'm just going to go in circles and be exhausted and take years off my life. So for me, the future of education starts with critical hope that so much is possible through education. (personal communication, May 4, 2021)

The authors couldn't agree more, as so much of our process writing this book relied on our collective hope for what's possible in and through education. If the only things educators can see are challenges, roadblocks, and broken or ill-conceived systems, and we let that drive our work, we will educate from a place of deficit rather than opportunity and limit students' horizons through our own disillusion. That won't be good for students, teachers, administrators, or families. Only when we have hope can we envision and work toward inclusive prosperity.

But hope without courage may not lead to the sorts of transformative work we need to see in schools, and which the landscape model encourages. And d'Erizans at the Millennial School also believes that education requires a great deal of courage if we actually want to see it improve:

> To really make things happen, you have to be courageous, having some difficult conversations or pushing some paradigms. And that can look small, and it can look big. . . . It could be a small conversation, or making inroads with a parent, or rethinking what inclusion means in the classroom. Being courageous is about questioning your own assumptions, or questioning other people's assumptions. (personal communication, June 1, 2021)

Many educators already embody these broader tendencies of hope, optimism, and courage, focusing on the whole child whether or not they've been formally trained to do so. We have all learned with and from an educator like this at least once in our lives, and the best educators channel their educational memories into best practices in their own classrooms. As hooks (1994) writes:

> I have always been most inspired by those teachers who have had the courage to transgress those boundaries that would confine each pupil to a rote, assembly-line approach to learning. Such teachers approach students with the will and desire to respond to our unique beings, even if the situation does not allow the full emergence of a relationship based on mutual recognition. Yet the possibility of such recognition is always present. (p. 13)

Every strategy explored in this book hinges on that recognition, on that willingness to respond to each student as an individual, and on the embodiment of joy, optimism, hope, and courage in all we do.

PERSPECTIVES ON WORD CHOICE
Teacher Versus Educator

Early in Jennifer's career, she taught a closeted gay student in a conservative country and school, a young man who had already attempted suicide three times before he entered her tenth-grade classroom. Through courageous conversations on identity and constant space for safe written reflection, Jennifer built an environment that helped him find his way out of the closet. Many years later, when his father thanked Jennifer for helping his son at age sixteen, he made a distinction that's been a guiding philosophy for Jennifer ever since. There is a difference between a *teacher*, he told her, who teaches a subject area, and an *educator* who sees, fosters, and supports the growth and well-being of the whole student.

Reflective Questions

Respond to the following questions alone or with your school team.

- Which of the eight principles best reflect the way you currently view education and your work with students, whatever your role? Which principles offer a new perspective you find helpful, and why?
- Which of these principles are lived values in your school community? Do any of them elicit resistance? If yes, where have you (or might you) encounter resistance, and why?
- How might you help encourage colleagues and families in your community to see value in these principles? Who are your allies,

and how might you leverage their commitment to get more of your community to buy into these principles?

- Were any of these principles at play in your own education? Explain why or why not. How did their presence—or absence—impact your educational experiences?

Takeaways

The following summarizes key ideas from the chapter.

- While embracing all eight principles is not a prerequisite for success on the landscape, they are through lines that support its successful implementation.
- All eight principles position students in the center of their own learning journeys and honor who they are as individuals and members of groups.
- Research supports these principles as the building blocks of meaningful, engaging, and equitable educational experiences that encourage student growth.

Synthesis Tool, Part 1

Use this reproducible to capture core insights and help with planning toward implementation of the landscape model. Please explore the following questions as you reflect, ideally in small leadership or faculty teams.

- Which elements of the landscape model, as chapter 1 (page 23) defines, does your school or classroom already use and to what degree? How well do you believe they are working, and do they serve all students?

- Which elements of the landscape model are not in use already in your classroom or school? How receptive do you believe your community will be to their implementation?

- Which principles from chapter 2 (page 45) align to the mission, vision, and values of your school? How might you leverage those connections to spark growth?

- Which principles feel most challenging in light of the mission, vision, and values of your school? How might you develop commitment to those ideals?

- Who might resist these shifts, and how might you develop commitment across the community?

- Who are the core allies, early adopters, and other champions already in your community, who you might leverage to ensure success with this work?

- What next steps do you need to take as a team and individually? How will you monitor implementation?

The Landscape Model of Learning © 2022 Solution Tree Press • SolutionTree.com
Visit **go.SolutionTree.com/diversityandequity** to download this free reproducible.

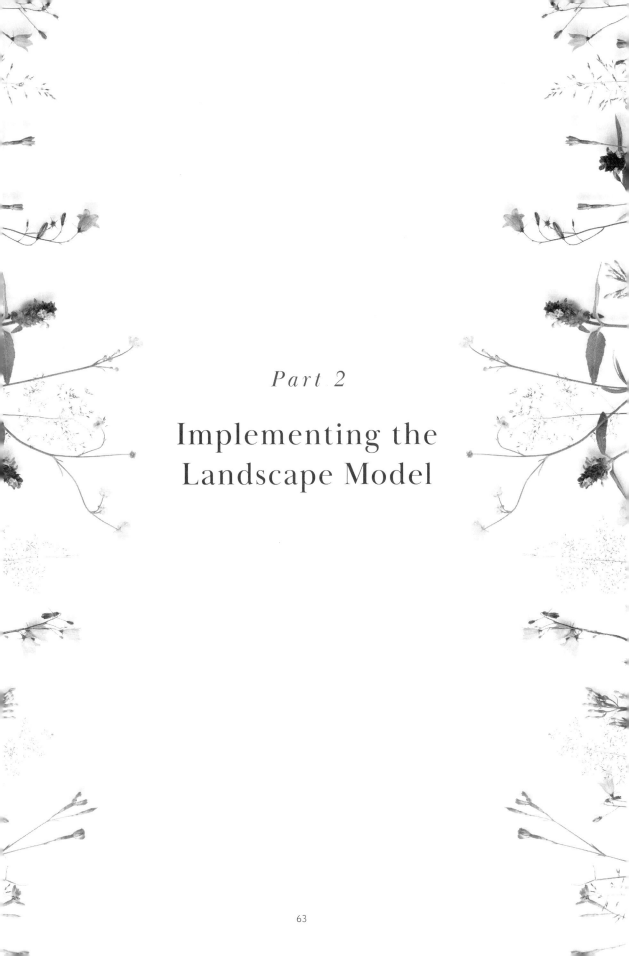

Part 2

Implementing the Landscape Model

CHAPTER 3

The Ecosystem

This debris of historical trauma, family trauma, you know, stuff that can kill your spirit, is actually raw material to make things with and to build a bridge. You can use those materials to build a bridge over that which would destroy you.

—Joy Harjo

All educators naturally pick up on elements of students' broader home contexts when they enter the learning ecosystem for the first time, through signals as subtle as the quality of a student's clothing or backpack, and as obvious as how well they speak the language of instruction. In Latin American countries with uniforms in common use, students' shoes still give away their socioeconomic status the moment they enter the classroom. Educators tend to focus first on getting to know students in the context of the disciplines they teach, using quizzes and other measures to check on previous learning of content and skills. Most educators naturally *want* to understand their students' cultures, identities, and backgrounds as well. Whether they can always accomplish this, however, is another question.

Developing a deep, meaningful sense of students' context outside of school that allows educators to build for and leverage each student's strengths and background is a lofty goal on which the rest of the landscape model depends. The educator's exploration of student context is much more than a survey of grades received in different subject areas and much more than a conversation with their previous advisor or homeroom teacher. It is an understanding that requires meaningful conversations, careful work to recognize and overcome deficit thinking, a great deal of intercultural savvy in some contexts, and, above all, an authentic curiosity to understand each student. But we don't believe it's impossible to accomplish, even in larger schools, and this chapter provides the tools to make it possible.

Jennifer recalls working with a White principal at a predominantly White institution early in her career, who struggled with understanding the very different contexts his scholarship students, largely students of color, came from. After years of workshops and conferences on diversity and inclusivity, it was a visit to the home of two Latina sisters that shifted his view of the students. He had previously considered the students "smart but lazy," and he believed the stream of uncles, aunts, and cousins at school events belied a lack of commitment from the girls' parents. However, the visit showed him that the girls had set up a homework space in their family bathroom, the only room with the quiet and privacy they needed, as they lived in a small multigenerational home with several members of their extended family. He also discovered the commitment they and their family had for high-level learning and for the scholarship their girls had earned, which they knew would open doors for the future of their family. During that visit, the principal discovered that extended family members knew the history of the school he led, that they clearly wanted to be a part of that history, and that they stepped in whenever the girls' parents couldn't attend because of their work schedules. How this principal led the education of these young women changed completely after this visit, and for the better, as it came from a less deficit-based assumption about their motivations. Instead, the principal's approaches began to come from an asset lens, a more authentic understanding of their home and lives, as well as their support and potential.

An in-person home visit may not be possible for every student or family, but the example helps illustrate how much more we can learn about students when we connect with their home and community. Regardless, your goal is to understand students' contexts from within an asset lens and to gather information that helps you determine what each student brings to the landscape of classroom and curriculum. Your goal is to understand as much as you can about their prior learning, their cognitive gifts and challenges, their family cultures, languages, socioeconomic circumstances, race, religion, and other dimensions of identity, all of which play a key role in learning. Gather this information not to label or track, but to respond to the whole student in your classroom and to open space for their rightful presence in your learning community.

This chapter discusses several goals at the core of understanding what students bring into the learning ecosystem, and for each we offer corresponding strategies that will help educators accomplish those goals. The goals include holding space for identity development, which serves the dual purpose of helping students understand themselves and helping educators know how students see themselves; integrating students' broader contexts into learning units, which focuses on leveraging students' strengths in the learning experiences we design; and developing inquiry to understand where students are in the learning ecosystem so that educators can establish appropriate horizons and pathways.

Holding Space for Identity Development

One tool for growing our understanding of context as educators is to simply ask. There are many ways to ask, and asking does take skill. Identity is personal, and to call out certain elements of identity can be easier or harder for different people in certain settings, depending most on the skill of managing open dialogue. As a result, inventories and surveys, while only a first step, have an important place in understanding a student's broader context. Inventory resources like the following can help students and educators better understand their strengths. (Visit **go.SolutionTree.com/diversityandequity** to access live links to the websites mentioned in this book.)

- **CliftonStrengths** (Gallup, n.d.; formerly StrengthsFinder; https://bit.ly/3yat4dV) helps identify specific talents in the domains of execution, influence, relationship, and strategy. It ranks strengths in order to give respondents a clear picture of each student's potential which, according to the tool, leads to greater performance.

- **DiSC** (www.discprofile.com)—short for dominance, influence, steadiness, and conscientiousness (Marston 1928/2015)—helps respondents gain a sense of their personal style in teamwork, communication, and productivity.

- **The Kiersey Temperament Sorter** (Kiersey, n.d.; www.keirsey.com) identifies individuals' core personality traits and, by extension, their dominant temperaments. True Colors (www.truecolorsintl.com/what-is-true-colors) is an interactive activity, an adaptation of the Keirsey Temperament Sorter.

While many inventories are psychometrically validated to ensure they are valid and reliable, a start-of-the-year questionnaire is a simple, homegrown way to ask about interests, experiences, strengths, and areas of growth. It can be a similarly powerful starting place for educators and students to build context before they jump into the content of learning, without the cost of purchasing a third-party tool. Pausing and taking the time to engage in these protocols almost always pay dividends in time and energy later.

But it is not just a question of creating a questionnaire and having students fill in boxes about themselves, either; it's about weaving the search for understanding into many learning opportunities. Regan, who was beginning to understand their nonbinary identity as a teenager, recalls a point in their education when they sensed their teachers were attempting to be responsive to their identity with a check box. They saw their professors "thinking that knowing the language [of their students] amounted to knowing how to truly meet students where they are" (personal communication, May 4, 2021). Regan has since had time to reflect and identified strategies that are most important in helping an educator learn about the context of the students while simultaneously helping the student to develop their own identity in a genuine and healthy way (personal communication, May 4, 2021).

For LGBTQ+ students in particular, Regan feels that an educator's goals shouldn't necessarily be to dig into students' identities or to try to figure out who is LGBTQ+; it should simply be to create a safe space for students to understand *themselves*. Doing so is often as simple as offering time for written reflection, through small-group dialogue and journaling. It also means holding space for multiple identities by, for example, offering non-gendered feedback on student work. For example, non-gendered feedback might mean responding to a student's use of *they* to describe a love interest with "It's fine if you want to be vague here, but consider being more specific about gender so the reader can see the love interest more easily, whatever their gender." As chapter 1 (page 30) explores, LGBTQ+ youth are particularly at risk of bullying, violence, homelessness, and even self-harm, so outing students should never be the goal—on the landscape or otherwise (CDC, n.d.). Instead, when educators hold space for identity development, LGBTQ+ youth often build the confidence needed to come out by their own choice, and are better equipped to handle the challenges which arise as a result. When the classroom is an affirming environment instead of a threatening one, LGBTQ+ students—and frankly all students—are more easily able to manifest and live as their true selves (Youth.gov, n.d.). See GLSEN (www.glsen.org) for information and resources that identify how educators can support LGBTQ+ students.

PERSPECTIVES ON DEFINING THE HORIZON
Testimonial by Sandra Chapman

Sandra Chapman is an educator, leader, facilitator, and equity consultant.

I'm a collectivist. Simply put, my cultural orientation is toward the group, not the self. Since I was born, I have been learning about equality, inequality, marginalization, and dominance. Yet, I still have a rudimentary understanding of systems of oppression. I say *rudimentary* because things are constantly changing. The following is an example of the importance of an analysis of bias that aids my solidarity work and teaching with people of all types of social identities. I am a light brown-skinned queer and racially Black Latina who is a cisgender woman. I experience racism, homophobia, and sexism. However, I don't experience the kind of fear and threat that a darker-skinned (colorism) Black (racism) transgender (transphobia) woman (sexism) would.

School is one place where students receive exposure to a dominant cultural approach. The presence or absence of culture in classroom life impacts children's sense of self and their learning opportunities (YWCA Minneapolis, 2021). Teachers, who are also products of their culture, rely on patterns that are culturally relevant, meaning that they make sense to the person delivering the content. Our cultural patterns determine what is of value and who is or isn't falling in line. When educators operate from an unexamined cultural pattern, they may attempt to fix what is perceived to be cultural deficits in students, believing that the sooner students assimilate into the patterns of behavior that the dominant school culture praises, the sooner they will reach cognitive, social, academic, and emotional success. Instead, this creates cultural discontinuity for students rather than a learning environment that affirms and sustains the child's unique cultural identity.

The development of self begins in infancy and continues into late adolescence and adulthood. Two factors influence students' self-concepts (DeDonno & Fagan, 2013).

1. **Familial:** These include parents, siblings, and extended family and strengthen students' sense of self—including racial, ethnic, and cultural identity—through a socialization process that involves the gradual acquisition of cultural values and patterns of behavior. For students of color, there are explicit family practices that encourage racial-ethnic and cultural pride.

2. **Nonfamilial:** These include school, peers, and community and also have an impact on students.

Both factors can contribute to positive, negative, or neutral messages that, over time, begin to inform students' individual and group identity and the feelings, thoughts, and stance toward self, their own social groups, and the groups to which they do not belong. In addition to these two external factors, there exist other conditions that affect how students learn, develop, and relate to others.

Race and racism are organizing principles in the United States, and this is seen in overt and covert ways in our educational system (Budhia, 2017). Through an anti-bias and anti-racist pedagogy, teachers actively engage in developing and shifting their own mindsets while simultaneously creating lessons and opportunities that attend to anti-bias educational goals. One aspect of anti-bias education is the development of cultural competency and cultural intelligence. A teacher who exhibits an understanding of culture as different and not negative and is developing their cultural archival knowledge about groups of people is able to effectively adapt to culturally based situations and interactions.

Cultural intelligence, then, is the awareness, knowledge, energy, and actions (Ren-Etta Sullivan, 2016) a teacher employs when encountering cross-cultural differences. Instead of seeing students as inherently lacking in a particular skill set, a culturally competent educator relies on teacher-efficacy to address the matter. Debra Ren-Etta Sullivan (2016), president of the Praxis Institute for Early Childhood, states, "Teacher efficacy can be defined as a teacher's belief in [her/his/their] ability to successfully affect children's academic performance in spite of any challenges they may face" (p. 68). Specific to race, Ali Michael (2015) coined the term *microproficiencies* to capture the understandings, statements, and actions that members of a privileged group can demonstrate, which support and empower members of the marginalized group. Developing microproficiencies and cultural intelligence takes a lifetime, and this positively contributes to teachers delivering fewer racial and cultural microinsults and microinvalidations toward people of different social identities.

Developing one's cultural knowledge is essential for all teachers, but not for the purpose of "visiting" other people's cultures, such as through holiday celebrations with clothing and food. While these aspects of a person's past and present way of living are relevant, they only address one level of culture, the concrete level, which is visible and tangible (Hidalgo, 1993). What makes it possible for a student to redefine their horizon with each new experience? Well, it is partly due to the adults in the home who contribute what researchers Luis C. Moll, Cathy Amanti, Deborah Neff, and Norma Gonzalez (1992) call *funds of knowledge*. Knowledge is socially constructed, and families have abundant knowledge from which schools can learn. When educators step back from controlling the learning path, they leave room for students to bring forth this family knowledge and define their own horizon, to be fully embraced for the varied identities they have and the ones they are still discovering.

Source: S. Chapman, personal communication, September 26, 2021.

Strategies for Holding Space for Identity Development

Strategies for holding space for identity development include journaling; activities called the iceberg model of culture, cross the line, and brave space; and affinity groups.

Journaling

The simple act of journaling can hold a personal space for identity development. It holds other benefits as well, including boosting self-confidence, honing emotional intelligence, and inspiring creativity (*10 Ways Journaling Benefits Students*, 2020). In schools, educators often think of journaling as either solely academic or solely personal, rarely interweaving the content and concepts of what they teach and learn with personal narrative and reflection. Of course, this oversimplifies the fact that many who might teach English language arts (ELA), or any primary language for that matter, use journaling as a tool for developing the skill of writing and for exploring thoughts and ideas. Project-based learning encourages reflection as a consistent strategy in any student-centered classroom, and journaling is an obvious place to house written reflections. Though educators often relegate journaling to the language arts, the authors feel that schools can and should use journaling as a reflective tool across all courses, and good journals can include any combination of academic learning and personal exploration, according to the needs of the moment. Using journaling for identity development in the context of academics is something we develop over time, successfully creating a space in time and on paper for students to develop and share their identity. Consider using a journaling protocol specifically for identity development, ideally as it connects to their growth in target disciplines. While this may stand out as awkward or odd in the context of a chemistry class, for example, we have seen the following formula for academic journaling used successfully in multiple content areas to support context building and identity development.

Keep in mind the following best practices when using this strategy. You can use journaling throughout the school year, particularly for reflection points before and after significant learning experiences like a provocative speaker, activity, empathy interview, or other experience students need to process fully. John Dewey believes that we learn more from reflecting on experience than from an experience itself (as cited in Lagueux, 2014), and the authors encourage regular journaling from grades 1 or 2 up, with age-appropriate questions and expectations.

- **Journaling as part of the learning process and used at regular and predictable intervals:** As we've established, journaling can be valuable at many moments in the learning journey, as it is a core tool for written reflection in any class. Weekly or biweekly journaling helps students come to see reflection as a natural and consistent part of the learning process. Educators can also use journaling as formative evaluation at strategic milestones or checkpoints.

- **Clear expectations for whether the teacher will read every journal entry or not:** In some settings, this is not a private journal, but a space for communication between the teacher and student or between students. In other settings, this can be a private journal and safe space for a student to get things on paper without being assessed or judged. Whatever the case, make sure students understand the expectations before they write. As a high school English teacher, for example, Jennifer allowed students to fold over pages where their reflections got too personal, and students knew she would not read those portions.

- **Clear expectations of the level of response to a journal entry:** This can range from an expectation of a simple one-sentence response that lets the student know their thoughts were read, to in-text feedback to academic content, or even to a full dialogue where the reader replies in depth to help develop conceptual or content knowledge and to support identity development.

- **Questions that are grounded in a concept:** Concepts are broader than content, and are more conceptual than skills. Concepts are ideas like *pattern*, *interdependence*, and *justice*. Concepts can be found in every discipline; for example, the concept of equity can be addressed in social studies (historical social equity and inequity), and literature (equity as explored through text, either informational, fictional, or poetic), and mathematics (exploring the mathematical property of equality, and the difference between equality and equity, or even using statistics to explore issues of quantitative inequity).

- **Questions are posed to students to connect the concept to themselves personally, their family, and (or) their community:** An example of a science question exploring life science and the concept of species interdependence in primary school might go something like the following.

  - *Journal 1*—How are flowers and bugs dependent on each other in a garden?
  - *Journal 2*—How is interdependence in a garden like our school community?
  - *Journal 3*—How is interdependence in a garden like your family?

Through this process of journaling, an educator may get a clearer idea of how a student understands the concepts being learned, as well as giving the student space throughout the unit to explore their own identities and contexts, and to share those thoughts with their teacher. When teachers read their students' journals, it also gives them an opportunity to speak with students more directly about their reflections and identity, and even to sound the alarm with counselors if teachers notice patterns that suggest a student is headed for self-harm or violence toward others. However, there are times when sharing journal entries with the teacher should happen only by the student's choice, particularly if reflection questions hit on sensitive topics. While this choice-based journaling approach may give the teacher less opportunity to learn about students, it provides more opportunity for students to learn about themselves without fear of an adult seeing their writing unless they choose to share. In the authors' experience, the safer students feel to explore their identities in private, the more likely they will begin to share their thoughts more publicly.

The Iceberg Model of Culture

One way to unpack educators' and students' cultural identities is to turn the iceberg model of culture into an interactive activity. First developed by Edward T. Hall (1976), the iceberg model of culture suggests that only 10 percent of a person's culture is external and as such observable, just as we only see 10 percent of an iceberg above the surface of the water. Meanwhile, 90 percent of culture—what Hall (1976) calls *deep culture*—is more internal and difficult to observe, as it lies beneath the surface. Visible culture includes things like dress, food, language, customs, or race, while beneath the surface lie an individual's core values, attitudes, beliefs, priorities, assumptions, and perceptions.

Following is an eight-step activity Jennifer developed for sharing deep culture through the iceberg model. This activity is appropriate for students as young as grades 2 and 3; the older the students, the deeper their understanding of culture and ability to make meaning with the metaphor will be.

1. Ask students to form groups and brainstorm words they think are elements of *culture*.

2. Give each individual student a simple iceberg drawing, with 10 percent above a water line and 90 percent below, but with no words on the sheet.

3. Display an image of the iceberg model, which includes categories of visible and deep culture (Visit https://bit.ly/3HjMu2S for an image of an iceberg model). Talk it through with students, to make sure they understand what we mean by visible and deep culture. If any students feel they don't have a culture, clarify that *family life is culture*, including things like the religion we practice, the foods we like to eat or the daily rituals of our household, and ask them to base their ideas on what is visible and hidden in the things their family cares about.

4. Give students five to ten minutes to fill out their own cultural icebergs, including the elements of culture that people see on the surface, and the elements of their culture that are less visible.

5. Once they've finished, ask "Are there any things above the waterline on your iceberg that are misunderstood by other people sometimes? Are there things below the waterline that feel more important to who you are?"

6. Give students ten to fifteen minutes to journal about their answers to the questions in the fifth step.

7. Have students get into pairs or trios, encouraging them to connect with someone they don't know as well in the class. Have them share their cultural icebergs with each other (five minutes each), to the degree each student is comfortable sharing; make sure all students know they don't have to share everything on their icebergs if elements don't feel comfortable.

8. If necessary, educators can collect iceberg drawings and read journals for deeper learning about how students see themselves and their family, broader culture, or both. A teacher or counselor should address any signs that a student is struggling with his, her, or their identity—not to "fix" anything, but to continue the conversation with the student and help him, her, or them feel heard.

Cross the Line

Kivel (2002) developed and made famous the process he calls *cross the line*. The goal of cross the line is to help participants notice inequities of experience within any given group. The protocol is particularly powerful in diverse contexts because it helps participants visualize the advantages and disadvantages experienced by each group member. The questions are based on a variety of points of privilege and marginalization, from the subtle to the obvious when it comes to how they can impact a student's starting point in the ecosystem. Processes like this one can bring up significant feelings for participants, so as with all interpersonal protocols, training on how to facilitate the process is necessary. Cross the line is most appropriate for high school students, potentially valuable for middle school students if facilitated with support, and not as appropriate with elementary students.

The process, which requires a culturally responsive facilitator, has participants follow two steps.

1. Students line up, shoulder to shoulder, across the middle of a space—sometimes a classroom, sometimes an auditorium, sometimes a field.

2. The facilitator asks participants to take either one step forward in acknowledgment of an indicator that gives them privilege, like having parents who have graduated from university, or take one step backward

to acknowledge an indicator of lack of privilege, like going to bed hungry or seeing people who look like you primarily in service roles in your community or on television.

Specific prompts might include the following options, or educators might choose or adapt questions to ensure relevance to the local context and what they hope to learn about their students (for an excellent list of thirty-eight questions facilitators can choose from, see Westmont College, n.d.).

- If your ancestors were forced to come to this country or forced to relocate from where they were living, either temporarily or permanently, or restricted from living in certain areas, take one step backward.
- If you grew up with people of color or working-class people who were servants, maids, gardeners, or babysitters in your house, take one step forward.
- If you were ever embarrassed or ashamed of your clothes, your house, or your family car when growing up, take one step backward.
- If you studied the history and culture of your ethnic ancestors in elementary and secondary school, take one step forward.
- If you started school speaking a language other than the language of instruction, take one step backward.
- If your family had more than fifty books in the house when you were growing up, take one step forward.

Participants complete the entire exercise in silence; and as the line splits, some participants advance forward and others fall behind. After the last question, the facilitator generally says, "The front wall represents your goals and dreams," maybe college admissions for a senior, for example, and on the count of three, asks participants to race to the wall. Inevitably, those in the first half of the group run, feeling they have a chance at their imaginary goal. And inevitably, those at the back half of the room stay put or try for the wall with little to no effort. While running is not a required step in the protocol, it provides a visceral demonstration of how more disadvantaged students tend to give up when their circumstances make the goal feel unachievable.

Debrief questions can vary, however many facilitators find success with the following questions.

- How are you feeling after this activity? Why?
- What did you experience? What did you observe?

- Which statements were the hardest to answer? Why?
- What surprised you? Why?
- Did you try to run to the finish line? Why or why not?
- How can we apply this activity to our lives?

The debrief is an absolute requirement for cross the line, whether or not facilitators ask the students to run to an invisible finish line. This activity can bring up challenging emotional reactions in students, as well as discomfort with the stark visibility of students' different experiences, made all the more salient when participants realize how far they have to run to get to the same goal as their peers. But what makes this protocol challenging is also what makes it powerful. Facilitators should be prepared to support students as needed, and may want to include a school counselor in the room. It would also be helpful to take an opt-out or challenge-by-choice approach, so that students don't feel forced to share if it gets too uncomfortable.

When Kapono and Jennifer ran the protocol with adults in a workshop at the National Association of Independent Schools (NAIS) People of Color Conference in 2017, we had several women of color pressed against the back wall of the space and a lone White male against the front wall by the end. Instead of having participants run, we asked them to look around—and we did the full debrief from our positions around the room. While uncomfortable for many, the process of unpacking privilege was supported by community norms around privacy, use of "I" statements, and respect for all experiences. However you structure the last steps, cross the line is a powerful process that demands the facilitator be able to engage participants in ongoing discussions of power and privilege, to ensure that those who feel they lack privilege find their power. It is most powerful for peers to understand that privilege is real, and that privilege provides real advantage that is not inherent in the individual, but rather a product of circumstance.

Brave Space

Brave space is a strategy that creates space for honest, brave sharing of students' perspectives and opinions, and as such can give educators a window into students' minds and lives in ways that can help them understand what students bring into the learning ecosystem. Kathy Obear (2013) proposes we evolve from the trauma-addressing practice of *safe space* to a new tool she calls *brave space*. Brave space is meant to foster growth by refocusing dialogue protocols from protecting participants, and shifting those protocols to ask participants to engage in more meaningful and productive ways to push through real issues. For example, brave spaces include inviting in both those who have privilege and those who come from a marginalized identity to participate together in a challenging dialogue.

While protocols such as affinity groups allow for a degree of safety in discussing, for example, issues of race by ensuring that all participants identify the same way, brave space uses facilitation and norms that ensure respectful participation in intentionally diverse situations that may be uncomfortable or connect to conflicts participants are already experiencing. A brave space might be used to help improve communication and respect among third graders who are teasing a peer about his well-worn shoes, among middle schoolers who are using the word *gay* as an insult during recess, or among high school students who are struggling with racial divides during their study of slavery, just to name a few examples. Brave space demands training to facilitate well, as the facilitator helps participants navigate potentially explosive and, by definition, controversial and sensitive issues.

While this activity can be used with adults, students from elementary to university can and should participate in these spaces. Topics and the depth of participation will vary, in part based on the age of participants, and the most productive brave spaces are practiced regularly as a component of a community protocol, such as grade-level meetings or town hall meetings. Schools might consider using this protocol with students to tackle issues of class, for example. A private school with a small proportion of scholarship students might facilitate a dialogue that explores class and privilege including students from all socioeconomic backgrounds. By using norms of participation and skilled facilitation, students would be asked to participate in potentially uncomfortable ways; as with restorative practices and other strategies geared toward deep and potentially difficult dialogue, norms like *leaning into discomfort* allow students to see that discomfort helps move them toward better understanding of and communication with their peers. Brave spaces also give educators a window into students' hearts and minds, helping them understand students' broader contexts and what they bring into the learning ecosystem. While this is more of an approach than a strategy, effective brave spaces prioritize the following (Anti-Defamation League, n.d.).

- Acknowledge privilege.
- Embrace candor as a gift.
- Find ways to respectfully challenge the perspective of others.
- Honor confidentiality.

This is a strategy that pushes out of the realm of academics in significant ways. If used without proper facilitation, there is a risk of asking participants to be "brave" and then causing more damage than growth. For example, having a sensitive discussion around sexual orientation without proper facilitation can leave students emotionally hurt, leading to serious issues of depression and self-harm, particularly if any students are accidentally outed. However, if used correctly, for example when students may have cheated *en masse* on a test or when a major community norm was violated, brave space can and should play a role in holding space for identity development and context building.

Affinity Groups

Educators use affinity groups to bring together people who share a similar identity to provide a shared, safe space for conversations that don't include explaining themselves to people of other identities—and that *do* include shared understandings, experiences, and even perspectives. In the case of schools, affinity groups occur regularly, such as biweekly or monthly meetings, so students know they can count on this space of shared experience when shared challenges arise. This could include affinity groups based on identities of race, ethnicity, gender, sexual orientation, religion, family status, and so on. The groups are designed for group members to participate from the "I" perspective, meaning that to be a part of the group, you must have lived the identity being discussed, and that includes the adult facilitator. It is not a group designed for allies and advocates who support the identity but cannot participate from the "I" perspective. Affinity groups can be run for participants of all ages; while they are more commonly seen in middle and high schools, the authors have seen effective use of affinity groups in upper primary as well.

Affinity groups help build relationships among peers (Columbia Social Work Review, 2020), helping students find others who relate to challenges they believe they are experiencing alone:

> A group of students who share an identity are going to relate to each other in ways they can't with peers who can't or don't understand their experience. It's about safety and, in some cases, about fundamental issues of injustice. (Bell, 2015)

Affinity groups also help students practice agency, especially around identity markers that can leave them feeling marginalized. For example, "Gathering in safe spaces around shared identity allows students to engage in conversations about how they can subvert the structures that push them to the margins" (Bell, 2015). Putting students in charge is an affinity group best practice; if an adult is needed, they must share the identity and should simply be present to support student leaders.

There are many resources available on affinity groups. Most share the following core features.

- **Groups are convened around a single or specific identity element:** You might organize groups around, for example, being an Asian American or being an African American woman.
- **Groups convene around norms of participation:** The group agrees on norms for all group members. Group members co-construct

norms or the facilitator presents them for members of the group to actively agree on.

- **The group may or may not need a facilitator:** This depends on the level of comfort of the participants to self-facilitate, but a facilitator should also be able to speak from the "I" perspective, meaning that the facilitator should always share the same identity as that of students.

- **There can still be spaces for allies:** The group can create spaces for allies (supporters who do not share the identity) in tandem but in a different space and time from the affinity group.

- **Meetings occur regularly:** Affinity groups meet regularly over an extended period and do not report to any external body. The goal and output of the group is the experience itself.

We highly recommend that any school organization interested in beginning affinity group work with students seek training prior to launching them, as they are a powerful and sharp tool that benefits from expert guidance.

Integrating Students' Contexts Into the Classroom

The strategies this section explores come from pedagogical structures like project-based learning and other student-centered practices, and all of them have a common goal: they allow us to understand students' lives and identities because they leverage who students *are* in the learning process. Ackers-Clayton calls on us to consider PBL as a powerful and holistic tool to integrate the understanding of a student's context into the curriculum:

> It's hard to separate . . . project-based learning from the inclusivity piece because the heart of who you *are* is in the work that you do. Everything is personal. Every time the lead touches the paper or your fingers touch keys, it comes from you. We try so hard to separate the human from the work that we've lost the humanity in learning. (personal communication, May 12, 2021)

This chapter expands the concept of PBL to include practices that come from other sources as well, such as design thinking, the engineering design process, and Socratic seminar. Each of these practices, in their own way and with their own strategies, elevates and prioritizes student voice and agency in the learning process and therefore, as Ackers-Clayton reminds us, allows us to see students *through their work*.

Strategies for Integrating Students' Contexts Into the Classroom

This section is not meant to be a how-to for PBL, design thinking, or any of these larger practices; however, several strategies are explained here as a starting point. Strategies for integrating the context into the classroom include empathy interviews, concentric circles (place-based learning), and virtual and in-person home visits.

Empathy Interviews

Design thinking, which you'll recall from earlier in this book, was created by the Hasso Plattner Institute of Design at Stanford University (n.d.) as a tool to spark innovation and to accelerate human-centered design. The empathy interview is one protocol from the design-thinking process that allows participants to explore how simple conversations and observations can inspire actionable opportunities for design (Lucas, 2018). Educators can use the empathy interview to better understand students, and students can use them to better understand each other, and any time they are solving a problem for someone beyond their immediate community.

Educators or students conduct empathy interviews in five steps.

1. **Define a challenge or problem:** The interviewer establishes the primary question that students need to answer, like How might our school encourage healthy eating? How might a student create a more effective study guide for themselves (or a peer)? How might our school community better include and welcome new students?

2. **Create an interview time limit:** Usually, for empathy interviews, the time limit is short—approximately five minutes per interview.

3. **Provide prompts that encourage the interviewee to recount stories:** The interviewer does not ask the design challenge question. For example, if the design challenge is about encouraging healthier eating in the cafeteria, rather than asking "How might we encourage students to eat healthier?" the prompts would be more like, "Tell me a time when you were excited about healthy food . . ." and, "Tell me about a time when you had a hard time controlling your food choices and regretted it."

4. **Avoid asking participants to interpret data during the interview:** The process is meant to build human-centered context around an issue *before* getting to the solution to the challenge.

5. **Reflect on and analyze themes that emerged during the interview:** Once the interview is complete, look back at the notes and start creating themes or buckets to put quotes and ideas into. These themes or buckets will serve as the starting point for the design of a solution.

Best practices for using this strategy are as follows (Lucas, 2018).

- **Establish trust:** Listen patiently, avoid interrupting, and allow pauses to give participants time to think. Use culturally appropriate cues (such as eye contact, nodding, and smiling) to reassure the interviewee that the interviewer is engaged and interested in what they are saying.
- **Get personal stories:** Try to use open-ended questions, such as *why* questions, to prompt stories that are memorable, interesting, motivating, and challenging.
- **Listen:** Let the interviewee lead the exploration. Build questions off what the interviewee says.
- **Capture:** Take notes; practice taking quick notes with key words and highlights; quotations are great for representing the interviewee's point of view.
- **Observe:** Watch for the interviewee's facial expressions, hand gestures, body language, emotions, and reactions—and respond accordingly.

The empathy interview is a specific component of design thinking, but it does not always need to be used as part of the design-thinking process (Hasso Plattner Institute of Design at Stanford University, n.d.). Use it *à la carte* as a tool to build significant understanding of context in multiple situations. It is often used by PBL teachers as part of the problem-solving process, particularly if students are solving for people other than themselves, to help them understand the needs of those they are solving for. If students are designing a playground for another grade level, for example, they will need to conduct empathy interviews to know what those students want out of their playground. The more you practice the empathy interview, the easier and more successful it will be.

Place-Based Learning—Concentric Circles

The concentric circles is a quick exercise Kapono developed for educators to ground their units in a sense of place, which we adapted to use with students. Place-based learning is an important tool that helps ground the act of learning on the landscape. Benefits of place-based learning include increased engagement and skills such as problem solving and creativity (Ormond, 2013; Ross, 2019). While place-based learning is a broader field that we will not explore in detail in this section, its features include the following (Getting Smart, eduInnovation, & Teton Science School, 2017).

- Being learner centered
- Being inquiry based
- Using the community as the classroom
- Starting with an interdisciplinary approach

Place-based learning leverages the power of the group to identify and utilize resources for learning in the community through grounding student learning in a sense of place. Place-based education leverages the assets of a community, and when students come from that community (or even if they don't), it allows students to see learning in context and acknowledge their own environment. Simultaneously it allows the educator to leverage the contexts of the students and community during the learning experience.

Schools use place-based learning in different ways. Many schools have successfully leveraged key community partners and regularly take students to a site to learn *in-situ*. For example, the American International School in Egypt (www.aisegypt.com), through a process like concentric circles, identified a refugee school as a community partner that could support regular visits and learning. Students regularly visit the school, several times a year, engaging in multiple projects that range from traditional service learning, to collaborative academic endeavors.

Concentric circles helps students identify potential partners for learning, both inside and outside the schoolhouse, and is best conducted with the class divided into groups of three or four students each. The goal is to use the following four steps to map resources in the community, near and far, that can serve as context to enrich learning.

1. Students start with a large piece of chart paper and one marker per person.
2. Each group draws three concentric circles on the chart paper.
3. The teacher prompts the group three times, based on the three locations the teacher identifies in the figure.
    a. In the innermost circle, brainstorm and write all community resources you can think of *on your campus* that might support your learning in this unit. (*This unit* is used as a placeholder for whatever topic you choose.) For example, is there a historic or cultural site that is part of your campus? Are there people, like potentially a teacher or staff member, who personally experienced a war? Are there natural features on campus like gardens, streams, and so on?

Are there historic items on campus that can serve as context for learning? Students themselves are resources as well.

b. In the next circle, brainstorm and write all community resources within *walking distance* (or easy transit, if you live in a more rural community) from your campus. Are there businesses that you know will partner with schools? Are there community parks that can be used as learning sites? Are there museums, historical sites, religious buildings, or other sites that can be visited? Are there natural phenomena nearby that can be used for learning, such as streams, lakes, and so on? Are there parents who can be tapped for expertise?

c. In the next circle, brainstorm and write all community resources that you could take a day *field trip* to in your broader community. Are there businesses that you know will partner with schools? Are there community parks that can be used as learning sites? Are there museums, historical sites, religious buildings, or other sites that can be visited? Are there natural phenomena nearby that can be used for learning, such as streams, lakes, and so on?

4. Once the map is complete, take a step back and observe. What's missing? What is most exciting? What connections do you have already? How might these resources help you learn?

See figure 3.1 for a sample concentric circle.

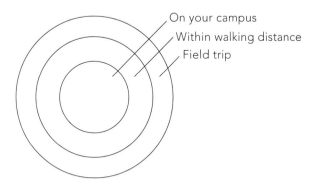

Figure 3.1: Sample concentric circle.

Now that the map is complete, there are several next steps that one can take. Teachers can integrate resources identified into their learning units. Students may leverage resources into their group's projects. They might create and share an enduring list schoolwide. You can modify this strategy several ways, including adding an outer circle to explore national or global resources that students might connect with virtually. In all cases, the list of community partners, learning sites, and people acts as a valuable resource, pointing out the power of the community and the place in which we live.

Virtual and In-Person Home Visits

Home visits are one of the most powerful tools in education. They allow the teacher a direct window into the ecosystem that the student comes from. During home visits, teacher can truly meet the child where he, she, or they come from; probe more deeply to understand culture, family structure, and other important information; and give families a chance to share what they feel are the most important parts of their children's backgrounds.

Most educators never conduct a home visit, yet those who do usually celebrate them as some of the best moments of their year (Wright, Shields, Black, & Waxman, 2018). A home visit takes grace and humility. It takes being vulnerable and understanding the vulnerability of those being visited. Yet when done in a way that honors students and their families by staying focused on assets, home visits can catalyze understanding the context of a student and transform how an educator teaches them and, therefore, how they learn.

The COVID-19 pandemic shifted the practice of home visits significantly, from more traditional in-person visits to more virtual ones. Like traditional home visits, virtual home visits allow a teacher or trusted adult to understand the context of a student's life by visiting the home, albeit in a slightly more limited way. A virtual home visit allows educators to accomplish more visits in a shorter amount of time and with a lower level of intrusiveness, and it does still function as a face-to-face conversation. However, the barriers of technology can hinder virtual visits; whenever possible, families without technological access should receive an in-person home visit so they are not excluded from the process.

Virtual home visits usually begin with an invitation to meet with the teacher and a statement of purpose. In the context of the landscape model of learning, the purpose is to learn about the student's home and family life, but in ways that emphasize their assets. Educators can use home visits with students who are new to the school or at the beginning of each school year. Some schools make visits part of the post-admission process, while others ask teachers to have parents sign up for visits at back-to-school events or use an online platform to facilitate scheduling at any point in the school year.

Visits are generally short—ten- to twenty-minute sessions, depending on the amount of time available. Prompts and questions for use in a virtual home visit might include the following. As appropriate, visiting educators might provide the choice to opt out of more sensitive questions about religion or race, or might send the questions in advance to allow families to think through their answers. If an educator is concerned about addressing a topic with the student's parents, it would be appropriate to talk with previous teachers or counselors first, to understand how best to approach the conversation with a particular family. As we have noted earlier, the topic of a student's gender identity or sexual orientation is *not* an appropriate question for educators to ask parents during these visits—or ever—because not all families are open to the conversation and because accidentally outing the student could result in homelessness or other harm if the parents are not aware or supportive of their child's orientation (youth.gov, n.d.).

- "Tell me about your child's strengths."
- "Tell me about what growth you hope to see in your child this year."
- "What is your child interested in these days? What really gets their attention?"
- "What three words describe your child best? Why?"
- "What languages are spoken at home?"
- "What religion is practiced at home, if any?"
- "What is your child's awareness of race and ethnicity? How do they self-identify?"
- "Is there anything else I should know as your child's teacher that would help me be the most effective educator possible for them?"

Virtual home visits usually end with a statement of gratitude and an invitation to remain in contact. A well-conducted home visit should create lasting connections to the home and build understanding of students' context, which educators can then use to inform their work in the classroom.

Developing Inquiry to Understand Where Students Are in the Learning Ecosystem

Many authors write about inquiry and its many levels. Trevor MacKenzie (2016) clearly outlines the different stages of inquiry, which range from a higher level of teacher control (dipping your toes into the waters of inquiry) to a higher level of student agency (students swimming in the deep end of the inquiry pool on their own). Collectively, these approaches support the goal of student-as-protagonist. In MacKenzie's (2016) model, the educator supports the student growing into his, her, or their ability to own more of the learning, slowly releasing control (allowing students into the deep end of the pool) as students metaphorically "learn to swim" and begin to see inquiry as a tool for learning that they own (MacKenzie, 2016; Wilson, 2020).

Inquiry strategies are helpful to understanding what students bring with them into the learning ecosystem as well. When done effectively, inquiry strategies allow the student and educator to live more from the student-as-protagonist model and move away from rigid teacher control. Classroom inquiry helps educators enter the broader context a student brings into the learning ecosystem (MacKenzie, 2016). At its simplest level, inquiry is simply a tool of engagement (MacKenzie, 2016; Sotiriou et al., 2020). However, when structured properly, inquiry-based learning can be the key to student protagonism on the landscape. When students can see how a question led to an educational adventure, so to speak, they willingly seek out new learning on the landscape, often with only gentle guidance from the teacher (MacKenzie, 2016; Sotiriou et al., 2020). A great inquiry-based unit lets the teacher know students and their interest and abilities, allowing the teacher to observe what each student already knows and what interests the student.

A great inquiry unit therefore sparks and fuels intrinsic motivation. Intrinsic motivation comes from within the learner rather than external to the learner. For example, an intrinsically motivated student has a personal drive to deepen learning, while an extrinsically motivated student studies for a grade, a sticker, or the praise of a teacher (Rheinberg & Engeser, 2018; Turner, 2017). True inquiry allows students to explore what *they* are curious about. Inquiry is the action that inspires and powers the intrinsic motivation to explore their own landscape.

Strategies for Developing Inquiry to Understand Where Students Are in the Learning Ecosystem

Strategies for developing inquiry to understand the broader context and understandings students bring into the learning ecosystem include KWL and RAN charts, the Question Formulation Technique, and Socratic seminars. The three simple techniques of KWL charts and RAN charts, the Question Formulation Technique, and Socratic seminars are simple entry points into the inquiry practice. These are logistically easy to implement and, at the same time, powerful for teachers and students.

Every successful inquiry technique turns control over to students and gives a window into where they are with a concept, topic, or idea. And every successful inquiry strategy allows educators to leverage more of the context students bring to the learning process, if they are willing to look, see, and validate that context. An example of this is the structuring of student-generated questions. While teachers truly should, and do, have a clearer idea of what students need to learn than the students themselves, this teacher-prescribed pathway places students as passive passengers on the journey of schooling. When students begin to generate their own questions, albeit inside of a teacher-generated topic or concept, the teacher benefits by understanding the student better (the student's current skills, knowledge, and what the student is curious about) and gets the added plus of having a list of questions that the student may actually be interested in investigating (Ciotti, 2020; Ogle, 1986; Stead, 2014). An example of this can be as simple as the following KWL chart activity. When learning is not about filling in worksheets and answering the teacher's questions, the student-as-protagonist approach motivates intrinsic, effortless, and powerful learning.

KWL and RAN Charts

Know-wonder-learn (KWL) charts (Ogle, 1986) are one of the simplest ways to start and track the inquiry process in a way that builds our understanding of students' context and helps us visualize where they are in their learning process, particularly with students in preschool and the primary grades. The KWL chart is usually a whole-class activity that facilitates inquiry and sparks curiosity; it includes three columns.

- **Know:** As a unit launches, students chart all the things they know about the topic. Those things can be correct or incorrect. In fact, part of the purpose of charting knowns at the start of the unit is to later reflect and see if anything we believed to be true or false was not so.

- **Wonder:** Also start this column at the launch of the unit. These are all the questions and wonderings that come from students regarding the unit, topic, or concept. Wonderings guide educator facilitation of learning; expect the list to grow as students' curiosity grows throughout the unit.

- **Learn:** Use this final column to record new learnings from throughout the unit as it progresses. As students chart what they learn, make connections to assumptions in the Know column about what students thought they knew that may have been wrong, and reinforce those things they did indeed know beforehand.

No column is complete until the unit is complete—and sometimes not even then, as we want to encourage students to see learning as a lifelong process. Placing the KWL chart on a classroom wall during an entire project or other learning experience, and addressing it for five minutes a day, is a simple yet powerful way to better understand how students think about the concepts of a unit, how the unit impacts them, and what students bring from home to affect the learning experience.

The reading-and-analyzing-nonfiction (RAN) chart (Stead, 2014) is similar to a KWL chart but offers a more nuanced and personalized approach to tracking and visualizing the learning process for older learners, as follows.

- **What I think I know:** This column establishes what students believe they know, without asking them to be certain of anything.
- **Confirmed:** As students engage in inquiry and investigation, they move information they discover they *were* right about into this column.
- **Misconceptions or oops:** As students engage in inquiry and investigation, they move information they discover they were *not* right about into this column.
- **New information:** As students engage in inquiry and investigation, they will discover facts they weren't even looking for, but that feel important. Their unexpected new learning goes into this column.
- **Wonderings:** As the students engage in inquiry and investigation, new questions will emerge; those questions go into this column, but students can move them as inquiry progresses.

Teachers can use RAN charts as a full-class tool, but they are most effective when students use them in small groups or as individuals, as they can serve to track each student's learning process and can even provide evidence for formative assessment checkpoints, particularly when applied to reading and analyzing nonfiction, as it was designed to offer insights into students' understanding of a text. The RAN chart is particularly useful with secondary-level students, who may approach learning as though they already know everything. These charts force those students to dig deeper and more explicitly than the KWL into what they *think* they know and then encourage students to use inquiry to validate—or disprove—those assumptions. Some teachers use different colored sticky notes to help identify which groups or individuals contributed which ideas on collaborative RAN charts, while others ask students to put their names on any contributions they make (see figure 3.2). Other teachers have individual students or project groups maintain their own RAN charts as they investigate.

Question Formulation Technique

The Question Formulation Technique (QFT) scaffolds students' comfort with and skill at asking their own questions, helping students grow in their agency and learn to practice inquiry, while enabling the educator to understand what students individually and collectively bring to the learning ecosystem (Right

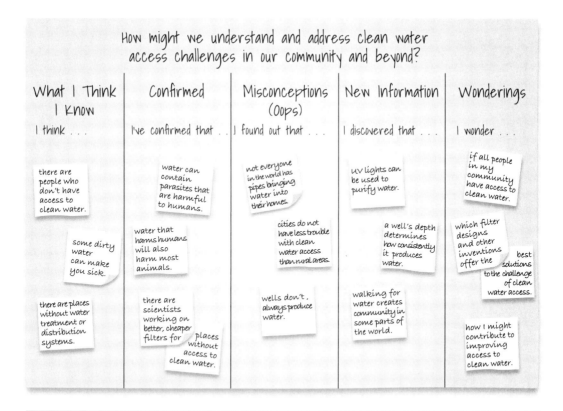

Figure 3.2: Sample RAN chart.

Question Institute, n.d.). This protocol allows educators to understand what students' most important inquiry questions are, which by extension allows educators to make instructional choices that directly address students' goals, needs, and next steps on the landscape. The QFT also serves as a tool for fostering students' inquiry skills and deepening investigation, as well as teaching them to articulate their thinking.

This activity is best done in small groups of three to five students, with groups sharing their top questions at the end for the whole class to explore (Right Question Institute, n.d.). Use the following seven steps.

1. Have students ask as many questions as they can about a topic. The goal is to get students comfortable with asking questions and to grow their desire to know more.

2. Do not stop to discuss, or critique, or answer any question students pose, and ask students not to stop to make judgments. Just ask the questions. There's no wordsmithing or commentary on the quality of any given question. In fact, teachers should avoid saying "good question," as that refers to a question's quality and implies that there are bad questions.

3. Teachers or students should write every question down and capture it exactly as students state them. This allows the educator to see exactly where the students are in their thinking without putting a scaffolding lens on the question.

4. Have students work in groups to rephrase any statements into questions. The goal is to ensure students approach learning with an inquiry lens, which can only happen through questions.

5. Have groups turn all close-ended, easily answered questions into open-ended questions. For example, change What is a historical site? to Why do historical sites matter? This process helps students recognize the difference between questions that are worthy of investigation and those they can easily answer with an online search engine.

6. Each group decides on the three to five questions they consider most pressing. This step helps students learn to prioritize during the inquiry process, and to honor any common interests they discover.

7. Have groups share their top questions and document them in the classroom for everyone to investigate. This step helps spark new questions in other groups, recognize common interests across the whole class, and organize the next steps in the inquiry process. Perhaps even more important on the landscape, it allows educators to understand exactly what students are curious about, and to plan accordingly.

What happens next? That's really up to the educator and is based on what the unit demands. Other benefits of using the QFT include the way the protocol amplifies student agency, how it teaches students to assess what they see in the news and online with a critical eye, how it helps them frame problems and challenges in a way that leads to action and investigation, and how it helps students feel more empowered as protagonists in their learning journey.

Socratic Seminars

Socratic seminars are a structured form of discourse that leverages inquiry to create an environment where seminar participants own the discussion, develop their own meaning, and create a new and shared understanding of a topic. The term as used in K–12 education grew out of the work of Mortimer J. Adler (1984) and the Great Books program, and therefore usually involved text-based discussion (meaning participants use one or more texts as the content of the discourse).

The process asks participants to think together, which means the following (Graybill, 2019).

- A Socratic seminar is an interactive discussion where replies, follow-up questions, and probing for specificity are as important as initial ideas. Socratic seminars are not a round-robin sharing of loosely connected ideas.

- Students' thoughts and ideas are a starting point, and teachers do not assume anyone's ideas or positions are final.

- Participants own the discussion. Socratic seminars are often facilitated by the teacher in the beginning until participants become comfortable with the process but are then turned over to the participants who own and shape their own discussions.

Similar to Socratic seminars are Harkness method discussions (Phillips Exeter Academy, n.d.), and spider-web discussions (Wiggins, 2017). The Harkness method uses large oval tables designed for collaborative inquiry and dialogue, putting students in charge of their discussions and emphasizing effective democratic processes. The table facilitates a visual mapping of dialogue, often drawn by a student but also monitored by the educator in the room, which provides additional opportunities for students to reflect on their participation and notice when it's important to draw in a peer or ensure that no group members dominate the discussion. Additional tools the teacher and students employ include time-tracking tables, to understand who spoke for how long, and capture tools for student comments and body language.

A spider-web discussion is very similar but without a table. The word *spider* serves as an acronym for the goals of this approach, which are to create dialogues that are *synergetic* in their inclusion of all participants, *practiced* repeatedly over time, *independent* of the teacher's control, *developed* in the sense that dialogue digs deep and goes somewhere, with *exploration* of a text or concept as the main goal, and a *rubric* that allows students and teacher to assess their participation. While Socratic seminars, Harkness method, and spider-web discussions are most often seen in middle and high school classrooms, educators can adapt them to encourage both autonomy from the teacher and collaboration toward meaning making at any age.

Investing time and energy in the element of the ecosystem is one of the most valuable investments an educator can make. As we have noted, students are not a *tabula rasa* or blank slate. They bring strengths, challenges, qualities, and identities that are all their own to the learning ecosystem. These strengths, challenges, qualities, and identities play a role in how a student learns and how an educator teaches, whether or not they are made explicit or planned for. In fact, students' differences have the potential of enriching the learning experiences for every student in the room. Exploring the element of understanding the broader context students bring into the learning ecosystem is the first step in the learning journey for the landscape model, a powerful first step that is a prerequisite for the rest of the journey.

Reflective Questions

Respond to the following questions alone or with your school team.

- How well do the systems in your school or classroom allow you to get to know your students currently? What are the strengths of those systems now, and what would you like to improve?
- How might you employ some strategies shared in this chapter, to understand who your students are and what they bring into the classroom? Which might be challenging in your context, and why?
- If you asked your students how safe they feel to express who they are and what they care about at school, what do you think they would say? What might you learn from their answers?
- How much were you able to bring your whole self to your learning experiences when you were a student? Were there any elements of your homelife that you wish teachers had understood, and how might that have changed your learning journey?

Takeaways

The following summarizes key ideas from the chapter.

- Knowing students deeply matters to their learning. When we understand who students are and their broader experiences outside of school, we are better able to understand what they bring into the learning ecosystem and where they stand on the landscape.
- Creating space for personal identity development is just as important as the subjects we teach, and such space can also allow educators to better understand their students.
- There are many ways for educators to learn about their students beyond just a questionnaire or survey, including strategies that connect their lives to the classroom and learning process.

CHAPTER 4

The Horizon

If a man does not keep pace with his companions, perhaps it is because he hears a different drummer. Let him step to the music he hears, however measured or far away.

—Henry David Thoreau

Schools often underestimate what their impact really is. That sounds strange to say. If you're reading this book, you probably believe in the imperative and massive impact of education. However, as educators, we are too often asked to measure that impact in standardized tests and in short-sighted, yearlong chunks. The 1-in-60 rule helps us understand how our goals actually lie over a horizon line. The rule comes from experts in air navigation and states that an error in one degree of flight path causes you to be off target by one mile for every sixty miles flown (Hyatt, 2019). While pilots will tell you horror stories of the dark side of the 1-in-60 rule, there is a powerful positive lesson. Making changes in *how* we do school often leads to frustration, as the impacts of those changes take time to see.

Many leaders make changes that are too bold, ninety-degree course shifts that cause a metaphorical sense of motion sickness. Remember that change is a vector. It is both the direction you're going *and* the speed at which you make the course correction. A one-degree course correction over a prolonged period of time can bring about profound positive change over time. When we apply the idea of slow change to students' learning experiences, the horizon is about the learning goals we set with students, the horizon they'll work toward their whole lives when we think of them as lifelong learners. But when we apply the landscape model more practically to the school experience, establishing a student's horizon might be as small as what we hope to accomplish by the end of the week or learning unit, or as big as what we hope to accomplish in a school year or by graduation from elementary, middle, or high school. Instead of being a fixed point, like we see at the end of a racetrack, the landscape model invites educators to work with students to define the most appropriate end point for *them*. At the same time that a horizon can feel unreachable, the landscape model asks educators to cultivate a comfort with the idea that mastery takes time, patience, and practice—for educators as much as students.

Robert d'Erizans asserts this idea with regard to school improvement (personal communication, June 1, 2021). In our conversations about his work to bring inclusive prosperity into the practices of his faculty at the Graded School, he continually emphasized long-term outcomes. The vision of inclusive prosperity that he wanted to see at his school was not possible in a year, but he knew he would see significant progress over three to five years. He extrapolates this to address student learning as well, asking us to reconsider and redefine success and growth, thinking in longer swaths of time, and charting growth longitudinally rather than through event-based assessments (R. d'Erizans, personal communication, June 1, 2021). How might educators define the horizon with students in a way that honors the broader context students bring into the learning ecosystem and every complexity of the journey, and that leverages each student's strengths, addresses his, her, or their growth areas, and allows for *all* students to succeed? This is the challenge and benefit of the horizon element.

In a more traditional setting, goal setting is generally the work of educators, not students, and goals are most commonly based on whatever standards or other academic outcomes the teacher needs to cover by the end of the unit or year. When we shift the responsibility for goal setting to students, with the support of their teachers, we create an opportunity for metacognitive processes that benefit students not just in terms of how empowered they feel to define their own horizon as protagonists but also in terms of how likely they are to *reach* those goals, even when such goals connect to the same sets of standards and outcomes. The more intrinsic the desire to reach the goal, the more likely the student will reach it, so involving students in goal setting helps ensure students will challenge themselves and strive for mastery and excellence (Fischer, Malycha, & Schafmann, 2019). In the authors' experience, a student who hates geography, for example, won't reach high levels of mastery and excellence if merely complying with the teacher's demands, while that same student, if part of conversations and processes wherein he or she identifies end goals and next steps, will be far more likely to reach excellence. Rather than a process that relies on students' compliance with teachers' demands, the horizon invites us to co-construct ideas about students' learning and growth goals, in both the short and long term, based on the experiences, strengths, and challenges they bring into the ecosystem. Leveraging students' assets is also key to defining the horizon, as teachers must avoid putting limits on students' goals, albeit accidentally, through their own implicit bias, as we explored in chapter 1 (page 23).

This chapter talks about goal setting to support the horizon, including aspirational processes that support defining the horizon, and defining the horizon for academic excellence; it includes corresponding strategies for each.

Goal Setting to Support Defining the Horizon

A simple starting place for defining the horizon is goal setting. Goal setting is often underestimated in its power and neglected in terms of investing the time needed to maximize its benefits. Studies show multiple benefits of goal setting, including greater chances of goal attainment, higher levels of satisfaction, and greater long-term retention of outcomes (Gardner & Albee, 2015; Riopel, 2019). Many schools implement goal-setting processes with students in homeroom or advisory, only to get rid of the practice a few years later, citing a lack of true results and the need to use the time in better ways. However, Sarah Gardner and Dave Albee (2015) show that by engaging in structured goal setting, students can nearly double their chances of accomplishing those goals.

Moreover, most efforts for goal setting do not include students in meaningful ways. On the landscape, involving students is core, as are the scaffolding, support, and gradual release of control that teachers need to provide during the process, to increase students' autonomy over time, and to build students' skills as protagonists. Rohit Kumar of the Apni Shala Foundation reframes goal setting from being a student activity to being a systems question, asking, "How do we make systems that enable teachers to set aspiring goals for young people?" (personal communication, May 4, 2021). The authors would add a second question: How is this the work of the systems versus the work of an educator? These questions inspire the strategies and tools that follow.

PERSPECTIVES ON WHAT STUDENTS BRING TO THE LEARNING ECOSYSTEM

Testimonial by Jan Iwase

Jan Iwase is the former principal of Daniel K. Inouye Elementary School and author of Leading With Aloha: From the Pineapple Fields to the Principal's Office *(2019), and* Educating With Aloha: Reflections From the Heart on Teaching and Learning *(2021).*

Empowering learners to explore, discover, create, and share is the vision of the Daniel K. Inouye Elementary School, a public K–5 school located on Schofield Barracks, a military base in central O'ahu, Hawai'i. Nearly all the students at the school have at least one parent who is serving in the military, and school can be challenging for these families (Strive HI, 2021). Every change of duty station means transitioning to a new environment—new home, new community, new school, new friends, new teachers, new routines, new curriculum—and change often happens in the middle of a school year. For military-impacted schools, the challenge is to begin building relationships immediately with new students so they can be contributing members of the classroom.

When I was first hired as the principal back in 2003, my hope was that our students and their families would embrace the culture, history, and values that make Hawai'i a special and unique place to live. When our students moved to a new state or country, they could take what they had experienced and learned at our school and become ambassadors of *aloha* to spread love, compassion, empathy, and respect to make this world a kinder place. That goal evolved over the years to become more meaningful and focused on real-world learning.

Hawai'i, which comprises eight islands in the middle of the Pacific Ocean, is a unique place to live. As such, resources are finite, and much of our needs and wants must be imported. An emergency such as a natural disaster, a shipping strike, or a pandemic can wreak havoc on our economy, and worldwide issues such as energy efficiency, climate change, food shortages, and economic challenges are magnified when the closest state is over two thousand miles away. We in Hawai'i realize the need to resolve challenges that impact the quality of our lives.

As a school, we chose to involve our students in addressing these types of challenges, even though they would probably not be lifelong residents of our state. Using project-based learning to tackle problems in our community, our students were much more than ambassadors of *aloha*; they were change agents. Students were invested and passionate about sharing their learning. Consider the following examples.

- Kindergarten students were concerned that the playground was too hot during recess. After learning about the many benefits trees provide, they worked together to plant saplings on the playground.

- First graders, while researching ocean animals, discovered that trash in the oceans was a huge problem and that the actions of humans were affecting ocean plants and animals. So, they worked in groups to create prototypes of trash-cleaning machines and proudly shared their models at a public exhibition.

- A garden provided second graders with real-life lessons on growing food and self-sustainability, a concern in Hawai'i where much of our food is imported. Students shared recipes using vegetables they grew, tried new ideas to increase productivity, and learned marketing strategies to keep their garden profitable.

- The school has a high rate of transiency with students coming and going throughout the year. Third graders learned about communities and researched about Schofield, where they lived. They then created websites to share information about the many services and activities available for families in their community.

- Hawai'i is addressing issues of climate change and its impact on native plants and animals. A National Oceanic and Atmospheric Administration grant allowed fourth graders to learn about the effects of climate change and rising sea levels on albatross nesting areas at Kahuku Point. These students, along with NOAA volunteers, cleared an area of invasive plants and replaced them with Native Hawaiian plants so the albatross could nest safely on higher ground.

- Fifth graders worked in groups or individually on projects they were passionate about. Topics included homelessness, inclusion, animal rights, bullying, and school safety, and students proudly shared their projects with the school community.

There is a Hawaiian saying—*Malama 'aina*—which means to take care of the land so it can continue to give back what we need to sustain ourselves now and in the future. When our students of military families depart, they may never return to live in Hawai'i, but while they are at our school, they learn that they can make this world a better place for everyone.

Source: J. Iwase, personal communication, October 6, 2021.

Strategies for Identifying Aspirations to Support Defining the Horizon

Before we begin to build concrete goals, students often need opportunities to think about their aspirations and to envision, predict, and set their sights on what those goals could be. The following are several activities easily run with students of all ages, with adaptations as necessary, and all help students imagine what's possible on a broad scale before they begin to craft more specific goals with their teachers. And while one activity is meant to remain private for students, the others can help educators understand just how far students might want to reach in their work, which helps ensure educators don't unintentionally limit students' horizons.

A Letter to Myself

This activity is particularly useful if done at the beginning of a school year or a significant new phase of learning and growth. The goal of the letter to myself is for each student to write a letter, which only that student will see, in which the student addresses his, her, or their future selves and establishes his, her, or their aspirations for the year. These aspirations can be personal, academic, sports, or arts related—but the teacher can also guide the focus, if they have goals in mind. Just beware of a teacher-driven prompt like "How will you get better at following the teacher's instructions?" as we want students to think bigger than your hopes for their behavior. Instead, make sure prompts are open-ended even if they're discipline specific, such as "How far do you hope to go with your writing, reading, and thinking skills by the end of the year?" Even better are wide open prompts, such as "What are your aspirations for this school year?"

Following are basic instructions, which you can adapt as necessary. For example, some classes might prefer to do this as an audio or video product, and teachers of preschool and kindergarten might have their students create letters through drawings and simple words they've been learning to write. Keep in mind that preschool and early primary students will generally have more difficulty with abstract goals, and may need to define their aspirations more concretely. Teachers should take the following five steps.

1. Give students advanced warning that you are going to run this activity; providing a day of notice or even the chance to journal before they craft their letters will help ensure they demonstrate deep thinking. Teach them the word *aspirations*, and encourage them to think big. Provide the prompt in advance, something like "What are your aspirations for this school year? Write a letter to yourself about all the things you hope you will be able to do, and all the ways you hope to grow and learn, in the course of this year."

2. Have students write their letters (or whatever form you choose with them). Give students as much time as they need to express themselves.

3. Have students seal physical letters in envelopes for privacy or upload digital products to a thumb drive or private cloud storage space. *It is essential with this particular activity that the teacher does not break the seals;* that is, the educator should not break students' confidence and read their letter or view their videos. The whole point is that this is a letter to *themselves*, not to you. Preschool, kindergarten, and early primary teachers will have to see students' letters to support the process but should try to avoid impacting its content.

4. At the end of the year or phase of learning, educators should return the letters to their students, again privately, so students can see and reflect on what they wrote to themselves.

5. As appropriate, discuss the letters in small or large groups, to provide an opportunity for deeper reflection on what students accomplished or not, and what the letter suggests might be appropriate goals for the following year.

The Headline of My Year

A much simpler activity, again appropriate for all ages, is the headline of my year. Teachers often use this activity at the beginning of specific projects, to get individuals and groups thinking about what success might look like. Teachers should use it for short-term aspirational thinking as well, so that students can define *the headline of my project*, for example.

The protocol is simple—students write and share an imaginary headline that the local newspaper or school paper, as we imagine it, will publish when each student reaches his, her, or their horizon. The idea is for students to capture their highest aspirations, their ideal end point (horizon) for whatever learning process the teacher chooses to focus on—or for the school year as a whole. Keep in mind that this is a perfect opportunity for students to think about their sense of personal purpose in a given learning experience as well. For example, a student beginning a project on healthy lifestyles might write a headline like *Fourth Grader Develops Antidote for Diabetes* because their sense of purpose in the project connects to a parent with diabetes. Similarly, a student entering her last year of high school might write a headline like *Basketball Star Receives Athletic Scholarships to Top Universities*.

The goal of this activity is to think big, and students should recommit to classroom norms before they write and share, to make sure no one suggests such high aspirations are silly or impossible. The whole point is to envision the most extraordinary horizon possible, so that students and educators know what their highest aspirations really are.

Storyboards and Vision Boards

Teachers often use storyboards to plan out steps in a project, or to plan the plot of a film or short story, so they can be very useful on the pathway as well. But when we think of storyboards as aspirational tools, they have the same impact as vision boards: they help students imagine a successful end point, as well as a few of the steps they'll take to get there.

Storyboards work well with students of all ages. While upper primary, middle, and secondary students can learn to use them with minimal support, preschool and kindergarten students can draw pictures in the boxes and write (or have the teacher help them write) a word or two to describe each step toward greatness. The combination of images and words makes storyboards a great tool for envisioning the best possible horizon, as well as the pathway to it.

Similarly, vision boards are usually assembled as a collage, using words and images cut from magazines to craft a board filled with each student's ideal future. Unlike storyboards, which include steps toward that future, vision boards simply ask students to envision where they want to be—at the end of a unit, at the end of a year, at the end of middle school, and so on. Educators should collect magazines and other materials for collaging in class, to make sure students have equitable access to resources, and display students' vision boards in the classroom to encourage conversation. Vision boards work with students of all ages, with small modifications for emerging writers and readers.

Strategies for Goal Setting to Support Defining the Horizon

The following strategies help students set more concrete goals and define their own horizons, with the scaffolding and support of their teachers: WOOP, SMART goals, ANCHOR, and student-led conferences.

WOOP

Psychologist Gabriele Oettingen (with Kappes, Guttenberg, & Gollwitzer, 2015) developed the WOOP goal-setting protocol in response to the fact that many goal-setting protocols don't yield the results that practitioners hope they will. It is designed to tap into the psychological elements that attract us to goals, and to address those psychological elements that keep us from accomplishing difficult things. WOOP can be used at the beginning of the school year, but will be most effective at the beginning of projects or other learning units, to help students define—and teachers see and plan for—the horizon they want to reach (represented by the W of *wish* and the O of *outcome*). By having students prepare for potential *obstacles* (O) and develop their own *plan* (P), WOOP facilitates a metacognitive process that empowers learners as protagonists—and makes it more likely they'll reach their horizons.

WOOP is a four-step process that educators can and should integrate into existing programs. Many WOOP practitioners use the protocol embedded into academic units (to set academic goals), into advisories and homerooms (to set personal growth goals), and with adults (to set professional goals). The four steps of WOOP are as follows.

1. **Wish:** What do you really want to accomplish?
2. **Outcome:** What is the best outcome that would happen if you accomplished your goal?
3. **Obstacle:** What personal obstacles are or will get in the way of you accomplishing your goal?
4. **Plan:** What is your action plan and road map to get there?

WOOP is not an action-planning template, and practitioners should supplement it with other action-planning resources that help students think through their steps, such as storyboarding or other organizational protocols.

While teachers can use WOOP goal setting with all ages, they will find it is more developmentally appropriate for students in kindergarten through third grade, particularly when compared to other popular goal-setting protocols like SMART goals.

SMART Goals

Using SMART goals (Conzemius & O'Neill, 2014) allows upper elementary, middle, and high school students to dig much deeper into goal setting in more advanced ways. Because SMART goals use complex language and require more complex thinking and planning, the authors recommend the use of WOOP in kindergarten through third grade, and believe that SMART goals are more appropriate for use from fourth grade up. SMART goals, by their nature, require students to identify more specific outcomes and how they'll measure success.

Teachers can use this strategy in almost any setting, but it is particularly useful at the beginning of projects to help student teams plan out their goals and, by doing so, define their horizons for the project. For example, students working to improve their algebra skills through a project in which they need to propose an appropriate minimum wage in their city might use SMART goals at the beginning of their planning process, as they think through what they want to accomplish and how they'll know they've reached their goals, and they might touch back on it at key checkpoints or milestones, to communicate their progress to their teacher and each other.

In order to encourage student protagonism and increase the likelihood students will work toward their goals with intrinsic motivation, students should do SMART goal planning, with scaffolding and feedback from teachers who can leverage what they know students bring to the ecosystem to support reaching for the highest levels of success possible for each. The teacher's role is to provide feedback and help encourage challenge, but not to edit students' SMART goals, which include the following characteristics (Conzemius & O'Neill, 2014).

- **Strategic and specific:** This step asks students to offer as strategic and specific a goal as possible. In a project on defining a dignified minimum wage, for example, "We will improve our algebra skills" is very general, while "We will make sure our algebraic formulas accurately identify the gaps between income and spending" is specific and strategically oriented toward the project goals.

- **Measurable:** This step asks students to plan ahead for how they will measure their success; for example, "We will demonstrate our progress with algebraic formulas through an Excel sheet we will use to track our findings and identify contradictions or challenges encountered," or "We will consider ourselves successful if we can share our argument for a more dignified minimum wage with two people who have the power to do something about it."

- **Attainable:** This step asks students to write realistic goals so they are attainable; for example, students who try to determine an appropriate minimum wage for all members of a country will encounter far more complexity than one project can withstand, whereas determining an appropriate minimum wage for one city makes the goal attainable.

- **Results oriented:** This step asks students to focus their energy on results, not just ideas; here, students are identifying their own best outcomes, with support from the teacher, which might look like a series of artifacts they'll produce as they work toward a final product. An artifact might be the same Excel sheet with their formulas, their written argument for a minimum wage, or even a presentation to a local policymaker involved in setting the local minimum wage.

- **Time bound:** Teachers usually manage scheduling and timing, but this step asks students to hold themselves and each other accountable for reaching results on a timeline. While teachers may want to set due dates, it is important to create student agency over the more moveable checkpoints they will work toward along the pathway, such as completing their investigation of incomes by a certain date, their investigation of the cost of living by another date, a written argument by another, and so on.

The SMART goal approach serves as an action-planning framework that helps students establish concrete and realistic goals based on the horizon they want to reach in their work. They also increase student autonomy (Ryan & Deci, 2018) and help both students and teachers understand where they want to go (horizon) and how they hope to get there (pathway).

ANCHOR

ANCHOR, which stands for appreciations, news, concerns, hopes, obscurities, and readings, is a simple protocol for checking in with students (World Leadership School, 2020). Used in experiential and outdoor education settings to help improve group dynamics and allow students to get to know each other, share fears, and set goals, ANCHOR is appropriate for students from second or third grade and up. Used daily by the World Leadership School (2020) on student- and teacher-immersion programs around the world, this protocol should be run entirely by students whenever possible, to increase agency, but may require modeling and scaffolding the first few times teachers use it.

We recommend the use of ANCHOR in advisory-type classes, at the beginning of field trip expeditions, and any time educators want to push students out of their comfort zone to help them understand where they are and help them define their horizon with an aspirational orientation. The ideas explored in concerns, hopes, and readings can all help students reflect on their aspirations and goals.

- **Appreciations:** An opportunity to verbally appreciate the people and experiences students want to recognize publicly, like "I appreciate how open Deborah was during the discussion about our families yesterday"
- **News:** A chance to talk briefly about the schedule, the purpose of upcoming activities, or other need-to-knows
- **Concerns:** An opportunity to voice fears and concerns that are coming up on the learning journey (such as "I'm worried about sharing my work for peer evaluation because . . .")
- **Hopes:** A chance to set goals for the next phase of learning and identify aspirations, such as, "I hope my prototype works at the next test phase because I worked really hard on it," or "The speaker last week inspired me to consider a career in . . ."
- **Obscurities:** Stories, weird facts, and highlights from recent experiences that may not relate to the goals of the moment, such as, "I keep thinking about that TED Talks video we watched last week because it was so moving"

- **Readings:** Chosen by the student facilitator, from any source, to inspire the group, such as a poem, a short excerpt from a novel or other piece of literature, and so on

While ANCHOR was originally designed for outdoor education and international immersion experiences, it is appropriate as a less formal discussion tool when students are about to undertake something new or particularly challenging, so that they can define their horizons in ways that address those challenges.

Student-Led Conferencing

A student-led conference is a meeting between a student, the educator, and the adults who are important in the student's life. Students lead the meeting with their significant adults as their audience and partners, with the purpose of reviewing progress toward setting and achieving goals, securing adult support along a goals-oriented journey, and encouraging lifelong learning. While part of the goal of a student-led conference is for the student to identify and articulate where they are in their learning currently, the other central goal is that they articulate their current challenges and identify where they want to be at the end of a given unit or grading period—or by the next conference date.

The real power of a student-led conference is that, when done well, it demands the orientation toward the student-as-protagonist. Chief academic officer for EL Education, formerly the Expeditionary Learning Network, and professor at Harvard Graduate School of Education Ron Berger (2014) writes:

> What may seem like a small change—parent conferences run by students instead of teachers—can change the entire culture of a school in powerful ways. When students must report to their families what they're learning—what skills and understandings they have, what areas still challenge them, and where they hope to get to—they must understand their own learning and progress. They take pride in what they can do and take responsibility for what they need to work on. Education stops being something *done to them* and begins being something that *they are leading*.

Student-led conferences are an excellent strategy for building students' ability to accurately reflect on and communicate about their own learning. Student-led conferences are a good strategy for tracking student growth as well. This makes sense in the landscape model of learning, since, "If the student can process how he or she is achieving, the student is more likely to develop goals and use an ongoing monitoring system to track improvement" (Muic, 2020). Kapono has worked with students as young as four years old who have successfully led their own conferences, presenting work and then setting and reflecting on goals with their parents or other significant adults.

One simple version of these conferences focuses on the four Cs (Battelle for Kids, 2019), whereas the EL Education model includes all academic courses in the conference discussion *and* the four Cs plus other competencies (Berger, 2014).

1. **Creativity:** The extent to which a student can think in innovative ways and approach both academic and social challenges creatively

2. **Collaboration:** The extent to which a student can collaborate effectively with their peers on projects, whether academic or social

3. **Critical thinking:** The extent to which a student can think critically about texts, concepts, and other elements of their academic and social experience

4. **Communication:** The extent to which a student can communicate their ideas through a variety of forms and to a variety of audiences

A four Cs conference is what we describe here. Other versions could be adapted to focus on academic skills, or social-emotional learning, for example. In the week before the actual conference, students are asked to think through their progress on each of the four Cs, and to write down what they want to share, both in terms of strengths and in terms of next-step goals. Some teachers find it useful to have students employ a set of questions or a checklist relevant to where they are in the school year or the specific goals of the conference. For more on tools and particular strategies for student-led conferences, see Berger's (2014) work and a collection of resources on student-led conferences for educators from *Edutopia* (Cronin, 2016).

Before the conference, the participants do the following six actions (Ciotti, 2012).

1. Teacher clarifies the conference's purpose to students in class and to parents through written communication as necessary.

2. Students gather evidence from the period they're discussing that demonstrates their strengths, growth, and challenges in creativity, collaboration, critical thinking, and communication, and their previous goals. Students look for at least one piece of archival evidence that shows their strengths, and one that shows where they need to grow next. These might be in the same piece of work.

3. The student reflects in writing on each domain (four Cs and their goals), writing or documenting in some other way their successes and ongoing growth areas (see resources from Cronin, 2016).

4. Students use the WOOP or other protocol with scaffolded adult support to create a single important goal for the next semester, based on their reflection.

5. Teachers ensure that the goal is correctly scaffolded and in the student's Zone of Proximal Development.
6. Students and important adults like parents and guardians both receive the student-led conference protocol.

During the conference, the participants do the following six actions.

1. Students present the purpose of student-led conferences. The important adults respond only by expressing gratitude and excitement for the conference.
2. Students present their work and reflection for each domain and goal, one at a time.
3. Parents respond by saying:
   - One thing they would like to positively acknowledge
   - One thing they aspire to for their child's continued growth
4. Repeat for each domain and goal.
5. Students present their new goal and ask their important adults what help they can provide to support the student accomplishing this goal, taking notes and preparing for next steps.
6. Students thanks important adults for their attendance.

After the conference, the participants take two actions.

1. Students reflect on the conference and take notes for reference at the next conference.
2. The domains and goals are revisited no less than once per month to ensure they remain relevant. The teacher supports students with regard to course corrections and feedback, to keep the journey toward the goal progressing.

Putting students in charge of their own conferences, with the structures and tools to support their doing so effectively, eliminates a significant amount of potential for educator bias to impact grades—while simultaneously positioning students as central protagonists in their own learning process.

When student-led conferences are done well, they tend to have the following qualities:

- *There are clear agendas and structures.* Students know exactly what they'll be sharing, for how much time, and how to facilitate the discussion so parents are actively involved.

- *Students have strong reflection and presentation skills.* They prepare and practice in class until their courtesy, speaking skills, and ability to reflect on their learning are solid.

- *A teacher helps each student* prepare for the conference. At the elementary level, this is the classroom teacher; at the secondary level, an advisor.

- *Students demonstrate how their work is evidence of meeting learning targets.* . . . They also reflect on their progress in habits of scholarship, character, and artistic pursuits.

- *Student portfolios anchor the conference* and tell the story of student growth and learning. The portfolios contain early and final drafts of student work, formative and summative assessments, and evidence of meeting learning targets.

- *Students set goals* for academic, skill and character growth, with support from their teachers and families.

- *Student accomplishments outside school are honored*, be they in sports, arts, or service learning.

- *There's a schoolwide approach to conference logistics and structures.* A student-led conference handbook can lay out all the details for scheduling, outreach, and other key decision points (for example, how often and when to hold conferences, what work to share, and how to prepare). (Berger, 2014)

As an example, students at Gimnasio Los Caobos collected work samples in advance to help illustrate the growth they wanted to spotlight. And on conference day, educators and parents listened and asked questions, guiding a bit more in the early years but trusting the student-as-protagonist to provide the core information accurately. In the experience of educators at Caobos, parents were less likely to blame the teacher when students shared their own learning journey; they were more likely to encourage autonomy with schoolwork at home and less likely to do their children's homework for them, recognizing that students were, in fact, capable of this level of challenge and self-evaluation at all ages (Nauss, 2010; Yauch, 2015). Most importantly, students developed regular habits of self-reflection, metacognition, and the articulation of needs and strengths—useful throughout their educational and professional lives (Nauss, 2010; Yauch, 2015).

PERSPECTIVES ON HONORING STUDENTS
Every Gift Matters

A mentor of Kapono's, Puanani Burges, a teacher, social worker, and *kupuna* (elder), was once working with a group of seven high school boys in a senior special education class in a predominantly disenfranchised and Native Hawaiian district on the island of O'ahu (Burges, 2017). Whenever Burges, who goes by Auntie Pua, works in a social-working capacity, she starts her sessions by asking participants to tell three stories: one about themselves, one about their community, and one about a gift and strength they bring. She finds that personal stories and stories about their communities tend to be easy to tell, but stories about their personal gifts are more challenging. On this occasion, as Auntie Pua facilitated the opening session with these seven boys, things were no different. They easily told stories about themselves and their communities. As expected, when she asked them to tell stories about their gifts and strengths, they started to struggle.

The seventh boy in the circle became more and more agitated as it drew closer to his turn. By the time the group turned to him, he had become red-faced and heated, almost angry. Auntie Pua pushed on, and the boy shouted out, "If I had any _____ gifts, I would not be in this _____ class" (using the full color of the profanity, of course). Auntie Pua pushed him further, like a social-working Jedi, yet at the exact wrong moment the bell rang, and the boy sprung up from his seat and disappeared into the crowd and down the hall, angry and embarrassed.

Auntie Pua knew she would have to wait an entire month before her next session with these boys and lamented every minute of the time between, regretting the situation she had facilitated this boy into. Yet every community has a certain place where you bump into people you either really want to or really *don't* want to see. This community was no different, and the next week, Auntie Pua came face-to-face with her student in the local supermarket. As he turned and caught her eye, she expected a scowl or frown. Unexpectedly, he bounded toward her with a smile and exclaimed, "I've been thinking about your question. I know my gift. Every time I go fishing, I catch fish and can put food on my family's dinner table. And when I go spearfishing, and the shark swims up to me, I look at him and say, 'I'm only taking what I need. I leave the rest for you.' And the shark always swims away. I know what my gift is!" The boy hugged her and ran back to his parents, waiting in the checkout line.

At this point in retelling the story, Auntie Pua asked Kapono, "Why did this boy need to wait until his senior year to know he had a gift? What role did schooling play in his feelings of inadequacy? What if schools were places where every student could learn from a place of strengths rather than be berated for their deficits?"

Defining the Horizon for Academic Excellence

As we note in the introduction (page 1), achievement, success, and excellence are concepts we may need to rethink to use the landscape model in ways that honor who students are and all that they are capable of. Modern education tends to tie ideas of success to mastery of standards, both the content and skills connected to our academic disciplines, with a fixed timeline for when students need to achieve it. The PBL or design-thinking teacher might also prioritize the essential competencies for our times, such as collaboration, critical thinking, or self-management, when they set objectives for learning. But the element of the horizon invites us to think of achievement as a lifelong journey that may be significantly different for different students, depending on their aspirations, talents, areas of challenge, and even their family culture. Defining the horizon for academic excellence requires educators to consider all that we have learned about what students bring into the learning ecosystem, and to involve students as protagonists in determining the right horizon for *them*.

If we are defining the horizon for each student, and if we are saying that horizon is not a fixed point all students work toward but a journey and an ever-progressing goal, how might we manage this with a class of thirty, for example, or a school of two thousand?

Not every student should be a doctor, just as not every student is the world's next Picasso. Defining the horizon means that every student gets to be the protagonist in defining his, her, or their *own* aspirations, both in the short and long term, for it is a personal aspiration that truly holds the power to motivate. Therefore, students should have the tools to define their own horizons with the help of their families and communities. The horizon element does not mean that curricula should not be well rounded. But it does mean that students do not need to be. Every student should receive endless opportunities. Yet not every student should end up in the same spot as a result of his, her, or their education. This is why one strategy we explore in this section, the portrait of a graduate (page 111), is so powerful and so dangerous at the same time. It helps us define the traits of learners we want to foster in students, but educators too often view it as a template that all students should fit into. The power and potential of using tools like the portrait of a graduate is to inspire students to determine their *own* definition of the horizon.

PERSPECTIVES ON HONORING STUDENTS' HORIZONS
How We Define Success

Springer Fyrberg, an environmental scientist and educator, was a high school friend of Kapono's (personal communication, 2000). A year older than Kapono and brilliant, her junior year Springer was accepted to Wellesley College a year early, without even having graduated from high school. Springer transferred to Pomona and then graduated with a degree in science, returning to rural Hawai'i to serve as a teacher in the predominantly Native Hawaiian community of Kahuku.

It was her first year, and career day was a couple of weeks away. A sophomore girl in Springer's chemistry class approached Springer for advice on a career day job shadow. The student wanted to be a doctor; and Springer saw in her a passion for science, a talent for academics, and the long road ahead of her. She was female, first-generation college-bound, indigenous Polynesian, belonging to the Mormon Church, and living in a rural and disenfranchised community. Springer was inspired to help. Fortuitously, both of Springer's parents were self-made doctors. Springer's mom put herself through university and medical school, then supported her construction-worker husband to do the same. Springer knew that the opportunity for this student to shadow her mother could not be missed.

Springer provided the student with a healthy dose of inspiration and a permission slip, telling her that it was up to her to bring in that signed permission slip; the road for her would be long, and she needed to practice self-advocacy early. Day one: no permission slip. Day two: no permission slip. Day three: another pep talk, and yet on day four, still no permission slip. Springer told the girl that to become a doctor, she needed to be responsible and get this done herself. Yet on day five, still nothing.

Springer didn't want this opportunity to slip away, so that weekend, she called the student's mother. "It's an opportunity that can't be missed," Springer said, explaining how this opportunity could be life changing. To Springer's surprise, the student's mother said, "I have the permission slip. My daughter has asked me for it nightly, and I won't sign it. I don't want her to go." Springer was taken by surprise, as the mom continued eloquently and clearly, "Becoming a doctor for you may seem like success. For me, I see my Samoan daughter moving to the mainland for college, moving away from our multigenerational household where her culture and family history is strong and grounds her in tradition and community support. Being forced to work on the Sabbath as a medical resident takes her away from God and her faith. And there are few Samoan male doctors, making it unlikely she'd marry someone who would bring her back home at some point, meaning her children will most likely not know their roots, either. She'd most likely move away, make money, and by your standards, be successful. But by cutting her cultural roots, separating her from her faith, and breaking a multigenerational chain of support in our community, you may be creating success for one, but not for our community or family."

When Kapono tells this story, he is often asked if the girl ended up going on the career day job shadow. No, she didn't. And for years, this seemed like a failure. After all, isn't the goal of education to help students realize their endless potential? Yes, it is! Yet, the real failure was not the student attending or not attending career day. There would be other opportunities in the future to inspire career and learning. The real failure was that Springer and Kapono were at the start of their careers and didn't have the tools to help the student and her family define their own horizon instead of trying to do it for them.

Strategies for Defining the Horizon for Academic Excellence

This section has concrete strategies to help define the horizon on the landscape: portrait of a graduate, SOAR model for appreciative inquiry, and capstone projects.

Portrait of a Graduate

EdLeader21 (n.d.) has made popular the portrait of a graduate (www.portrait ofagraduate.org) as a tool for schools and school systems to help support a flexible horizon of learning outcomes that are broad, not overly prescriptive, yet powerful. (Visit **go.solutiontree.com/diversityandequity** to access live links to the websites mentioned in this book.)

EdLeader21 (n.d.) presents the portrait of a graduate as an articulation of the horizon-linked goals for students that are specific to your school and your community. The tool supports the collaborative multi-stakeholder creation of the portrait of a graduate, which is grounded in the following three questions:

- What are the hopes, aspirations, and dreams that our community has for our young people?

- What are the skills [and mindsets] that our children need for success in this rapidly changing and complex world?

- What are the implications for the [design of] learning experiences [and equitable access to those experiences] we provide in our school systems? (Garza, 2017)

Schools can engage in portrait of a graduate work in many ways. The What School Could Be Innovation Playlist (https://whatschoolcouldbe.org/innovation-playlist) encourages a community process by which representatives of all major stakeholder groups form a portrait of a graduate task force, decide on the key traits your school nurtures in students, and publish a visual of these key traits. By engaging in this process, a school can expect to define a community horizon—the cardinal direction that education is facing—leaving room for each student to plot his, her, or their own destination along that horizon.

What School Could Be (n.d.b) also provides essential questions to support schools in successfully moving through the portrait-of-a-graduate process:

- What are the skills and character traits you believe your graduates need? Why?
- How well does our current education system foster these competencies? How well does your school currently foster them?
- If you were to shadow several students in your school (something we recommend!), would you observe they're developing these competencies?
- How well do your assessments capture progress on these essential competencies? Foster them? Impede them?

A cautionary note we previous alluded to is that the portrait of a graduate, at its lowest common denominator of implementation, can be perceived as a sort of silhouette that all students should fit into, or a cookie-cutter version of an ideal student. That is quite contrary to its true intent, yet it's a pitfall many schools succumb to. To avoid this common issue, consider a portrait of a graduate that is bold, aspirational, and leaves room for each student to create and own his, her, or their own outcome (horizon). For example, Mid-Pacific Institute in Honolulu, Hawai'i (www.midpac.edu) aspires for its students to be innovators, artists, and individuals. This type of portrait of a graduate focuses the school, giving cues that the program it offers must provide opportunities for innovation (potentially in the realm of science and technology) and opportunities for artistic exploration, but it leaves significant room for students to define their own goals within that focus.

SOAR Model Analysis

Students of all ages are capable of reflecting on their strengths and aspirations; it's just a question of adapting the questions and communication strategies to match the capacities of the group, whether because of age or because of what we were able to learn about the broader talents and challenges they bring into the ecosystem. The SOAR model analysis (Stavros, Cooperrider, & Kelley, 2003), described in chapter 8 (page 204) for use by teachers and leaders, is a metacognitive process that can also help students work intentionally toward their own highest level of academic excellence. Metacognition is one of the most powerful tools for ensuring that learning happens in deep and meaningful ways, especially with regard to long-term retention and application (Perry, Lundie, & Golder, 2018). Designed to encourage an appreciative inquiry process, the protocol invites students to consider their strengths, opportunities, aspirations, and results, and can be used at any point in the year to help students—and educators—home in on students' assets and set goals for growth (Stavros & Cole, 2013; Stavros et al., 2003).

Consider questions such as the following, adapting the questions to a *we* format when students are reflecting on their work in groups. Visit **go.SolutionTree.com/diversityandequity** for a free reproducible version of this SOAR model analysis.

- **Strengths:** What can I build on? (Peregrine Global Services, 2020)
    - What am I most proud of as a learner?
    - What makes me unique?
    - What is my proudest achievement in the last year?
    - How do I use my strengths to get results?
- **Opportunities:** Where do I see opportunities to grow and improve? (Colorado State University Extension, n.d.; Otte, 2015)
    - What are the top three opportunities for growth that I should focus my efforts on?
    - Who are possible new partners and allies for that growth?
    - What are new strategies I might try for improving in these areas?
    - How can I reframe challenges, to see them as exciting opportunities?
    - What new skills do I need to move forward?
- **Aspirations:** What do I care deeply about? (Colorado State University Extension, n.d.)
    - What am I deeply passionate about?
    - Who am I, and who would I like to become?
    - What is my most important aspiration for the future?
    - What strategies might I use to reach my aspirations?
- **Results:** How do I know I am succeeding?
    - How might I measure my progress toward my goals?
    - What specific achievements would indicate that I'm making progress?

- What resources do I need to reach my desired results?
- Who are the supporters and partners who can help me reach my goals?

The authors have seen the SOAR method not only help students identify and define their horizons and aspirations early in the learning process but also celebrate their successes at checkpoints and reflect on their growth as they near the end of their learning journeys. We encourage the use of SOAR as an iterative part of the learning process, one that positions student protagonism as the most powerful and effective way of defining aspirations and goals—without the potential impact of implicit bias.

Capstone Projects

Capstone projects are a tried-and-true way to encourage the student-as-protagonist paradigm, and are particularly well suited to defining what excellence looks like—and might look like in the future—for each student. Capstones can take many forms and have many names, including defenses of learning, senior projects, and culminating projects, but regardless of the title, a great capstone project culminates learning in a demonstration of mastery that is rooted in students' passions and firmly grounded in their voice (Ha, 2017).

What's different between a normal unit-based, inquiry-based project and a capstone project? A unit-based project allows a student to explore the concept or concepts of a specific unit; a good capstone project asks students to innovate and *kulia i ka nu'u* (strive for their highest peak) in a demonstration of mastery that spans multiple units, a year, or even multiple years (R. Peters, personal communication, October 2017). The capstone project asks students to apply learning in novel ways and to demonstrate mastery of multiple concepts and skills with a highly significant archival leave-behind as a marker of learning. Often considered an opportunity for students to defend their readiness for the next phase of education, as measured against the school's portrait of a graduate, capstones are a powerful tool for helping students articulate their current horizon as they close one chapter, and for identifying future goals as they move into the next.

Capstone projects do not have one specific formula, but great capstone projects share the following traits (Ha, 2017).

- **Culmination of learning:** Capstones help to culminate the learning that took place over an extended period of time—multiple units, a year, or possibly an entire degree program.
- **Inquiry driven:** The inquiry should span multiple concepts, skills, and disciplines and ask students to bring something into being that did not exist before.

- **Self-directed:** While capstones are possible for students of all ages, teachers most often use them with students in high school and beyond, as they should require students to work in a highly autonomous way, with the educator-as-coach intervening as little as possible. Many schools implement different levels of capstone projects as exit-point experiences, such as at the end of primary school, the end of middle school, and the end of high school. Teachers also use them with students as young as second or third grade, depending on when students exit lower primary to move to upper primary, or even as part of graduation from preschool or kindergarten, as long as younger students are given scaffolding and the opportunity to practice student-as-protagonist autonomy early in their learning.

- **New idea or ideas:** Capstone projects are not just final essays in disguise. A great capstone may be a piece of writing, but it will bring new ideas and have a real audience that it impacts (besides the educator).

- **Archival leave-behind:** Most good projects will do this, but a capstone leaves behind something that the student can come back to years into the future. While this might be an aspirational goal of every project, it's just not practical for this to happen for every project a student engages with. A capstone is the opportunity for students to leave behind significant evidence of their learning, and most importantly, the impact of that learning.

All the strategies this chapter explores have the same goal: to involve students in co-constructing their horizons in ways that honor who they are and who they want to be. The authors believe that defining each student's horizon is an essential step that helps ensure students—and the educators who work with them—strive for limitless growth and potential. Once students know where they hope to go, and what success might look like for them, they can embark on the pathway of growth toward that horizon.

Reflective Questions

Respond to the following questions alone or with your school team.

- How well do the current systems in your school or classroom allow students to be part of defining their own goals and aspirations? What are the strengths of those systems now, and what would you like to improve?

- How might you employ some of the strategies connected to working with students to define their own horizons? Which might be challenging in your context, and why?

- If you asked your students how much they feel like you consider their strengths and challenges when defining learning goals, what do you think they might say? What might you learn from their answers?

- How much were you able to define your own goals and aspirations growing up? Did you experience other people deciding for you, and how well did their ideas align to your own thinking and the values of your family? How might more space for your own protagonism have changed your learning journey?

Takeaways

The following summarizes key ideas from the chapter.

- Having students involved in defining their own goals matters to their learning. When we involve students in the process of defining their horizon, we honor who they are and want to be, and avoid the limitations educator bias might have on their aspirations.

- Defining the horizon and associated goals improves student motivations and outcomes, as well as providing a tool for assessing progress toward checkpoints and milestones.

- Defining a student's horizon should include other important adults in students' lives, including the student's family, and should recognize what excellence means to that student, not just how the school or teacher defines it.

CHAPTER 5

The Pathway

*It is good to have an end to journey towards;
but it is the journey that matters, in the end.*

—Ursula K. Le Guin

The landscape model asks educators to break down the mindset that learning should be teacher controlled. It places students as the main actors (protagonists) of their learning on the landscape. How does the teacher support each student becoming his, her, or their own main character in the learning story? How is each student's Zone of Proximal Development honored as chapter 2 (page 47) describes? What is the personal (and personalized) pathway that facilitates the growth that each student deserves and is capable of? And how might each student find success (growth and mastery), rather than merely access (basic achievement)?

These are huge questions that can be daunting to address, especially at the classroom level. However, there are simple tools that can support protagonism along students' personal learning pathways. It is also important that educators understand the three terms *differentiation*, *personal* learning, and *personalized* learning, as chapter 2 (page 56) explores.

Moving away from the simplest form of differentiating content for students and toward shepherding learners on the pathway is a necessary paradigm shift to make. The shift from a racetrack metaphor to landscape metaphor allows us to do so quite organically. As explored in chapter 2 (page 45), at its lowest form, differentiation starts with content or skills and modifies them or offers additional supports to make them accessible for the student. For example, a mathematics lesson on fractions may be modified "lower" for one student, using single digit numerators and denominators, or increased in rigor for another student using triple digit fractions. Similarly, teachers might offer an audio recording to a struggling reader to support comprehension or give the student more time to complete a reading quiz. This is a noble and logistically doable starting point, but one we aspire to move beyond.

The pathway asks us to create the boundaries of the landscape based on big concepts and essential transdisciplinary skills, rather than planning based on discipline-specific skills and content. If one student comes to a persuasive writing unit with, say, significant ability in standard written English, but the need to hone persuasion skills, while another student may enter the unit as an English learner with limited standard English, but with strong storytelling and critical-thinking abilities in that student's home language, the path to success will be different. Starting from the student, knowing what he, she, or they can do, and determining what the student's next stage of development might be, is the essential paradigm shift of the pathway, as it allows educators to bend the curriculum toward who students are and what they need. Charting our course along the learning pathway means acknowledging that students are at different starting points and therefore their path toward the horizon will be different.

This chapter will discuss the importance of asset-based thinking and communication along the pathway, supporting student growth in discipline-specific skills, planning units that put students at the center of their educational journey, and shifting educational outcomes, as well as corresponding strategies for each.

Leveraging Asset-Based Mindsets and Communication

This element relies heavily on educators functioning from an asset mindset when it comes to students' skills and strengths, leveraging what students are good at, and being interculturally intelligent in our dealings with them. In its essence, asset-based thinking is about assuming the best about students' inherent capacity to grow and learn, and planning accordingly, while asset-based communication means that *students* know we believe in them because their strengths are at the heart of how we interact with them. Unfortunately, an educator who charts the course along the learning pathway with a student, but with a pervasive focus on that student's weaknesses, will never plan a pathway capable of bringing out the best in that student.

Equity and intercultural expert Rosetta Eun Ryong Lee speaks often on the challenges of developing an asset lens not just in educators, but in students themselves. While it is natural for the human brain to see things based on the void they leave behind, we know that it is also within the human capacity to shift our perspective beyond deficit thinking (Cherry, 2019). At a presentation at the Mount

Vernon Presbyterian School in 2018, Lee told teachers and leaders that "identity models are like a map, but it doesn't actually determine the path that a young person will go through. It turns out we go through different journeys depending on which assets of identity we're talking about" (as cited in Van Rossum, 2018). Given the dissonance between students' experiences in different contexts, particularly for those who experience marginalization for socioeconomic, racial, or other elements of their identity, Lee believes it is the role of educators and parents to prepare students for the reality that their assets may not always be recognized (as cited in Van Rossum, 2018). Lee offers the following language to recognize this dissonance with students:

> I wish we lived in a world where people saw you just as beautiful and capable and wonderful as I do, and many people will. Many people in the world are good and kind and fair and will see you as capable. Every once in a while, though, you're gonna encounter somebody who may not feel this way, and this is not your fault. It's not your fault, and you shouldn't have to deal with this in the world, but you may have to, in which case I want you to be strong and prepared. (as cited in Van Rossum, 2018)

But as Lee points out often, there *shouldn't* be such a big difference between the love and affirmation we receive at home, and the way our educators treat us in school (as cited in Van Rossum, 2018). As a long-term mentor and teacher for marginalized students on scholarship at predominantly White independent schools, Jennifer saw that deficit thinking, however unintentional, easily translated into dangerous comments and actions that injured students' sense of self.

Jennifer's mentee Jessica, a Mexican American girl who entered a predominantly White institution through a scholarship program in sixth grade, had myriad experiences with teachers misunderstanding and underestimating her in ways that eroded her sense of self. Early in Jessica's first year of the scholarship, a teacher suggested to an entire study hall that they should talk to Jessica if they had questions for Spanish class, mispronouncing her last name completely and telling the class, "She speaks Mexican." One of very few students of color in her grade level, Jessica reflected, "I already felt different as it was because I didn't look like everybody else. And then knowing that the *teachers* noticed that, it made me feel even more insecure. It made me not want to be there anymore" (J. Portillo, personal communication, December 6, 2016). When offered support services such as tutoring, Jessica would fall to pieces because, from her perspective, the tutoring sessions felt like indications of her academic weaknesses in comparison to her peers, not attempts to support her growth:

> The tutor made me feel like everything I did, I needed to work on. Like I could do better on *everything* I was doing. She wouldn't really tell

me when she thought I was doing a good job; there was just always something I needed to work on. (J. Portillo, personal communication, December 6, 2016)

Jessica's breaking point came when a high school mathematics teacher told Jessica, in front of the whole class, that she needed to try harder and get things right so she could get into college. Jessica's peers could feel the sting of the comment as well, several approaching her after class to make sure she was all right. Jessica was devastated, paralyzed, and quiet in the moment but quick to seek out Jennifer's advocacy immediately after the class—for the first time in the five years she'd been enduring these microaggressions. In the following weeks, in spite of Jennifer's advocacy, Jessica stopped trying altogether, putting only minimal effort into any of her schoolwork and allowing her grades to drop in almost every subject. This teacher's presupposition of weakness, in the form of a public assertion that she would be a hard-luck case to get into college, was directly related to Jessica's decision to drop the scholarship and leave the predominantly White private school at the end of tenth grade (J. Portillo, personal communication, December 6, 2016). It was the last straw in a pervasive pattern she'd felt since the first day of sixth grade—and which most elements of the school's system and culture had served to ingrain, not relieve. As Jessica put it, "I was the one always getting pulled aside and talked to, not just about my grades but about how I felt, and it made me feel more *different*, not more supported" (J. Portillo, personal communication, December 6, 2016).

It's important to point out that when Jennifer confronted the mathematics teacher about his mistake, he broke down completely—he hadn't considered how the comment would land, really *did* care about Jessica and her academic future, and never intended to make her feel stupid or inadequate. His mistake came from a lack of understanding, not malice, and a tendency to perceive weaknesses before assets—but the impact on Jessica's self-worth was the same as if he had intentionally sabotaged her performance. He was a perfect example of a well-intentioned educator who simply lacked the training and orientation necessary to interact with his student in a strengths-based manner that leveraged her assets. After all, Jessica had won the scholarship because of the excellence and potential she'd shown in elementary school—she was far from being a hard-luck case. But even if she had been, she deserved interactions that honored who she was and what she was capable of, not interactions based on assumptions about her deficits.

The approaches and strategies we describe in this chapter all hinge on avoiding a story like Jessica's by focusing on students' strengths and leveraging them to improve on areas of weakness. When we support students' growth in discipline-specific skills, how are we engaging students in improvement by starting from what they care about and do best? How might we shift our thinking about educational outcomes to adapt to the landscape model and the idea that not all students will be on the same learning pathway? The following sections will offer strategies that help us bring out the best in every student, whatever path the student may be walking.

Leveraging Assets Along the Pathway

Schools supporting students in finding, knowing, and practicing their strengths is not that far-fetched. In fact, many of you probably do this within your classes to some extent already. This strengths-based work must be at the core of a student's experience in school, and developing student's skills as self-advocate is one clear way to do this (Learner Variability Project, n.d.).

Kristen Pelletier, former head of student support services at the International School of Brussels and director of redefining access, asserts that personalized learning along the pathway hinges on schools preparing and supporting students to self-advocate, particularly in special education—a largely inadequate term when we remember that *all* students learn differently across a spectrum from the most challenged to the most gifted, not to mention we have many students who show excellence in one area and challenge in another (personal communication, April 23, 2021). The systems for inclusion at ISB focus on students as self-advocates, and are designed to build students' skills over time so they learn to advocate for what they need, using a continuum of self-advocacy that starts in kindergarten. This continuum is not tied to particular grade levels or ages, but to the developmental and personal readiness of each individual child; Pelletier cites examples of second graders ready to advocate for their needs with teachers and peers, and of ninth graders still working to understand their own learning needs.

In the early stages of the developmental continuum at ISB, students learn to understand their identities as learners, including their assets, challenges, and the strategies that can support them to leverage their assets to support growth in their areas of challenge. The process is taught and guided very specifically until each student reaches the developmental stage where he, she, or they are ready to take on more of the student's own advocacy. Further along the continuum, educators coach students to develop their own voice and, as they are personally ready to do so, to be more in charge of articulating their strengths and needs. As students reach this stage, Pelletier describes students on personalized learning plans leading their own meetings and embracing their roles as protagonists, all of which prepares them to articulate their needs and strengths throughout their lives. The skill of self-advocacy demands a teacher—and a *system*—that supports students in the role of protagonist along the learning pathway. Additionally, the entire continuum requires collaboration with parents, who may need support as their children learn to define their own selves and learning journeys (K. Pelletier, personal communication, April 23, 2021).

There are simple strategies that teachers can use to leverage an asset-based model as students move along the learning pathway, as the ISB continuum suggests. Self-advocacy means that it's not the educator defining students' next steps alone. In fact, the student experience should focus on the student-as-protagonist as much as possible, recognizing that students will need scaffolding and practice to reach the highest possible levels of autonomy and self-awareness. We aspire and work toward students on the landscape being aware of their own strengths and their own next stage of development. While this is a tall order, the following strategies support this goal.

Strategies for Leveraging Assets Along the Pathway

Leveraging students' assets simply means that we ground learning in what students care about and already do well, as a means to motivating their growth in areas needing improvement. By honoring what students care about and are good at, we improve their confidence along the pathway and motivate them toward more significant growth (Fischer et al., 2019). For example, a student who excels in the visual arts but struggles with mathematics might receive an artistic role in a project such as the dignified minimum wage project that chapter 4 (page 101) describes. While he will still be asked to learn the same algebraic concepts and processes, his artistic role leverages his strengths and will motivate him to excel in mathematics as well.

The following strategies help leverage assets on the learning pathway: passion projects, affinity mapping, design thinking as a PBL structure, and student portfolios.

Passion Projects

Passion projects are short projects either independent from or loosely tied to the curriculum, where students receive leeway to accomplish something they are personally passionate about. Bishop T. D. Jakes (2017) says that "If you can't figure out your purpose, figure out your passion. For your passion will lead you right into your purpose." Passion project examples might include students exploring an area of interest, such as a second grader who wants to learn everything he can about race cars, or it might focus on a particular talent students want to grow, such as a fifth grader who wants to improve her soccer play through learning about and practicing new strategies. When Jennifer offered space for passion projects in middle and high school electives, the students who gravitated toward the opportunity generally came with their passions already defined, from the eleventh grader fascinated with programming who came to work on the design of a new application, to the three ninth-grade girls obsessed with Korean culture and K-pop who used the time to build a plan and argument for a semester abroad in South Korea. The project outcomes do not need to support standards per se, and there is no pressure for the project to necessarily support a school-driven outcome. Students receive a little structure, such as the following questions and steps offer, and some time, and they bring something into being that didn't exist before.

Passion projects are small starting points to try when transforming an entire class or unit is not possible. Teachers use them in corporate settings where innovation is a goal; for example, the company 3M is credited with something it calls *15 percent culture*, where it allows employees to spend 15 percent of their work week investigating ideas they choose (3M, n.d.). Passion projects, like scaffolded inquiry, wherein educators pose questions and challenges to help students move through the inquiry process, allow students to dip their toes into the process of leveraging their strengths, and allow educators to give students the room to progress toward their own horizon, even when the school as a whole may not be ready for this type of radical change (McKenna et al., 2019; Serin, 2017). Passion projects have a particularly important impact on students' learning experiences, as Director of Programs for WakeEd Partnership Douglas Price and middle grades teacher Dino Mangano (2019) note, "Passion projects are built as an endeavor to engage students more directly with their own process of learning. Through these projects, students engage in two primary facets of learning: ownership and creativity."

There are many ways to accomplish a passion project, but one version is as follows. Other approaches include elements of design thinking or other inquiry structures, while passages at the Open School in Colorado are structured around six core areas of preparation for life, including *logical inquiry*, *creativity*, *career exploration*, *global awareness*, *adventure/survival*, and *practical skills* (Posner, 2009). See more on passages in chapter 8 (page 219).

Six steps to a good passion project (What School Could Be, n.d.a) are as follows.

1. **Brainstorm:** As a group, brainstorm and document the answers to the following questions.

    ◆ If we could learn anything, what would we want to learn?

    ◆ If we could spend our time doing something fun and useful, what would we want to spend our time on?

    ◆ What do we want to get better at? What do we want to be good at?

Students take all the ideas from the group brainstorm and identify their top three options. Then, with scaffolded support, students choose one topic, as small groups or individuals, to guide their passion projects.

2. **Create a question:** From the topic, create an essential or driving question. What problem are you solving? What questions are you answering?

3. **Research:** Spend some time seeing how others have gone about successfully or unsuccessfully trying the same or similar undertakings. What can we learn from their efforts?

4. **Plan:** Write down the big steps you will take to accomplish your goal and answer your questions.

5. **Create:** Use the time allotted to create, coming back to your plan often to ensure you are on track. Don't be afraid to modify the plan if you need to along the way.

6. **Reflect and present:** Reflect on your accomplishments, and present what you've created and your reflections to an audience that cares, such as parents or peers.

Other protocols, including the following, are similar in that they play around with the structure of how teachers might leverage students' passions and strengths. No matter which tool you choose, you'll have a good starting point to give students the opportunity to leverage their strengths and define their own horizons as they move through their learning experiences.

- **20Time** (20Time.org [n.d.]) came from the 20 percent of time that leading software companies dedicate to passion and play. 20Time projects all include autonomy, mastery, and purpose, and are based on the thesis that we must give students the time to pursue future-ready projects in a less controlled environment.

- **Genius Time** (What School Could Be, n.d.c) is a block of time where students get to pursue their passions and interests with support, but with no direction from the teacher. This can be done in as little as one class period, and a powerful addition is asking students to teach each other what they have learned.

Affinity Mapping

Affinity mapping, or affinity diagramming, can use slightly different steps, but always with the same goals: to allow students to explore their interests and talents and, through that process, to organize them into *working groups*, for projects and otherwise, with peers who share their goals (Kent, 2016). It is not the same as asset mapping, which we explore in chapter 8 (page 206), a practice designed to help us recognize and leverage assets across a community. However, assets are sometimes leveraged as a way to create affinity groups for projects, so that working groups share similar assets. To explore a variety of ways to structure affinity mapping, search the free protocol banks from the School Reform Initiative (www.school reforminitiative.org) and the National School Reform Faculty (https://nsrfharmony .org). Since affinity mapping is based on students' ideas and existing knowledge, and is designed to help them hone in on the topics they're most interested in exploring, it can be done effectively with all ages, with varied levels of scaffolding and support depending on students' ages and needs. This process also allows educators to ensure students recognize and honor each other's talents and ideas, as well as their own, which helps leverage all students' assets across a given classroom or school community.

Following are instructions for the *chalk talk* version of affinity mapping in the adapted form Jennifer uses with student and teacher groups to get them into interest groupings. While the base of the chalk talk was designed by the School Reform Initiative (n.d.), this adaptation offers a simple last step that makes it a form of affinity mapping: it moves students into groups based on what they find most compelling during the activity.

The following three-step process is easy to run with primary, middle, and high school students; and it can even work well with four- or five-year-olds if teachers speak the questions and students draw ideas instead of writing.

1. The teacher prepares several butcher block papers on walls or tables, each with a question related to a possible area of focus for a project or other investigation. For example, if the class is studying the United Nations's (2015a) Sustainable Development Goals, and curricular demands allow students to focus on the goal of their choice, the class might start by narrowing down the goals as a large group, choosing the five to seven it believes are most relevant to their community. Each goal will have its own piece of butcher block paper (the number of topics or papers should be based on the number of students in the class, so that final groups will have an average of three or four members each).

2. The teacher writes (or the students help generate) a "How might we . . . ?" question for each topic or paper, one that helps lead students toward whatever challenge they are trying to solve in their projects. (For example, "How might we support Sustainable Development Goal 2: Zero hunger in our own community and beyond?")

3. Depending on the number of papers, students have fifteen to twenty minutes to write their personal answers to the questions on *all* the

topics. At the end, the teacher asks students to stand by the paper with the topic they most want to work on, and the groups are set for continued work.

If this process ends with too many students interested in the same topic, allow students to organize themselves into two or more groups, based on the assets each student brings to the teams, so that each team has a balance of talents (a strong writer, a strong speaker, a good organizer, and so on). Ideally, if the group has already experienced some strategies involved in understanding the broader context they bring to the ecosystem, there should be little stigma involved in identifying talents—and even in identifying those students who need additional support.

If only one student chooses a topic, allow that student to decide—if another topic allows the student to explore something of interest, the student can move to join a group; but if the topic is an area of deep passion, allow the student to work alone, encouraging him, her, or them to collaborate with peers any time they see the opportunity to do so. This allows us to honor the needs of introverts as well, who will still have plenty of opportunity to collaborate at other moments during the project.

In another version of affinity mapping, an adaptation Jennifer has developed and used, based more specifically on grouping students according to their talents and assets, students write reflections about their strengths, their areas for improvement, and the role they want to play in their team, based on a list of three or four roles the educator prepared in advance or generates with students. Depending on how much time the teacher allots for the project, students might even prepare a résumé to apply for their role of choice in order to build additional asset-based and career-oriented skills. Then, the teacher invites students to form groups that include one person from each role, considering their assets and needs.

Design Thinking as a PBL Structure

While they are often taught and used separately, project-based learning and design thinking have more in common than not, and both are incredibly useful student-centered structures for establishing goals (horizon) and working toward them (pathway). Design thinking (Hasso Plattner Institute of Design at Stanford University, n.d.) is most often articulated as a five-step iterative process, similar to project-based learning in the sense that the following five steps rely on the protagonism of students and work toward a final product over time.

1. **Empathize:** Design thinking is a human-centered protocol that asks practitioners to understand how the "client" feels and what the client needs at a human and emotional level. The empathy interview anchors this stage (see more in chapter 3, page 80).

2. **Define (the problem):** Before we can solve a problem, it's essential that we truly understand the problem. Design thinking uses a problem statement protocol to ensure all participants have a shared understanding of the challenge being met.

3. **Ideate:** Suspending judgement and generating numerous solutions, including those that are ridiculous, ineffective, and downright silly, is a key component to design thinking. By sharing bold and wild ideas, practitioners learn what may work and why, as well as what may *not* work and why, before they implement the solution.

4. **Prototype:** Low-resolution prototypes allow for solutions to be tried, tested, and redesigned before participants invest so many resources in a particular solution that it becomes difficult to change a less-than-effective solution.

5. **Test:** Testing or using a solution and collecting qualitative and quantitative data allows practitioners to modify a prototype, suggesting small changes or taking the solution back to the drawing board, and never settling for *done* but instead aiming for *solved*.

Why incorporate design thinking? While a driving question in project-based learning might be something like "How might we design a solution to keep runoff from entering a stream?" a design-thinking project backs up further, giving students the wider horizon of "Runoff is a problem in our streams," and asking that students define the problem before designing a solution. The protocols used most commonly in design thinking, by definition, demand that the client and the design team drive not only the solution but also the definition of the problem. This activates the student-as-protagonist at a high level, as well as providing a wider horizon with more choices for students to leverage their strengths, gifts, and inspirations to solve real problems. Design thinking, as a process visualized in figure 5.1 (page 128), is a structure that can increase engagement, foster student agency, and develop complex skills such as creativity, problem solving, and collaboration.

In the authors' experience, project-based learning experiences are enriched by adding elements like the empathy interview, for example, which invites students to work to understand the client needs in design thinking, or of the people impacted by a challenge students are trying to solve in PBL. Similarly, design thinking is enriched by utilizing student voice and choice, or by including multiple opportunities for students to reflect on their learning. Ultimately, both pedagogies help students on the landscape because they allow learners to work toward

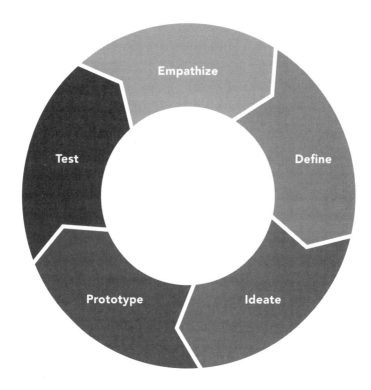

Source: Adapted from Hasso Plattner Institute of Design, n.d.

Figure 5.1: The design-thinking cycle.

*Visit **go.SolutionTree.com/diversityandequity** for a free reproducible version of this figure.*

different horizons or end points, and to chart a course along the pathway based on their interests, talents, and opportunities for growth. This allows students to work from a place of strength, from the assets they bring to the classroom, and to work on areas of challenge through authentic, motivating experiences connected to their interests.

Because design thinking provides protocols to address an issue, educators should not present issues in a clear and sanitized way. Students must instead use strategies of empathy to understand the issue. For example, a great design-thinking issue may be something like addressing student nutrition at school. Rather than presenting a narrow problem with hidden predetermined solutions (like "What might we do to get students to eat more vegetables and less pizza?"), a great design-thinking issue is broad and demands students themselves identify and define the challenge (like "How might we improve students' nutrition on campus?"). This five-step approach positions students as leaders of their own learning, allowing them to determine the horizon they want to work toward (one group might work on removing sugary treats from the vending machines, while another group might work on finding creative ways to get students to eat more fruits and vegetables, and so on).

1. **Define:** After a series of protocols, such as the empathy interview (chapter 3, page 80), students use other design-thinking protocols to define the problem. Some students may define the problem as the temptation of junk food, for example. Others might define it as the availability of healthy food. Yet others might define it from an economic point of view, addressing the price point of junk food as compared to healthy food.

2. **Ideate:** The stage of ideation then asks students to create multiple solutions that are vetted by their potential users. The feedback gleaned pushes students to iterate, possibly throwing out solutions they loved for those that are appreciated by the client. For example, one group may hear from clients (peers in this case) that the solution should address the cost of food, while another group may design a solution around a new menu of food choices.

3. **Create:** Once a group identifies a potential solution, the students create, using prototypes that don't demand a heavy investment in resources so they are more easily iterated, and so the group can integrate feedback without the designer feeling like his, her, or their work and resources were wasted.

4. **Test:** Students test the product and procure feedback from the intended audience, peers, partners for learning (experts who support the learning process), and the teacher.

5. **Repeat:** The cycle then begins again from step 2 until a viable and workable solution is designed and implemented. Many classroom experiences will stop at testing and not start the cycle again from step 2. However, the deeper learning truly happens in repeated reflection and application of the testing data.

Student Portfolios

Another approach on the pathway that positions students as protagonists is the consistent use of student portfolios. Often misunderstood as equivalent to capstone projects, portfolios are meant to be a collection of student work, collected by the student over time, which provides evidence of growth. And while a given course might include a portfolio of best work at the end, as art classes often do, the broader intention of portfolios is to collect work across all courses and over several years (Ciotti, 2012). In their essence, portfolios are a student-led representation of each child's learning pathway.

Student portfolios have been in use for a long time (Driessen, 2016). In fact, the idea of gathering samples of your best (or worst) work is part of nearly every trade, craft, and business. The use of portfolios in the classroom varies. However, great portfolio protocols usually include the following (Ciotti, 2012).

- Collection of student-selected work samples, based on predetermined criteria co-constructed with students
- Reflecting on those work samples (usually on what makes that example exemplary, or how they have learned from work that does not yet demonstrate mastery)
- A summary reflection about the portfolio and the growth it demonstrates
- Goals set for the next portfolio process

Also, as a central part of EL Education's (n.d.) approach to evaluation, high-quality portfolios are developed every year, across grade levels, so that students reach gateway points (elementary school graduation, middle school graduation, and so on) with evidence of the work they've done—not gathered at the end, but throughout the journey (*The Who, What, and Why of Portfolios and Passage Presentations*, n.d.).

If done consistently, student portfolios in high school provide a wealth of excellent work that students can share with universities, to help ensure the admissions process is equally authentic in its insights into students' strengths and potential. To be clear, students should develop their own portfolios; many educators keep folders of students' best work, but it's not a portfolio unless the *student* decides what goes inside and can articulate why. Regardless of where students might be on the landscape, the portfolio will help them communicate learning and celebrate success, as well as provide the sort of documentation of growth educators might need for evaluation purposes. Portfolios therefore act as the ever-bending horizon, adjusting in distance for each student.

Supporting Student Growth in Discipline-Specific Skills

In schools of the future, preparing students for their futures will certainly need to be structured differently. The ubiquitous nature of content and the rise of machine intelligence will mean that much of what we teach in schools will become irrelevant to a greater extent than it already is (Wagner & Dintersmith, 2016). In 21st century schools, however, small steps to big change are the realistic pathway to school reform, particularly in terms of how we develop students' discipline-specific skills. Teachers, principals, and even superintendents can't necessarily change the metrics by which their schools are judged and therefore funded, so ensuring that the landscape supports core disciplinary learning and discipline-specific skills is essential—skills such as numeracy, reading fluency, reading comprehension, and content knowledge.

Discipline-specific skills still have a place in the 21st century schoolhouse, and they are an important part of learning on the pathway. If educators can leverage simple strategies to support discipline-specific skill acquisition in a more personal way, we can free the educator to embrace the role of landscape-learning-facilitator, rather than sage-on-the-stage or skill-drill tutor. The strategies that follow can help you as the teacher do just that: support discipline-specific skill acquisition in ways congruent with the landscape model.

PERSPECTIVES ON WALKING THE LEARNING PATHWAY
Testimonial by Dwayne Priester

Dwayne Priester is the secondary principal at Mid-Pacific Institute in Honolulu, Hawai'i.

Since 2000, I have dedicated a significant amount of time challenging two fundamental untruths about teaching and learning. First, the traditional methods of measuring student learning are, at best, inadequate and fall short of their intended purpose. Second, the one-size-fits-all approach to delivering instruction has long become antiquated. This approach to teaching has divested countless students of a quality learning experience.

You may be asking what evidence I have to support these claims. For the past twelve years, I have collaborated extensively with our faculty and deans and counselors at Mid-Pacific as we engaged in a process of gathering and analyzing feedback from our students and their parents. Our purpose was to examine our current assessment methodology. As a result of our careful review of these data, we discovered two important facts that have dramatically changed how we approach teaching and report student learning. First, as suspected, we found that the traditional letter-grading system (As, Bs, Cs, and so on) did not comprehensively articulate what our students learned. Second, when asking parents and students if they could, with certainty, explain what their children's grades meant, they consistently responded, "No." However, as we moved away from simple grades toward a reporting system that integrated more specificity such as deep narratives and descriptors of learning and accomplishments, parents could speak more in depth about their student's learnings. Further, parents were able to interpret the grades their students received.

This reimagining of teaching and learning through the lens of assessment initiated swift revisions to our former approaches to delivering instruction.

> Rather than exclusively utilizing the traditional path of repeatedly teaching and testing, we approach learning as an ongoing journey. What this means is that we understand learning as a continuum of exploration—imagining and reimagining, risk taking, acquiring knowledge, and refining. On this same premise of learning as an ongoing journey, we took another radical step. We no longer assign a numeric value to a student's homework and class participation, nor demerits for late assignments. Additionally, we ended administering final exams. Instead, we created opportunities to make student learning visible. Rather than sitting for tests and exams, students had opportunities to develop projects (both individual and collaborative) and to engage in action research, a process by which research is conducted and improvements made as learning happens. Classmates, faculty, and community members provided feedback and evaluated student learning based on a clearly articulated criterion. While this process is extensive and requires a significant amount of work to develop, it reflects student learning both authentically and holistically.
>
> Our students and faculty were willing to adopt these bold but necessary steps to embark on a unique co-learning journey. As data were collected regarding each student and the student's learning, this created the capacity for our faculty and deans or counselors to explore designing and modifying instruction based on student needs. The fruit of this collaborative work of our students, faculty, deans, and counselors is that instruction became unique and relevant to our students' individual learning needs.
>
> *Source: D. Priester, personal communication, September 30, 2021.*

Strategies for Supporting Student Growth in Discipline-Specific Skills at a Personal Level

Many readers may be familiar with the strategies from the work of Lucy Calkins (2001; Calkins & Hartman, 2013). While the work has been popularized in English language arts, the strategies that make up the workshop are effectively used in all disciplines, especially when practicing and growing students' skills.

Workshop Model for Skill-Based Disciplines

The workshop model allows discipline-specific skills to be learned and applied in a manner congruent with the landscape model. Three specific strategies are used in the context of a workshop that allow educators to know what each student can do, and to support their next level of development: (1) conferring, (2) strategy groups, and (3) guided groups (Calkins, 2001; Calkins & Hartman, 2013). On a regular basis throughout the year, the teacher leverages these three strategies while students engage in independent reading or authoring (Calkins, 2001; Calkins & Hartman, 2013; Koesel, 2020). By using these approaches, educators can apply what they know about students' broader contexts, as well as the goals students have set, to co-construct the best pathway for each student (Calkins, 2001; Calkins & Hartman, 2013; Koesel, 2020).

Each tool has the educator working with a single student, or a small group of students, so what are the other students to do while the teacher's focus isn't on the whole class? The goal is that over the course of weeks and months, students build stamina to work independently or collaboratively as readers, authors, scientists, mathematicians, musicians, artists, and so on. While a teacher is working with an individual or small group, the students *do:* they create, design, build, write, calculate, inquire, and so on. In a language arts workshop, the students might be reading or writing based on a shared minilesson (a ten- to fifteen-minute lesson that directs the independent work time). This could be similar in a mathematics workshop, or a workshop in any other discipline. This approach allows educators to provide support where needed, in a variety of configurations, while simultaneously developing students' skills as protagonists on the learning journey.

Conferring

Conferring refers to one-to-one work between one teacher and one student. It is usually accompanied by a running record or conferring log, where the educator notes which skills the student is working on, records the student's progress, and those notes follow a student from conference to conference. Teachers track discipline-specific skills, noting what students *can* do and using a skills continuum to identify the student's next stage of development. In this way, conferring is both assessment and teaching. Conferring should happen ideally once per week, per student. In larger classes, it can happen as infrequently as once per month.

The three goals of conferring are the following.

1. Understand where the student is in his, her, or their learning and what the student can do right now.

2. Understand the student's next stage of development, being careful to maintain an asset mindset about the student's ability to learn and grow. Teachers identify what a student *can* do and use a predetermined continuum of skills to identify his, her, or their next stage of development.

3. Use the one-to-one setting to support students in moving forward. The teacher uses the next session to support the student one to one, or uses data collected from conferring to place the student in the correct

small-group setting for work with students at a similar level, or students working on a similar strategy.

Strategy Groups

Strategy groups are heterogeneous groupings of students where each group works on a single strategy. A strategy, by definition, has steps, and a strategy group leverages differences rather than similarities to support peer-to-peer learning as a supplement to teacher instruction and coaching (Koesel, 2020).

A strategy group's focus is usually curriculum driven. For example, in a specific mathematics unit, all students should understand how to divide by breaking down tricky numbers into friendly numbers. The educator gathers a group of students of varying skills and shares the strategy using an example that all students can access. Then, the group practices the strategy using examples of varying complexity, allowing students to support each other. The educator supports the group, listening and watching how each student is understanding and using the strategy, and provides light facilitation as the group works together.

Strategy groups are purposefully heterogeneous so students learn from their peers and have the opportunity to deepen their knowledge by teaching or explaining what they know to peers. Heterogeneous groupings are also helpful to ensure students broaden how they think through a challenge, exposing them to varying ways of approaching a problem (Wang, 2013). There are times where homogeneous groupings are preferable. For those times, the workshop model recommends guided groups.

Guided Groups

Guided groups are homogeneous groups of students where the educator works on raising students' skill levels. Students of similar skill level share the same group, and the educator works in their Zone of Proximal Development (Vygotsky, 1978). For more on the ZPD, see the Zone of Proximal Development as a Dynamic Model section later in this chapter (page 141).

Guided groups are usually convened using some sort of diagnostic data, for example, students of a similar reading level. The educator instructs students at their current ability level, and then at the next more challenging level, and individualizes the learning to best reach students where they are in their learning and needs. Similar to differentiation, this strategy starts with the student (in this case, a small group of students) and then provides them specific support where they are, regardless of where the rest of the class is. This strategy allows for personalized learning to happen in more efficient ways. Groups are reorganized regularly with different members to ensure they are always convened with students of the most similar level possible.

Student Shadowing

Shadowing a student is a powerful tool to gain empathy, build understanding, and gain insight into the realities of how students experience the learning pathway. Different practitioners articulate the process in different ways, but shadowing usually includes the following four elements (Schwartz, 2016; Zmuda, 2016).

1. **Prepare:** In the preparation element, educators shadowing students define their goals (for example, understanding what the experience of a twelfth grader is at your school or seeing the school through the eyes of a student with attention deficits). The preparation element includes securing permission from parents or guardians (ideally through a permission slip that explains the opportunity), stating intentions to the community (usually through a school bulletin, short video, or combination of media), and committing to post-shadowing sharing (with pertinent constituencies in ways that protect the anonymity of students).

2. **Shadow:** Shadowing is most effective when it is "door to door," meaning that the educator quite literally walks through the school day alongside the student, from the start of a student's commute to the student's arrival back at home (D. Espania, personal communication, 2019). This ensures the educator understands the entirety of a student's day. However, beginning and ending the shadow experience at a student's front door adds significant complexity and permissions, and therefore most experiences start at arrival to school and end at dismissal. The educator participates as the student does, in all activities.

3. **Reflect:** Soon after shadowing, the educator reflects in formal ways, capturing the experience, themes, questions, and insights. The reflection is most powerful when it is shared out with a broader community. Action steps are outlined and committed to.

4. **Act:** Insight gained is acted on. This step is important to close the loop and make the shadow experience worthwhile. When a community sees the understanding of its experience impacting the system, it's more invested in that system.

Shadowing a student for even one day can build a great deal of understanding of and empathy for what the learning pathway feels like for students, providing opportunities for educators to adjust their practices when they recognize a negative impact, such as low engagement, or to amplify a successful practice, such as activities students enjoy. For schools interested in immersing educators or other stakeholders in students' experiences over time, RESCHOOL Colorado has designed a game called REVOLVE that simulates a full year in a public school student's shoes (Fuller, 2020). While the game aspect may make the shadow element less concrete and visceral than physically following a student for a day at school, REVOLVE is designed on the basis of case studies from real students and the real factors in their lives. Described as "a card-based immersive experience that builds empathy for young people and highlights the valuable learning that happens everywhere" (Fuller, 2020), REVOLVE can take educators deep into the lives of young people, helping us understand their experiences in any context.

Planning Units That Put Students at the Center of Their Educational Journey

The Native Hawaiian proverb *Ma ka hana ka ʻike* says that through doing, comes learning. It is through *doing* that students become actors in their education. At a small level, it is disappointing to imagine yourself as the main actor in a worksheet, completed at your desk. However, once action has been added to the equation, the student-as-protagonist can truly come to life.

Putting students at the center of their educational journey is about honoring what we learned about their place in the ecosystem, understanding what their desired horizon is, and planning learning experiences that allow for student protagonism and appropriate personal challenge along the pathway. To plan for *Ma ka hana ka ʻike* (action in learning and learning through action), student-centered iterative unit planning and the Zone of Proximal Development prove to be powerful tools.

Strategies for Planning Units That Put Students at the Center of Their Educational Journey

Student-centered iterative unit planning and ZPD as a dynamic model are two strategies discussed in the following sections. Both provide approaches to planning that are deeply tied to students' strengths and interests, and which invite educators to design learning experiences that engage students' previous learning and curiosities, their learning styles, how we hope to measure growth, and where we might go next.

Student-Centered Iterative Unit Planning

Student-centered iterative unit planning does not ask educators to make individual units for each student, nor to leave infinite options and infinite changes driven by students as they engage with each unit. Student-centered iterative unit planning does not ask educators to design a unit on dinosaurs for student X and a unit on space for student Y. Instead, charting the pathway on the landscape is about developing plans that allow for perhaps five or six potential pathways through learning that connect with students' strengths and interests to motivate growth in their areas needing attention. It asks educators to be critical and prioritize the learning outcomes. It then asks them to consider the students (their strengths and their growth areas), capitalize on their curiosity, and adjust as they go along. This might look like a project-based experience in which students work on solving an authentic challenge. All students will need some of the same learning in terms of content and skills, but their solutions to the challenge can come from their own ideas and interests. The educator uses the prompt to create the boundaries of the landscape. All students engage in the same unit or project, but educators plan for differences in where students start on the landscape and respond to students' contexts and interests as they shepherd them through the landscape toward the horizon.

Many educators are familiar with the Understanding by Design (UbD) work of Jay McTighe and Grant Wiggins (2012). UbD is a backwards planning protocol that asks educators to plan units rather than discrete lessons, and to do so by first starting with the big ideas and concepts that are important for students to uncover through inquiry (McTighe & Wiggins, 2013).

- Stage 1 asks educators to start with the end in mind, defining the educational outcomes they are working toward with students (much like the horizon asks us to do).

- Stage 2 asks educators to design an assessment that will allow students to show their teacher what they have learned (similar to defining the horizon).

- Stage 3 is the lesson plan phase, where teachers plan the learning experiences necessary to support mastery of standards and concepts (akin to the pathway of the landscape).

While UbD helps teachers around the world to begin with the end in mind, student-centered iterative unit planning can even more powerfully support learning on the landscape because it begins with the assumption that students will enter the learning at different levels (R. Peters, personal communication, October 2017).

Student-centered iterative unit planning uses six questions in an iterative cycle, rather than the linear model of UbD (Ciotti, 2020; R. Peters, personal communication, October 2017). Unlike UbD, where a teacher plans the unit ahead of time and then moves through the unit following a series of lesson plans, student-centered iterative unit planning asks educators to design a unit that is flexible in structure and that can be (and should be) adjusted as the unit is in progress.

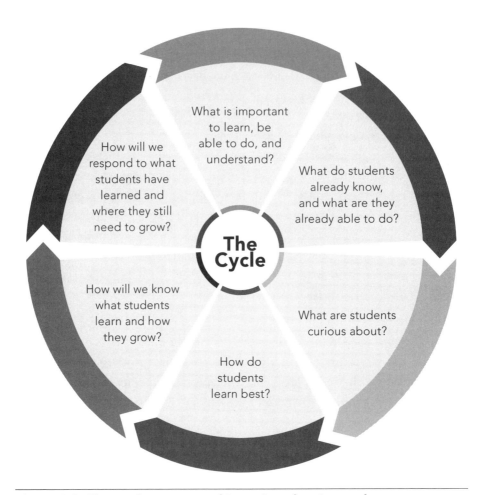

Figure 5.2: The student-centered iterative planning cycle.

A school that wholeheartedly embraces this style of unit planning is Hanahau'oli School, a small century-old unapologetic social-constructivist school in the hills above Honolulu, Hawai'i. Its former head of school, Robert G. Peters, led Hanahau'oli (which means *joyous work* in the Hawaiian language) for thirty years, embracing a pedagogy of progressive education that aligns well with the landscape model (Hanahau'oli School, n.d.).

During Peters's tenure, a kindergarten class at Hanahau'oli had planned a unit on its school community and interdependence: Who is part of our school community, and how does each person's role play an important part in our community being successful? This was a hands-on unit, steeped in student inquiry and student-as-protagonist pedagogy, and the unit was going amazingly . . . until the bees moved in. In the middle of the unit, everything ground to a halt as a colony of bees made its home in the tree at the center of the kindergarten play area. No recess, no outdoor play. The school needed to call a beekeeper to remove the dangerous bees. Worst of all, the students wanted nothing more than to talk about the bees buzzing around outside their classroom. Instead of letting the bees derail the unit, the educators iterated. They re-asked the question: "What are students curious about?" *Bees* was the new answer. And they shifted the inquiry in the unit from community interdependence to garden interdependence and studied the bees' role in garden interdependence. The students still explored the same big ideas, but the educators adjusted so that it was through the lens of what students were most curious about.

This type of on-the-fly adjustment to planning and pacing can seem intimidating in the context of linear planning. In most classes, there's a pacing guide, with standards and skills that students must accomplish in a certain order and in a certain window of time, or learning will get (even more) behind (than it already is). Wherever we go, in every school and across numerous countries, the educators we speak to share this sentiment, that educational pacing needs to provide far more flexibility to capitalize on unplanned events that spark curiosity and deep learning for students. Student-centered iterative unit planning allows for planning at a high level, ensuring the big ideas and concepts that are most important are touched on. Furthermore, it leaves room for students and their curiosity to be at the center, not the periphery, of the unit-planning process.

What Is Important for Students to Know, Be Able to Do, and Understand?

This first step is glaringly missing in educational systems around the world. Most teacher-preparation programs don't presume to educate excellent curriculum writers. And most schools subscribe to systems of standards that experts in their field create, people far more expert in mathematics, for example, than the average K–12 educator. However, these experts create these bodies of standards and curricula without knowing the context of *your* students, *your* school, and *your* community. This context is important, as is the fact that the standards contain more content than educators have time to teach and students have time to learn. Multiply that by the number of disciplines needing to be taught, and you have a recipe for rushed learning that is all breadth and no depth. This first question asks teachers to be the professional educators they are and not rewrite but *reprioritize* standards, benchmarks, skills, and concepts. What is most important for your students, now, in this context? By asking these questions and prioritizing, educators create the boundaries of the landscape.

The best answers to this question come from the *people in the room*. Experienced educators know what their students really do need to know. In conjunction with a critical examination of bodies of educational standards and facilitation by curricular and pedagogical leaders, schools can and should engage in this important conversation regularly.

What Do Students Already Know? What Can They Already Do? What Do They Already Understand?

Teachers ask these questions while planning the unit as well as throughout the unit as it is taught. These questions help us to understand the previous learning students bring into the learning ecosystem. Knowing what students bring to the landscape with regard to prior knowledge and skills helps ensure we calibrate the unit to best meet student learning needs and best leverage strengths. Educators re-ask this question throughout the unit, as they use the tools for understanding students' broader context, as described in chapter 3 (page 67), to better understand what students bring to the learning experience.

What Are Students Interested In? Curious About?

Again, teachers ask this question in unit planning and then throughout the unit as it is taught. During unit planning, the educator puts him-, her-, or theirself in the shoes of students and predicts what will excite them, what will cause them awe, and what will inspire curiosity. On the landscape, this question is answered in large part by the ongoing work educators do to understand the identities, strengths, and needs their students bring into the learning ecosystem, as well as the aspirations and concrete goals students develop. The answers become the source for inquiry, the essential question, and the inquiry-based assessments. Like the second question, teachers ask this question throughout the unit, using tools like the KWL or RAN chart, Socratic seminar, or other questioning or inquiry techniques (see chapter 3, page 86).

How Do Students Learn Best?

While this can seem like a high-level philosophical question, setting up a dichotomy of behaviorism versus constructivism, for example, it also asks a much smaller question, one much closer to students. Behaviorism is a theory that leverages rewards (and at times punishments) to influence a person's actions (Moore, 2011). Constructivism, by contrast, is a theory that sees humans as constructing their own understanding of concepts and knowledge through their unique experiences (Concept to Classroom, 2019). How do *your* students learn best? You may have your philosophy of learning set already; you may believe that students learn best through hands-on learning, inquiry, practice, and feedback. The authors believe that defining one's pedagogical beliefs is essential for all educators.

However, at the unit-planning level, the question asks how *your* students learn *this material* best. Given what you've learned about the experiences, cultures, and assets they bring into the learning ecosystem, how might *your* kindergarteners learn about interdependence best? Do they have a community partner that could serve as a hands-on learning site? Do they respond well to videos or collaborative learning? And how do we accommodate those students who might have a different preferred style as compared to the rest of the class? Again, you as a teacher must ask this question not only while planning the unit but also during its implementation.

What Have Students Learned? How Do We Know?

These questions, asked during the planning phases, press teachers to design assessments where students can show their understandings and tell us what they have learned. Rather than the teacher asking and the students responding, and rather than an assessment that asks the students to leave their learning on a piece of paper and walk away from it, how might an assessment allow students to demonstrate what they have learned and take that learning with them? Two tools that do this well are performance tasks and authentic assessments, where students not only demonstrate their mastery in the assessment, but extend their learning by engaging in the demonstration of learning (page 168). Teachers then ask these questions during the unit through formative assessments, informing adjustments that might be made during the unit to best reach students where they are.

Zone of Proximal Development as a Dynamic Model

As we explored in principle two (chapter 2, page 47), the ZPD is a vital strategy for putting students at the center of their learning, and it has connections to all of the elements; the ZPD helps educators understand where students are now in their skills and understandings (horizon), understand which goals are developmentally appropriate (horizon), and chart a pathway that challenges students appropriately (pathway). The authors believe the ZPD is particularly useful as a dynamic model that can help educators chart the most appropriate pathway through the learning experience. This tool is valuable for all students, not just those in special education.

In classrooms today, the ZPD is still being used as a lens to increase learning. Movements in problem- and project-based learning embrace the theory as a framework for supporting scaffolding and student autonomy and agency (Harland, 2003; Kurt, 2020). Twenty-first century students are also experiencing artificial intelligence software that aims to find their ZPD and provide learning and support targeted specifically for them. ZPD has gained traction and increased in relevancy as it has matured as a theory, and is vital to any classroom or school working with the landscape model.

To support teaching in the ZPD framework, educators Rob Wass and Clinton Golding (2014) created a checklist for educators to reflect on their teaching and to adjust lessons as needed. This checklist assumes that teachers are doing regular formative assessments, in varied forms and opportunities, to ensure they can correctly identify what students currently know and can do. These questions support student-centered iterative unit planning. The following are guiding questions that could improve ZPD delivery within a unit (Vygotsky Learning Conference, n.d.).

- Am I teaching in my students' ZPD?
    - What can my students currently do, and how do I know?
    - What can they potentially do with scaffolding?
- Would my assistance offer scaffolding for my students or mere structure? In other words, would my assistance make a difference in students being successful in outcomes and growing in independence?
- What are the most effective scaffolds I can provide?
- How am I providing a conducive teaching environment?
- What could I do to create a more conducive environment for student learning?
- What are the hardest tasks my students can do, if I provide the most effective scaffolds, in the most conducive environment?

Educators can ask these questions independently to reflect on the facilitation and evolution of a unit, or they could ask them within their collaborative teams to iterate a unit. Regardless, the ZPD helps us adjust the course as we move along the pathway, to ensure that we are challenging all students appropriately.

Reexamining What the Outcomes of Good Education Should Be

Roberto d'Erizans, head at the Millennium School, suggests that to best chart the pathway we need to redefine success when we're establishing goals—or before: "Fundamentally, we have to redefine what success means," he says. "Is success really measured in that kind of 'I got an A, therefore I'm a good kid' kind of way? What do we want out of students?" (R. d'Erizans, personal communication, June 1, 2021). The landscape model of learning aligns to this way of thinking about students' growth and educational outcomes, as it requires educators to work *with* students to define their most appropriate horizon, a process which requires that we think through what success looks like with students. Redefining success really means defining success as the journey across the landscape rather than the destination alone; in other words, *navigating* the course along the pathway. By shifting our definition of success to include progress as much as final results, educators can shift their thinking about educational outcomes so that they more fully capture who students are and how much growth they experience along the pathway, not just the end result of the journey.

Two specific tools support this type of redefinition of success: (1) progress-based assessment and (2) redefined educational outcomes.

Progress-Based Assessment

Progress-based assessments are critical and powerful in supporting a personally charted course along the pathway. While we take a deeper dive into assessments in chapter 6 (page 155), it's important to begin to understand their formative role on the pathway. To understand progress-based assessment, it's necessary to start by defining other forms of assessment. First, most educators experienced predominantly summative, achievement-based assessment while in school as students. We studied content and grew in our skills based on what a teacher taught us. Then, we took a test and got a percentage on that test, which was translated to a letter grade: a 75 percent would earn us a C, for example. However, that test was usually made up of multiple skills and lots of content. Did the C mean we had passable ability in all of the skills and knew 75 percent of all the content? Or did it mean we were excellent at some skills and had major needs in other skills? The C grade did not tell us this.

From there, the world began to embrace standards-based assessment and grading (Mahr, 2020). Rather than a C representing the summation of multiple skills and content areas, standards-based assessment and grading asks educators to assess each standard and skill, and to report on the mastery of that particular benchmark. A summative test might have six major skills and multiple standards embedded in it. A standards-based report would say which standards students mastered, which were approaching mastery, and which needed significant growth.

This is a huge evolution forward, giving students, parents and guardians, and educators more relevant information about what students can do and their next stage of development. However, while it offers significant advantages over traditional grading practices, it does nothing to capture the learning journey itself. What if a student comes to a course knowing 90 percent of the content already? What if they begin a Mandarin Chinese language class already conversationally fluent? Or, what if a different student starts the year two grade levels behind and grows a grade level and a half in the school year? In both cases, standards-based assessment and grading fails to capture the learning journey.

Progress-based assessment requires that the educator know what different stages of progress look like along a formative continuum. Education researchers Irene C. Fountas and Gay Su Pinnell (2017) offer the quintessential example of this type of continuum, where different reading levels or behaviors are plotted along a line to allow for the charting of advancement in skills by the student. Fountas and Pinnel (2017) delineate reading behaviors in multiple domains, and chart out what the next stage of reading might look like. Other continua have been created by schools like Hanahau'oli School (n.d.), which uses continua to track progress in all disciplines. Such continua allow educators to shift their thinking about success, ensuring that progress is as important as the end result when we define what learning objectives and mastery look like.

Teachers can use continua in any subject or discipline. They are most useful in showing progress in skills that build off each other, like writing skills, where students develop their abilities to write argumentatively, for example. Educators can also use them to track progress in demonstrating conceptual knowledge, like in science, where a student might develop a deeper understanding of a concept like *interdependence*. Figure 5.3 shows how a teacher might use a continuum to track growth in second-grade science based on a Next Generation Science Standard of structures of property and matter (NGSS Lead States, 2013). The continuum tracks the growing independence and consistency a student might demonstrate over a two-quarter unit.

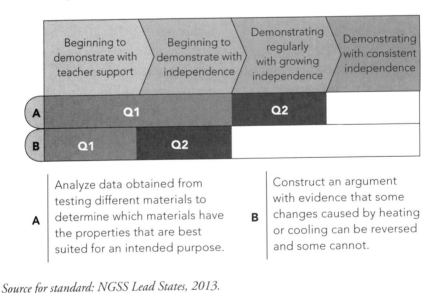

Source for standard: NGSS Lead States, 2013.

Figure 5.3: Sample continuum to track grade 2 science progress.

Progress-based assessment supports an educator knowing what students can do now, helps point them to their next stage of development, and honors the work done (and illuminates any lack of progress). A student who made fourteen months of progress in a single school year can be celebrated, even if proficiency is still below grade-level standards. And educators can identify and encourage the student who coasted through class, depending on his, her, or their prior knowledge and not growing to challenge themselves more.

Redefined Educational Outcomes

Great education considers outcomes that truly transform the student, helping the student grow to be future-ready with skills such as creativity, problem solving, and critical thinking. To further redefine success, we must look at educational outcomes in a taxonomy of four major categories.

1. **Content:** Content refers to facts and citable knowledge, things that one might find in an encyclopedia or on a search engine. Students can answer content-specific true-or-false and multiple-choice questions.

2. **Discipline-specific skills:** Discipline-specific skills refer to skills in one academic discipline like mathematics, language arts, or music, for example. They include things like the ability to multiply two-digit numbers, reading fluency, and playing a C scale on a clarinet. Discipline-specific skills are described as "Students will be able to . . ." and are specific to a single discipline.

3. **Concepts:** Concepts are big ideas such as interdependence. There is a factual definition of interdependence that is different than the conceptual definition. A conceptual understanding of interdependence would include being able to apply the new understanding from the context of the interdependence of organisms on a coral reef to the interdependence of organisms in a garden, to the interdependence of people in a town.

4. **Learning traits and complex transdisciplinary skills:** Traits of learning are complex traits that are actually patterns of multiple skills practiced over time. Examples of traits of learning are problem solving, creativity, and communication. Communication is a broad skill that one cannot measure in one single assessment but must rather assess as a pattern of multiple skills demonstrated in multiple contexts over time.

This list functions as an inverted hierarchy, describing increasingly complex outcomes for education. The first two, disciplinary content knowledge and discipline-specific skills, were the main focus of education in the past, and continued to be prioritized throughout the American No Child Left Behind (2002) era (and similarly continue to be the central outcomes of highly standardized baccalaureate systems and high-stakes testing). We know how to measure content and discipline-specific skills. The tools necessary to do so are readily available to educators, and assessing understanding is generally efficient and easy to manage. Administrators and school systems demand the results of such measurements and then measure one school against another. There's nothing wrong with teaching and measuring content and discipline-specific skills, except that content is ubiquitous. A student with a smartphone has access to more content than U.S. President William Clinton did during his presidency from 1993–2001. If you can search it, should it be the focus of students' learning?

This is not to say that content is not important. Content is the building block of good learning. Students need content knowledge they can use, building skills and growing in conceptual understanding and traits of learning. Schools should support students to be readers, authors, scientists, artists, musicians, athletes, and mathematicians, and each discipline has a specific set of skills that is necessary to be successful. But again, should learning stop here?

Concepts are the big ideas that power our world, ideas such as interdependence, justice, and equity (Ciotti, 2020; R. Peters, personal communication, October 2017). These concepts exist as content as well. There is a dictionary definition of interdependence, but that's not what we are talking about here. Do students truly understand the concept of interdependence, and can they make connections, for example, between interdependence of organisms in a garden, in a coral reef, and in an urban community?

Learning traits and complex transdisciplinary skills such as communication, collaboration, and creativity are not straightforward and therefore require time and multiple touchpoints to assess (Gibb, 2013). These are complex patterns of multiple skills that transcend any particular discipline and are demonstrated over longer periods of time. For example, it's not possible to assess the depth and breadth of a person's critical-thinking ability in a single assessment. Therefore, strategies like those in the following sections are essential.

Strategies for Shifting Educational Outcomes on the Pathway

Schools have successfully used the defining outcomes protocol to help schools redefine their educational outcomes to include conceptual learning as well as learner traits. It is a simple way to redefine educational outcomes to better support students in charting their course.

Collaborative Protocol for Defining Outcomes

The collaborative defining outcomes protocol supports clarification and redefinition of educational outcomes with the following six steps (Ciotti, 2020).

1. In a collaborative team, one teacher brings a unit to present for feedback and development.

2. The educator presents the unit, sharing the relevant essential question, assessments, learning plan, and other details to help peers understand the unit, its relevance, and its implementation. (Five minutes)

3. The presenter moves back from the group and turns his, her, or their chair to face the other direction, not responding to the conversation but just taking notes on anything relevant that the presenter hears.

4. The group discusses the following questions.

    * What content is important for students to have in order to best interact with this unit? What should students *know* that will support their navigating and sense-making in this unit? (Three minutes maximum)

    * What discipline-specific skills are being introduced for the first time, practiced and given feedback, and mastered and assessed for reporting? (Three minutes maximum)

    * What is the main concept that students should understand at the end of this unit? And how might they apply this concept outside of this unit? (Three minutes maximum)

    * What learning traits and complex transdisciplinary skills are students practicing? Specifically, how are students getting the opportunity to be: creative, collaborative, autonomous, interculturally savvy, strong communicators, and critical thinkers? (Three minutes maximum; note that schools should focus on the essential skills identified in their community's portrait of a graduate)

5. The presenter responds to the discussion by sharing the following.

    * What resonated with them and what seemed off base
    * New thoughts they have now from listening to the discussion
    * Further questions they have now from listening to the discussion
    * Next steps to ensure that all four categories of outcomes are present and strong in the unit

6. The presenter turns discussion outcomes into action steps.
   - List outcomes that need to be deleted from the unit.
   - List outcomes that need to be added to the unit.
   - Follow up in the next meeting to ensure continuity of action.

This is a collaborative discussion protocol that helps clarify outcomes of education. While it may force educators to adjust their planning as they go, based on what students actually need to work on, that is precisely the point—the process allows educators to bend the learning pathway toward the current needs of the students in their classrooms. Use it to redefine what outcomes you truly value for students, both in terms of their progress and their end result. These outcomes and the path to them are essential as you navigate the pathway along the landscape. (For more on adjusting curriculum, see chapter 8, page 195.)

Using Wise Criticism to Keep Challenge High

Professor Rachel Godsil, cofounder and codirector of the Perception Institute, and colleagues (2017) proposes *wise criticism*, a strategy for the pathway through learning that, rather than professing high standards alone or lowering standards for some, asks educators to clearly articulate to students that the bar is high, that we believe everyone can succeed in their own way, and that we are there to coach and support students to their highest potential. This sounds like: "I'm giving you this feedback because the bar is set high. I believe you can meet the goal, and I'm here to help." As such, it is a vital strategy for supporting high levels of challenge and success for all students at all points along the pathway.

Research shows that wise criticism helps students of disenfranchised races, genders, and socioeconomic status perform better academically (Godsil, Tropp, Goff, Powell, & MacFarlane, 2017). It also actively mitigates the implicit biases that we all carry, allowing educators and educational institutions to be more equitable in how learning is facilitated by ensuring that all students receive an unbiased level of challenge and support. Wise criticism is one concrete strategy that allows educators to break away from the paradigm of sameness as an educational outcome, while not lowering standards or creating inequity. This strategy then helps us as educators to define a horizon that is in the student's proper Zone of Proximal Development (ZPD; Vygotsky, 1978), meaning the most appropriate next level of challenge according to the student's current strengths and needs as a learner. (See more on the ZPD in chapter 2, page 47.)

Three wise criticism steps establish the following.

1. **The high standard of success and the expectation that you will give feedback to support the student moving from the current level to meeting or exceeding the standard:** This will sound like, "I'm going to be giving you feedback along the way, so that you will know how to grow your own skills and understanding."
2. **Belief in the student's ability:** This will sound like, "I believe you can work hard toward this goal and achieve success."
3. **A coaching relationship and expectation:** This will sound like, "Expect me to give you feedback. Expect my support. I'm here for you as you work hard to accomplish these goals."

However, as we undertake our work along the pathway, what is clear is that the learning experience needs to value progress and growth as much as final outcomes, and to honor where students are and what they need from us along the way. Recognizing that students come into the ecosystem with different gifts and challenges, and that their horizons may be significantly different, we believe that the pathway through learning should be as personalized as possible and should invite and encourage the highest levels of positive challenge possible for each student.

Reflective Questions

Respond to the following questions alone or with your school team.

- How well do the current systems in your school or classroom allow students to take different pathways through their learning? What are the strengths of those systems now, and what would you like to improve?
- How might you employ some of the strategies connected to developing more centered, personal pathways through learning? Which might be challenging in your context, and why?
- If you asked your students how much they feel like their learning experiences capitalize on their talents and interests in meaningful ways, what do you think they might say? What might you learn from their answers?
- How much were you able to determine your own pathway through learning growing up? How flexible were your teachers when you wanted to pursue a particular topic or skill that interested you? How might more space for your own protagonism have changed your learning journey?

Takeaways

The following summarizes key ideas from the chapter.

- Having students involved in charting their own pathway through learning allows educators to help them work toward success in more personalized ways.
- Redefining educational success to include both growth along the pathway *and* the end-of-unit outcomes allows educators to honor both as equally important.
- Planning units that include flexibility along the pathway and can shift according to the interests of students will encourage relevant, deep learning while still ensuring big concepts and transdisciplinary skills are developed.

Synthesis Tool, Part 2

This worksheet is designed to help readers capture core insights and help with planning toward implementation. Please explore the following questions as you read, ideally in small leadership teams, faculty teams, or both.

The Ecosystem

Questions to consider:

- Which strategies best suit the needs of your students?

- Which strategies best suit your needs as a teacher or leader?

- What are the potential challenges of implementation?

- What might be some solutions to those challenges?

The Horizon

Questions to consider:

- Which strategies feel best suited to the needs of your students?

- Which strategies feel best suited to your needs as a teacher or leader?

- What are the potential challenges of implementation?

- What might be some solutions to those challenges?

The Landscape Model of Learning © 2022 Solution Tree Press • SolutionTree.com
Visit **go.SolutionTree.com/diversityandequity** to download this free reproducible.

The Pathway

Questions to consider:

- Which strategies best suit the needs of your students?

- Which strategies best suit your needs as a teacher or leader?

- What are the potential challenges of implementation?

- What might be some solutions to those challenges?

Part 3

Leading the Landscape Model

CHAPTER 6

Student Growth Assessment on the Landscape

Masters are not experts because they take a subject to its conceptual end. They are masters because they realize that there isn't one. On utterly smooth ground, the path from aim to attainment is in the permanent future.

—Sarah Lewis

How might educators envision evaluation and grading in the context of a learning landscape? In the end, most educators do have to put something in the gradebook to document the extent to which students achieved the goal. So what might grading look like if students begin and end in different places rather than expecting them to be homogeneous? How might we help educators and students see evaluation and grading as distinct concepts, maximizing evaluation as a tool for growth and minimizing the negative impacts of grading? How might educators confront concerns about the expectations being different for individual students if they're working toward different goals? And what does it look like to manage formative and summative assessment with students at a wide variety of starting and ending points, particularly in larger classrooms? While it may feel harder and messier to evaluate growth more authentically, we believe that traditional approaches to grading, and even grading itself, are largely antithetical to our goals as educators. Once again, we find that student protagonism is core to developing systems of evaluation that motivate and communicate all forms of student growth, for all students, in any size school.

The industrial model of education, with students theoretically beginning and ending in the same standardized place, makes assessment significantly easier for educators—but far less authentic or effective for students. Assessing on the racetrack leaves students who struggle constantly feeling behind and *less than* because of what goes into the gradebook, which lowers motivation and often kills the love of learning entirely (Kohn, 2011; Stommel, 2018). Students with average- and high-achievement levels are also negatively impacted, as grades can cause endless stress or even become the primary purpose and motivation behind learning. Particularly grade-driven students often lose their willingness to take risks or be creative in high-stakes grade environments, as higher grades often suggest a certain compliance with and skill at meeting the expectations of the educator, but not always with thinking for themselves (Kohn, 2011). This has important ramifications for life beyond school, as cultivating innovators to meet future challenges requires building students' comfort with risk taking and creative problem solving, and on lowering their reliance on an authority figure to decide whether they "got it right."

The landscape model requires that educators develop assessment strategies that allow them to evaluate—and students to communicate—learning achievements along a personal (and personalized) pathway. This makes assessment messier but much more authentic and relevant. Student-centered evaluation is more likely to spur growth than decontextualized tasks not aligned to where students actually *are* in their learning process. That said, most educational systems around the world still rely on more standardized demonstrations of core learning, such as the SATs, ACTs, or country-specific national (or provincial) exams developed by ministries of education for use at the end of high school in nearly every country in the world, and the gatekeepers of higher education still insist on a specific body of knowledge for all applicants (Strauss, 2020). As a result, this chapter addresses how educators might evaluate on the landscape *and* prepare students for more traditional assessment expectations. Refer to the reproducible "Synthesis Tool, Part 3" (page 253) for help with this planning.

This chapter discusses student growth assessment on the landscape, offering several perspectives on the problems with traditional grading and providing a variety of ways to rethink how student protagonism might support a more student-centered approach to documenting the learning process along the pathway. We will also explore the importance of self-evaluation, co-constructed rubrics, and other strategies that allow us to de-emphasize grades and prioritize authentic demonstrations of students' growth. As with all elements of the landscape model of learning, educators still guide, scaffold, and adjust, but they give students a much more prominent role in evaluating their own growth.

Problems With Traditional Grading

We have worked in public and private schools, in U.S. and international schools, and witnessed a vast array of school cultures when it comes to assessment. The intention behind the landscape model of learning is to move away from a focus on grades and points, and to keep the focus on *students* and their growth along the pathway. This doesn't necessarily mean eliminating all teacher-centered assessment, or even grades, but it does mean amplifying other forms of feedback and evaluation that are more effective in sparking and measuring growth—and in the best of cases, it might include eliminating grades altogether. Even new movements like the use of achievement badges or microcredentials are just dressed-up versions of the same thing: an external judgment of student work that runs exactly the same risks as traditional grading does in terms of how it impacts students' motivation, performance, and sense of self-worth. To really shift thinking about assessment means getting rid of the bell curve and the need to compare students against anything other than their own previous performance. We know that students will have to face stakeholders comparing them for opportunities like university admissions, scholarships, and jobs in the future, but the authors believe that what should be prioritized in preK–12 education is growth more than competition. We recognize that many schools may find such a shift challenging, particularly those where competition, grades, and awards are central forms of recognition, but we believe a more growth-focused, student-centered approach is worth working toward, particularly when we think of learning as occurring on a landscape. It requires shifting away from a *transactional* relationship of power, judgment, and extrinsic rewards; and moving toward a more *relational* approach to evaluation where connection, understanding, and intrinsic motivation reign. And it means remembering that our real goal as educators should be to use evaluation to spark growth, not to fill a gradebook.

Although we can do a lot to frame the work of authentic evaluation as translatable for the gradebook, the most powerful way to make assessment equitable, and to ensure it doesn't limit students' sense of themselves, is to stop worrying about the gradebook entirely. This is far from a new idea. In the 1920s, while developing plans for The School in Rose Valley, founder Grace Rotzel (1971) visited several small private schools in the United States that had no systems of grades or other external rewards. The schools were designed around the pathways John Dewey (1938) suggests would allow education to adapt to meet rapid changes in communication, technology, and science. Rotzel (1971) finds that these gradeless schools were a "revelation," writing:

> Here were children, from kindergarten through high school, learning because they wanted to, without grades, marks, examinations, or prizes. . . . I was fascinated to see that rewards were completely unnecessary, that, in fact, they often got in the way, because the children interpreted the reward as the reason for doing a job, and concluded that the job itself was not worth doing. (p. 5)

The following sections discuss some problems with traditional grading that Rotzel saw as early as 1929: competition and grades as currency, extrinsic motivation, and the impact implicit biases can have on more traditional assessment practices.

Competition and Grades as Currency

In high-achievement public and private schools, students generally compete over grades not just with themselves, but with each other. The grade becomes the carrot that motivates achievement, or as Simon Sinek (2019) might put it, the currency that motivates performance in only a brief and extrinsic way. Whether the sense of competition comes from parents and guardians, educators, students, or some combination, it is particularly hard to shift a grade-driven school culture—and some schools intentionally cultivate a reputation for academic rigor and grade-based achievement, even taking pride in the number of students who can't succeed in their high-pressure environments.

Some of this pressure lessened with the COVID-19 pandemic, which required K–12 educators to shift their assessment practices away from traditional exams (because they were too easy to cheat on), and which required many universities to forego standardized entrance exams while giving them was impossible (again, because they were too easy to cheat on—a sign they rely more on content recall than higher-order thinking skills). The change resulted in a rise in university applications across the United States in 2020 and 2021, particularly among first-generation college students, which suggests that exams like the SAT and ACT had become barriers to higher education for many students (Dance, 2021; Thornton, 2021). Whether the shift to de-emphasize such exams is permanent remains to be seen, but at the very least most universities have had to recognize other forms of evaluation, such as portfolios and more authentic demonstrations of learning. The authors hope that the shift might signal a more long-term willingness to value more than just grades and exams.

PERSPECTIVES ON WORD CHOICE
Grading Versus Evaluating

As a product of ungraded public schools, Jennifer believes there's a very important distinction between *grading* (what goes in the gradebook), and *evaluation*, which can and should be a constant, iterative process designed to promote and track the growth of understandings and skills (the word *assessment* tends to be used as a catchall for both). The landscape model requires that educators focus more of their hearts and minds on evaluation. In Jennifer's experiences at the Open School growing up in Colorado, evaluation was any combination of self-evaluation, peer evaluation, teacher and advisor evaluation, family evaluation, and expert

> community-partner evaluation. Without grades, the impetus was to recognize excellence and areas for improvement, to provide real-time growth-producing feedback, and to have honest conversations about learning and growth with people who had deep relationships with the student. The metacognitive skills this education developed weren't even clear to Jennifer until many years later, when she found that most of her college and work peers, even in education, didn't demonstrate the same ability to speak what educational thought leader Guy Claxton (2017) calls *learnish*, the language of learning and growth. Jennifer's high school transcripts were more than fifty pages of her own written reflections on her learning experiences, a living transcript that in many ways resembled a modern student portfolio. As you can imagine, the model Jennifer experienced at the Open School relies on student protagonism more than teacher-centered assessment, and every evaluation session was about growth instead of judgment for a gradebook.

A scene in the film *Most Likely to Succeed*, produced by Ted Dintersmith and directed by Greg Whiteley (2018), illustrates what happens when grades and university admissions become the goal. In the film, students at High Tech High, a much-celebrated model of school transformation in California, are asked if they'd rather learn important lifelong skills or simply be prepared for college. To the surprise of the interviewer, the students all answered that they'd rather play the game of school and get into college than truly learn. This example illustrates the challenge and need not just to address *educators'* perceptions but to change the perceptions of *students* who enjoy and are successful at the game of school than they are at deeper learning. It's harder work to be the protagonist of the story; it's much easier to learn the formula for success and stick to it.

There are clear examples of grades impacting the depth of learning in classrooms around the world. The game of school and its rules are quickly learned by all—and those who come to school with matching skills find comfort in the rules. One student of Kapono's in a high school social studies class once asserted that discussing and making meaning in a Socratic seminar was too hard. "Why not just answer textbook questions?" he asked. But over the course of the year, the new rules of engaging in hands-on and minds-on learning became familiar. Students began to lean into the unfamiliarity of leading their own discussions, asking their own questions, and making their own meaning. The following year, that same student returned to Kapono's class to say how boring the textbook had become in his new social studies course. The student said he wished the school asked him to think.

In discussing this book with educators in a variety of countries, several remarked that the biggest problem with the landscape model and the idea of students moving through learning from their real starting points to their best horizon would be students' perception that their peers didn't deserve the grades they'd gotten for "lesser" work, and that parents would want to see higher grades for students taking on higher challenges. This obsession with fairness and efficiency in grading does little to improve education, notes educator and author Jesse Stommel (2018):

> Language around grading emphasizes "efficiency" (the word repeated incessantly) while reducing individual students to cogs in a machine that ultimately seems to have little to do with them. The work of grading is framed less in terms of giving feedback or encouraging learning and more as a way of ranking students against one another. Nods to "fairness" are too often made for the sake of defensibility rather than equity. What disturbs me is how effortlessly and casually this language rolls off Education's collective tongue.

The authors have also worked with schools where mediocrity reigns, where students have figured out the minimum required to pass and generally stick to that minimum because there's little motivation to do more. Educational thought leader Alfie Kohn (2011) writes:

> Impress upon students that what they're doing will count toward their grade, and their response will likely be to avoid taking any unnecessary intellectual risks. They'll choose a shorter book, or a project on a familiar topic, in order to minimize the chance of doing poorly—not because they're "unmotivated" but because they're rational.

On the landscape, students should be challenging themselves not because of the external judgements of their teachers, parents or peers, but because learning matters and because each new challenge is a step toward a horizon they *want* to reach. While the authors recognize that grades and exams have a long history as currency in education, and that eliminating them completely may be impossible for many schools, we hope that educators can at least shift toward prioritizing learning more than systems of extrinsic motivation, helping students see deep, meaningful learning as the real reward.

Extrinsic Motivation

Sadly, this extrinsic focus also comes from overprioritizing assessment for the gradebook and underprioritizing purposeful, meaningful evaluation and reflection focused on growth, personal (and personalized) evaluation that positions students as more than cogs in a machine and motivates them toward challenge in more intrinsic ways.

Kohn (2011) suggests that grades do significant damage to the entire learning process, tending to "diminish students' interest in whatever they're learning." Considering that some students quickly figure out the minimum level of effort required to get a passing grade—while other students quickly figure out the formula for high grades and stick to that—the deep, personal investment in learning and growth, and the potential to become lifelong learners, are hurt significantly by formalized grading systems. According to Kohn's research, grades can even reduce the quality of students' thinking. Kohn (2011) writes:

> A "grading orientation" and a "learning orientation" have been shown to be inversely related and, as far as I can tell, every study that has ever investigated the impact on intrinsic motivation of receiving grades (or instructions that emphasize the importance of getting good grades) has found a negative effect.

Table 6.1 shows grading orientation versus learning orientation traits.

Table 6.1: Grading Orientation Versus Learning Orientation

Grading Orientation Traits	Learning Orientation Traits
• Is teacher centered	• Is student centered
• Taps extrinsic motivator	• Taps intrinsic motivator
• Can favor compliance	• Favors *learnish* (Claxton, 2017) and metacognition
• Suggests lack of trust	• Suggests trust in learners
• Judges growth	• Sparks growth
• Calls for efficiency	• Calls for depth and complexity
• Emphasizes assessment *of* learning (Stiggins, 2005)	• Encourages challenge
• Can dehumanize students	• Emphasizes evaluation *for* learning (Stiggins, 2005)
	• Recognizes students' inherent humanity

Source: Adapted from Klein, 2022b.

Perhaps most importantly, grading is a minefield rife with implicit bias, particularly when teachers are assessing qualitative and subjective factors as the following discusses in depth. Yet, we know that the more subjective the skill, the more qualitative the evaluation has to be, and the more qualitative the evaluation, the more *growth* can occur (Gibb, 2013). We also know that some of the most important skills we teach students are what educator and thought leader Will Richardson (2012) calls *immeasurables*, skills such as empathy, curiosity, resilience, and passion for learning. But knowing they're important doesn't mean we've succeeded in ascribing them *as much importance* as more traditional measures of learning. Even transdisciplinary skills like collaboration are still called *soft skills* by most, which lowers their importance alongside more "academic" skills. Richardson (2012) writes:

> At the end of the day, as much as we may claim to value those other, more immeasurable things, we end up looking to old tests and scores to tell us how well our kids are doing. They're what we know. They're what we trust, because they're the same measures that were applied to our learning when we were in school. But those scores really tell us very little about what kinds of learners our kids are. And they tell us even less about what our children will actually be able to do in their lives. (Kindle location 596)

Whatever the extrinsic reward, whether it's the grade or that laptop a student's parents promised them for higher achievement, the landscape asks for deeper, more meaningful motivations to learn that come from inside the student. The authors believe that the process of defining the horizon with students will help make their motivations more personal and intrinsic, and even honoring what students bring into the ecosystem can build the kinds of relationships that lead to more intrinsic motivations for learning. And the more we can focus on student protagonism, the less educator bias will impact our evaluation processes, however unintentional such biases may be.

Impact of Implicit Biases

We believe in the power of more subjective, qualitative evaluation, but the moment we need to put something in the gradebook, our implicit biases as educators can have a significant impact on students. In their meta-analysis of twenty studies, researchers John M. Malouff and Einar B. Thorsteinsson (2016) find that teacher bias *consistently* impacts the grades students receive. They find that biasing characteristics appeared relatively evenly across the following categories, and they identify similar levels of bias from early learning through university (Malouff & Thorsteinsson, 2016).

- Race and ethnic backgrounds
- Education-related deficiencies
- Physical unattractiveness
- Poor quality of prior performance

Interestingly, Malouff and Thorsteinsson (2016) believe the problem comes from educators knowing too much irrelevant information about students. Their meta-analysis suggests that educators have work to do when it comes to deconstructing and avoiding bias, but it also suggests that knowing students is a bad thing—an assertion we find disturbing.

Most of us have experienced how just one low grade can impact our sense of self and potential, how easily one so-called failure can shift aspirations for the future. No one wants factors like students' race or attractiveness to influence grades, but Malouff and Thorsteinsson (2016) establish that they absolutely do; and the more students become aware of these biases, the more likely stereotype threat, the self-worry of confirming negative stereotypes about a group one belongs to (Steele & Aronson, 1995), will impact student achievement. Writer and activist Soraya Chemaly (2015) puts the broader social impacts of implicit bias into sharp focus, reminding us that *all* students are harmed by it:

> The issue of whose assertive qualities, self-expression, and imagination are being cultivated and whose are being penalized speaks directly to the broader harms of not taking a nuanced intersectional approach to the problem of education. Everyone's lives are impoverished by these bias and the stereotype threats they cultivate in children. When we tackle the ugly sexism of the tech industry, try to understand why young boys are killing themselves, or contemplate the aggrieved racialized and gendered entitlement at the heart of so much of our violence, we are fighting rear-guard actions. It's too little, too late.

Knowing more about students might seem like a double-edged sword, leading to the inevitable conclusion that only quantitative, non-subjective, or even blind assessments are effective at avoiding bias. While there are times identity-blind assessment can provide positive objectivity, educators work with human beings, not scantrons, and "right answers" aren't the only thing we educate for. We believe that what educators know about students *should* be part of their understanding of students as learners (Barshay, 2018; York, 2014). Educators should know as much as possible about who students are and what they carry with them into the schoolhouse, not to increase bias but to unpack assumptions and know each child as a whole person (as explored in chapter 2, page 45, and chapter 4, page 93).

No information is irrelevant; education is about *people*, not efficient strategies for measurement. And that means we need to approach evaluation through student protagonism. The authors' extensive experience with student-centered learning suggests that classroom practices that include self-reflection and dialogue with the student-as-protagonist offer a way to ensure equity in evaluation and lessen the impact of educators' implicit bias. By encouraging more dialogue and other strategies to understand who students are and what they bring into the ecosystem, and by involving student voice in evaluation processes, educators at the very least will be better able to balance their own perspectives on students' progress with their understanding of students' contexts and students' own opinions about their growth.

Student Protagonism in Evaluation on the Landscape

The landscape model is *not* about allowing some students to avoid challenge, nor rewarding those who do more with extra points. It's not about points at all. It's about understanding where students are and can or should go next; it's about accurately defining and working toward each student's Zone of Proximal Development; and it's about constant reflection and building a school culture that promotes self-motivation, a culture of challenge and growth for every student, wherever they are on the landscape. Above all, it's about students' authentic protagonism in the evaluation and documentation of progress, so educators spend less time on judgments for the gradebook and more time focused on supporting students' growth.

When we think about evaluation of growth, it is important to include a mix of formal and informal opportunities for students to demonstrate what they're learning and where they are on the pathway. More formal opportunities are usually graded; these might include written reports, formal lab demonstrations, oral presentations, and even more traditional quizzes or tests, so that students get practice with the more standardized assessments they'll confront in their educational lives. More informal demonstrations of learning are rarely graded, such as class discussions, active-learning protocols, and journaling; they provide a less punitive, more formative space for exploring new ideas, and as such are equally important to evaluation on the landscape. Both formal and informal demonstrations of learning can serve as formative assessment as we move along the pathway, helping us know where students are individually and offering the opportunity to scaffold and plan for specific needs. Furthermore, the landscape invites various sources of feedback along the way, from teacher feedback to peer feedback to self-evaluation.

In the following sections, we will explore the importance of non-punitive, student-centered formative assessment processes such as feedback and revision cycles, ways educators can maximize student-led documentation of growth instead of having all work channel through them, the power of self-evaluation to spark growth, and the importance of co-constructing rubrics with students. Each section provides ways to rethink traditional grading so that our evaluation practices align to the landscape, and all are appropriate as a complement to current practices, even in the most traditional of schools. While we are not suggesting that the teacher be removed from evaluation, and we recognize that removing grades entirely would be challenging in most educational environments, we *are* suggesting that educators emphasize growth more than grades, and that we keep student agency and protagonism at the heart of our work on the landscape.

Formative Evaluation and the Power of Feedback-Revision Cycles

Coupled with educator feedback and expert feedback from an authentic audience, student protagonism in evaluation can be particularly helpful for formative assessment during a project or unit and can help ensure the educator isn't the only one managing the evaluation process. Involving students in evaluating their *own* growth is perhaps the most important, as self-evaluation develops the metacognitive skills that are core to critical thinking and growth. Self-evaluation requires significant scaffolding, as students don't always know how to articulate or consider their own weaknesses without regular practice, but the skills can be developed at any age with the right practice and support. For example, educators who co-construct rubrics with students often find students are better at offering each other feedback on the basis of expectations they were involved in choosing. Education researcher John Hattie (2012) clearly outlines the benefits of feedback, showing that it is one of the most effective strategies teachers can employ. Similarly, Hattie and colleagues (2016) further assert that feedback, from self-reflection or the teacher, is one main factor in deepening learning and ensuring *transfer* of learning from one scenario to another.

Peer evaluation and feedback is another vital component, but these practices also require significant scaffolding before they become useful for growth. Simply put, students don't always know how to give each other growth-producing feedback. But if educators scaffold those skills and model them, creating repeated opportunities for students to get better at providing helpful feedback, we can build the kind of collaborative, supportive culture the landscape model asks for. For example, student-centered kindergarten teachers often display an image-based, age-appropriate rubric for the class and then walk the students through it, asking them to voice how well they think the group is doing for each element of the rubric. Teachers in upper primary, middle, and high schools can take this further, co-constructing evaluation rubrics with students (see page 172), and then having students use the rubric repeatedly to support each other's growth in peer review sessions over several weeks or months. Even when students are at different points in their learning, co-constructed criteria can help students identify where they are and give appropriate advice to their peers. (For a powerful example of students from kindergarten through fourth grade providing growth-producing feedback, see the video at https://eleducation.org/resources/austins-butterfly of

Ron Berger's famous talk with students about *Austin's Butterfly* [EL Education, 2016].) What we see in well-developed peer review practices are students working closely with each other to provide specific, helpful, and kind feedback that really does produce growth.

Feedback and revision cycles should happen repeatedly over the course of any unit or project, as should other types of formative assessment checkpoints, to ensure that *all students* are able to produce high-quality work. A concept with deep roots in constructivist educational design, feedback and revision in the context of the landscape should be a cyclical, repeated process that keeps student protagonism at its core. A feedback-revision cycle asks students to create and share a draft or prototype of their work in progress, to receive feedback for its improvement, and to use that feedback to revise and improve their work. Laur and Ackers (2017) suggest a minimum of three full cycles in the development of any product in a project-based classroom, and encourage the use of feedback from the teacher, experts, and other students, as well as opportunities for students' self-reflection and self-evaluation. These processes not only help students improve their work, but help to develop a growth mindset about their learning.

Feedback and revision cycles tend to boost students' confidence, self-awareness, and enthusiasm, as well as being "more strongly and consistently related to achievement than any other teaching behaviour . . . regardless of grade, socioeconomic status, race, or school setting" (University of Reading, n.d.). To be successful, educators will need to scaffold a classroom culture where honest feedback is good, a safe space where feedback is always growth-producing for the person who receives it. Educators should offer this feedback *just in time*, meaning that it should happen right when students need it most, usually at critical points in the draft or prototype development process. We believe there is nothing worse for student achievement and enthusiasm for learning than having no opportunities to receive feedback until the work is finished and the grades are in, a pitfall we see across much of education. We also believe that drafts should not be graded, meaning they should not impact the gradebook, to encourage risk taking and creativity. Still, students should track and document the iteration process to monitor their growth (and so the educator has something to put in the gradebook when necessary). As much as possible, feedback should be positive and framed from a "You're not there yet, but I know you can . . ." perspective when students are struggling.

In the authors' experience, involving students as protagonists helps avoid the impact of educators' implicit biases on grades, particularly with more qualitative work, because it helps balance teachers' opinions with those of other students and experts in the field. And while students may be too easy on their peers or too hard on themselves in their evaluations, it is always appropriate for the teacher to adjust when assigning an actual grade. For example, students of color in a predominantly White institution might be particularly hard on themselves in self-evaluations because of stereotype threat, and it behooves educators to adjust their grades accordingly—and to have conversations with students designed to build their self-esteem over time.

Student-Led Documentation of Growth

While many educators manage the bulk of assessment and progress tracking in schools, the landscape model invites educators to increase students' role in tracking and measuring their own growth. While this will require the scaffolding of students' autonomy, self-motivation, and responsibility, as well as the metacognitive processes involved in articulating their learning processes, even four-year-olds can choose their best work and, with scaffolded questions, can explain what they learned over time. This shift does not mean teachers aren't involved in evaluating both content and skills; the role of the educator's knowledge and understanding of learning objectives will always be important. But shifting some of the work to students not only empowers them as learners, helping us reach that inclusive prosperity we seek for every student, but also reduces the workload for teachers, making assessment along the learning pathway far more manageable, particularly in larger classrooms.

Trusting our students is the first and most important step to building better evaluation strategies, the kinds of approaches that will work on a learning landscape. As we explored in our discussion of student-led conferences in chapter 4 (page 104), our students can reflect on their own growth and needs as young as four or five years old, if educators scaffold the process with them. Similarly, self-management is a core skill fostered in project-based learning classrooms; and the more autonomous students become, from project to project and year to year, the more we can balance educator evaluation with student-led documentation to gain a more complete picture of where students are—and should go next—on their learning pathway.

Educators often load themselves down with grading that's really just checkwork designed to ensure students complete the activities assigned. Collecting homework increases the educator's workload significantly and is largely intended to ensure compliance with tasks that the teacher assigned. When we trust students to do more on their own and to be capable of understanding their own learning needs, scaffolding their skills and releasing teacher support gradually across the grade levels, as described by Pelletier in the self-advocacy continuum for students with cognitive differences at the International School of Brussels (see chapter 5, page 117), we can move a significant amount of this task tracking to the students themselves. A more student-centered approach might look as simple as having students work in small groups to compare their homework, teach each other where they can, and identify questions they need more learning to answer—and as complex as some of the systems we will describe shortly.

We don't need to dictate every step as educators, and we don't need to see or grade everything students do; building a culture of trust is the first step toward fostering the student-as-protagonist to manage the work of documenting and evaluating their own growth.

On the landscape, the learning *process* is more important than what students *produce* as a final product, whether that be a traditional exam or a more authentic demonstration of learning. This makes student-led documentation all the more important. Student-led documentation ranges from the simple to the more complex, including tools and processes such as the following.

- **Task logs:** Students track what they complete (or who will complete what as part of a group project). In doing so, they learn to work toward completion and establish goals, next steps, and roles. Many PBL educators have students use online task logs, which teachers check regularly, for example, in weekly team meetings where groups might report their progress to the teacher.

- **Group contracts:** Groups develop these at the beginning of a given learning experience, and they help students learn to collaborate effectively and resolve conflicts. Rather than relying on the teacher to solve all challenges that might arise, group contracts allow students to think ahead and identify potential pitfalls, as well as the strategies they'll use in response (that is, steps they will take if a group member isn't completing their work).

- **Milestones:** These include formative checkpoint-evaluation activities such as peer reviews, discussions, due dates for key elements of students' work, and active learning protocols to help educators check for understanding and allow students to reflect on their progress. Teachers can check several of the strategies in chapter 3 (page 65), such as KWL and RAN charts, and discuss them with students at such checkpoints. Milestones help students build more autonomy around deadlines and completion; in some student-centered classrooms, students even help set the dates for checkpoints, to provide additional protagonism in the learning and evaluation process.

Whatever the tools educators use, the goal is to position students as protagonists on their own learning journeys and, through scaffolding and experience, support the growth of students' autonomy and self-management.

The work of educators Silvia Rosenthal Tolisano and Janet A. Hale (2018) offers a wide array of strategies for educators who want students to document their learning process with technological tools. Additionally, Tolisano's online resources, which include webinars, blogs, and online tools for student documentation of learning, produced as @LangWitches over the course of her career, provide a wealth of strategies for student protagonism in documentation of the growth process. Describing documentation as a tool "OF learning, FOR learning and AS learning," Tolisano and Hale (2018) describe these three types of documentation as "a visible, interconnected, metacognitive approach for creating evidence of one's learning process" (p. 5).

- **Documentation *of* learning:** In this form of documentation, students provide snapshot artifacts (products or performances) that display learning moments and what students learned from them. It aims to help learners show others what they learned.

- **Documentation *for* learning:** In this form of documentation, students provide explanations and interpretations of purposefully collected selected snapshot artifacts to convey meaningful moments during and because of learning. It aims to raise awareness of a learner's changes, trends, or patterns over time.

- **Documentation *as* learning:** In this form of documentation, students use curation to capture and explain purposeful moments as evidence of learning. Going beyond documenting for learning, documenting *as* learning becomes a critical facet of the learning journey that uses critical thinking and purposeful decision making about what to capture to express core moments of the learning process (Tolisano & Hale, 2018).

Importantly, *the learner completes documentation of learning, for learning, and as learning, not the teacher,* though students of all ages will need scaffolding and support as they learn to use these strategies. The goal is for students to communicate their thinking and learning in ways that promote "visibility, meaningfulness, shareability, and amplification" (Tolisano & Hale, 2018, p. 4). This allows students to share their learning with teachers, parents, and community partners, and even to share learning more broadly across social networks as appropriate. This approach turns the educator into a central hub for information generated by the students themselves, and the teacher's job is to co-create structures and systems with the students so that growth is tracked consistently in visible, meaningful, shareable, and amplified ways. Educators can design such documentation structures to align with any given learning objective, learning experience, or stage of a project, and teachers need only interpret, validate, and adjust those results for the gradebook as necessary. As an added benefit, these approaches develop students' digital literacy, writing, and critical-thinking skills.

As a high school English teacher, Jennifer used journaling as a central formative evaluation strategy for almost two decades. Each entry prompt included some form of literary analysis (complex questions about the text students were reading), as well as personal reflections (how students felt about the themes explored in the initial questions, and how those themes connected to their own lives). She encouraged students to just *write* and not worry too much about spelling and grammar—the goal was just get their ideas onto paper. Students were allowed to sit wherever they wanted and to listen to music on their headphones as long as it didn't disturb others, all to create a culture of trust. Perhaps most importantly, students always had the right to fold over pages any time they let themselves get more personal than they were comfortable sharing.

The goals of journaling are many when we employ it on the landscape.

- Journaling teaches students to think through writing, an essential skill for their professions and personal lives, as the ability to use writing as a core means of expression remains essential in most careers and contexts (Fritson, 2008; Merrow, 2018).

- Journaling helps more introverted students prepare for class discussions, giving them the time to think about what they want to say in advance.

- Journaling helps educators discern who is and isn't doing the assigned reading, and enables them to assess reading comprehension quite easily when needed.

- Journals provide an informal space for self-evaluation, often more telling and useful than formal self-evaluation protocols during class.

- Journals become a resource for teachers to understand the raw skills and challenges of each student at the beginning of a learning journey. Further, journals provide an informal road map of growth over time, from which educators can glean a great deal of information about how much students' writing—and thinking—have advanced.

Perhaps the most important quality of journaling, especially when students know they can get personal but are not required to share, is the space created for the kind of deep, safe reflection that helps students know *themselves*. Using deep questions connected to the literature, questions about family, culture, values, self, and identity, journaling in Jennifer's classroom provided a low-stakes opportunity for students to grapple with some of the most important questions of their early teens: Am I just the product of my family culture and history, or do I get to decide which elements I carry on? Who am I, and how do others see me? Who do I love, and how do I want to live my future?

Questions like these always spun off from the literature itself: a short story about family history and what we carry on or don't, a novel about the birth of identity, a play about the loss of love because of self-doubt, a poem that sparked new understandings of gender or sexual orientation. And Jennifer didn't need to know everything about her students, nor did she read all the entries, but she had a resource when she needed to understand a student better. Best of all, students tended to let her read more of their personal entries as the semester progressed, letting her in on more elements of their identities and experiences. By the end of the course, when students created portfolios that manifested who they were and traced their growth, that sense of safety allowed most to share these truths with their peers, which increased the whole class's sense of community, connection, and interdependence.

Research supports the value of such work; adolescence is when young people are asking such questions, and the schoolhouse is a key place for exploring and understanding themselves. Education researchers Monique Verhoeven, Astrid M. G. Poorthuis, and Monique Volman (2018) write:

> School—a place where adolescents spend a lot of time—is an important context where adolescents' identity development can be supported: Here, teachers can help adolescents to explore the identity implications of new ideas, activities, or possibilities they are introduced to at school.

Given that so much of the landscape model hinges on knowing and understanding students deeply, and students understanding themselves as people and learners, practices like journaling are a powerful way to encourage self-reflection and identity development.

In the humanities classroom, teachers can easily connect most themes and content to students' own lives, as both language arts and the social sciences contain themes we experience in everyday life. In mathematics or science, a journal might be used for informal notes on points of frustration and success during the learning process, or perhaps reflections on personal connections to the learning, such as a journal entry reflecting on levels of salt intake in students' homes in connection to a biology unit on the impacts of sodium on body systems. Jennifer worked with a mathematics teacher for many years who gave particularly hard homework but asked students to stop after a limited amount of time and journal about their questions, to help them better internalize what had and hadn't worked for them. Whatever the approach, journals provide a non-threatening space for students to think—about themselves, about their learning, and about why it all matters.

Co-Constructed Rubrics With Student Protagonists

The authors definitely have a love-hate relationship with rubrics. While they can be a helpful tool for building students' vocabulary in *learnish* (Claxton, 2017), rubrics built entirely by educators can easily create teacher-centered judgment systems that students must adopt for success, just as badges and microcredentials tend to do. We are not suggesting that educators should exit the evaluation process, but we recognize that a teacher-created rubric can easily take us back to evaluation as compliance with the educator's demands, just as grades do. Furthermore, rubrics filled with numbers and points become, for students, much more about the numbers than the criteria they contain. Even worse, rubrics can limit what educators receive from their most proficient and creative students and can consistently demoralize struggling students. To combat this, we believe that student protagonism with rubric development is key; we recommend co-creating rubrics with students so that their criteria and personal horizons dominate the language and ideas those rubrics contain.

In other words, the expectations for excellence should come from *students,* with tweaks as necessary to ensure the educator's expectations are included as well. This approach has the added benefit of teaching students to define the goals and quality expectations for the work they're doing, which makes it more likely they will understand, internalize and reach those expectations (and makes the motivation to do so more intrinsic). We also recommend removing all points and numbers visually, at least on the rubric shared with and used by students, and ensuring all levels of quality include supportive language, even at the *not yet* level of a struggling student.

One seven-step process that Jennifer has developed for co-creating rubrics with students is as follows. It is appropriate for all ages, with additional scaffolding and support of preschool and early primary students during the process.

1. Students brainstorm all the things they're learning in the given unit or project, with the goal of identifying all content and skill learning that feels important to them.

2. With teacher support, the class narrows the list back to the most crucial knowledge and skills that will make up the rubric's criteria, such as that tied to standards or other objectives the course needs to meet. As

necessary, the teacher adds criteria the students didn't come up with themselves, which the educator knows are core to the unit or project.

3. Students move into small groups by affinity mapping based on their interest in defining a given criterion, and write down ideas about what different levels of quality might look like for this particular goal.

4. Students share their quality levels with the class for feedback and make any revisions (could be done as a rotation in which one group member stays in place to explain their ideas, and the rest rotate and offer feedback on the other criteria in the room).

5. After class, the educator takes students' descriptions, makes any adjustments necessary to meet school norms, curricular standards, or their own expectations, and builds the rubric.

6. At the next class period, the educator shares the rubric draft for final feedback from students. If students push back around elements the teacher has added or changed out of necessity, it is appropriate for the teacher to clarify why those changes are important in terms of the broader curriculum or systems of evaluation at the school.

7. Once the rubric has been finalized, it should be used by students as a tool for peer review and self-evaluation throughout the unit or project, each time the group does a feedback and revision cycle. This will help students internalize the criteria they were involved in developing, making it more likely students will reach the highest levels of quality in their feedback and work.

Rubrics can be general enough to encompass many learning pathways, such as a product rubric which doesn't define what the product *is* so much as the *quality* of work expected. However, the use of rubrics often presupposes that all students are working toward the same standards simultaneously, regardless of whether they are at the same level of mastery with the associated content and skills. And yes, many educators may feel they have to stay tied to this "move together" model if their school is designed that way. We will discuss different models for organizing curriculum in chapter 8 (page 195), but suffice to say that co-constructed rubrics can be valuable for both self-evaluation and peer evaluation processes, not just for educators.

PERSPECTIVES ON THE DANGER OF GRADES
From Open Schooling to the Ivory Tower

We've all worked with colleagues and parents who fear the eventual importance of standardized exams, and it is true that most countries require national or regional exams at some point during the preK–12 experience, in some cases quite often. Most countries require a major national or international exam for high school graduation as well, if not several. But why would we turn that reality into a reason to use dehumanizing practices *more* of the time? Yes, students need practice with the kinds of multiple-choice, high-stakes exams they'll need to get into university, and external tests can give us helpful validation of the learning we think we see, but that doesn't mean we should use them all the time (see more on the NWEA MAP Growth Test in chapter 7, page 187). Jennifer remembers Open School founder Arnie Langberg explaining once how he would take all the authentic data students produced and educators organized, translating it into what the district needed to see. He insisted that not even the teachers should feel the burden of interpreting authentic learning into grades, and that it was his role as principal to produce the traditional results the district was expecting.

It is no surprise that an educational system designed to move students through their education efficiently would have turned into a monster when it comes to recognizing and leveraging students' basic humanity. Even after a childhood of ungraded learning at The School in Rose Valley and the Open School, Jennifer struggled to keep from caring about grades in college. She found As and high GPAs infinitely appealing, and they quickly encroached on her love of literature, writing, and learning. As a different thinker with a high IQ, she found any grade under an A left her feeling reduced, unseen, misunderstood somehow, in a way her ungraded preK–12 education never made her feel. She even started to make choices based on what she thought her professors wanted from her, rather than on what she believed was important. Imagine if, additionally, her professors had let her alternative background in what they perceived as a "hippy school," bias the grades they gave her, or if her professors had let anti-Semitic views create implicit assumptions and related expectations about what she should be good at—and bad at—because of her Jewish ethnicity.

Jennifer's story has a happy ending because she didn't experience prejudice—and because her student-centered upbringing had given her the self-advocacy skills needed to find support and look for answers when she needed them. She stuck to her path in spite of the highly rigorous academic program creating a feeling of imposter syndrome she still struggles with—but too many assessment stories end differently. Too many end with students pulled off their potential career path or passion pursuit because of that lingering feeling of not being good enough. This is particularly true for first-generation college students, who often make extreme sacrifices to succeed and fit into the expectations of universities, only to spend their entire education feeling like they don't measure up. If the goal of education is to help students become whole people who are happy, successful, and contribute to their communities, we need to focus much more on collaborative formative evaluation and far less on an abstract number or letter to put on spreadsheets and grading platforms. It's our students and their growth we should be focused on, not on maintaining a bell curve. Sean Michael Morris (2021), senior instructor of Learning Design and Technology at the University of Colorado at Denver, puts it best:

> *We continue to talk about grades long after they've ceased to matter because they mark us indelibly.* And it's just as important to recognize that indelible mark as it is to recognize that if grades can cease to matter at some point in our lives, it might stand to reason they never really mattered in the first place.

As educators shift evaluation practices toward more intrinsically motivated, student-centered approaches, we recommend beginning from small steps, particularly in grade-oriented schools. There may be resistance to removing grades entirely, but even small shifts such as those described in this chapter can help make evaluation more meaningful and growth producing for students. On the landscape, students and educators should at least be focused on growth more than grades, and on offering appropriate, authentic challenges instead of the easy path to an A. We will explore bigger shifts and models in chapters 7 (page 177), 8 (page 195), and 9 (page 235), as we believe that the landscape of education is changing, as are the gatekeeping mechanisms for entry into higher education. However far you can push the practices of your own community, just remember what education is (or should be) working toward: evaluation that sparks growth and empowers students, not the kind that dehumanizes or demoralizes them along the learning journey.

Reflective Questions

Respond to the following questions alone or with your school team.

- To what extent is your school culture currently tied to grades and point systems? Where do you see opportunities to shift practices, even a little, toward more student-centered forms of evaluation?

- How might more use of feedback and revision cycles and other types of formative evaluation help your students move from where they are to where they might go? What are you already doing well, and where do you see opportunities for growth?

- If you asked your students how much agency they currently have in helping to establish learning outcomes, what do you think they would say? How might you amplify student protagonism in your rubrics and other evaluation processes?

- How much voice did you have in evaluation processes during your own education? Which evaluation practices really helped you grow as a learner, and which did not? How did your evaluation experiences impact your life beyond school?

Takeaways

The following summarizes key ideas from the chapter.

- Traditional systems of grades actually hurt students' learning because they emphasize external rewards and offer only extrinsic motivation, as well as being impacted by educators' implicit bias.

- Emphasizing evaluation as formative and student centered allows educators to spark growth and self-reflection, making students' motivations more intrinsic.

- Student protagonism in evaluation can help lower the workload for teachers, and can ensure that students feel empowered with and excited about their own potential for growth.

CHAPTER 7

Challenges of Implementation

Today, schools remain standing as one of the last institutions of the top-down, male-dominated management practiced in the 20th century. They are not broken, so much as oddly out of place as we work together across generations and genders to create a different future.

—Tim Kubik

As with all initiatives, implementation is a whole different animal than theory. What are the potential challenges educators might encounter as they begin to implement the strategies in part 2 (page 63)? What speed bumps must they anticipate, and how might they prepare to overcome these hurdles? Every educational context will have its own unique set of challenges, so the solutions may be unique to a degree as well. That said, being able to anticipate and design in response to potential roadblocks will allow schools to mitigate the impact of such obstacles, so this chapter offers school leaders and classroom educators insights into some of the most likely challenges to emerge—and our ideas about how to solve them.

This chapter tackles many of the challenges educators can face while implementing the landscape model of learning. These include challenges in private and public school settings, of understanding and discussing identity, of educational management technologies, of buy-in and accountability, in traditional and progressive contexts, in international school settings, of working with parents and other caregivers, and of policies and politics.

The Challenges in Private and Public School Settings

As we've established, the landscape model doesn't necessarily require costly resources beyond a commitment to professional development, which makes it accessible to schools across socioeconomic sectors. However, higher-income educational communities, whether public or private, local or international, are likely to see more pushback from educators, parents, and even students initially, at least in part because of the high-achieving, grade-oriented cultures that tend to dominate in this socioeconomic group (see chapter 6, page 155). Private schools may have more flexibility when it comes to how they allocate funds and design curriculum, but the intensity of grade orientations will be the same in public schools with a reputation for rigorous, high-achieving academic programs.

The good news is that many excellent schools have already started to shift these educational mindsets. Ivy League universities such as Stanford, Harvard, and MIT have shifted many departments toward design thinking, PBL, and other student-centered models where students are positioned as protagonists (Barshay, 2018). Many high-achieving college preparatory programs are also leading new ways of thinking about mastery and excellence, as we see in the Mastery Transcript Consortium (https://mastery.org), an organization founded by a small group of the United States' best college preparatory schools. The consortium reimagined the high school learning journey and resulting transcripts to focus on mastery of learning goals and curriculum standards more than grades. With 281 private schools using their method as of early 2022, as well as 124 public schools, the Mastery Transcript Consortium strives to reshape the thinking of schools around the world. This work can help any school trying to implement the landscape model, as it offers a new way of defining excellence and a whole network of top schools making it work already.

Based on what we've seen in schools around the world, we hope that the landscape model will be more easily integrated into middle- and lower-income public and parochial schools—but there will definitely still be challenges. Since public schools are subject to external regulations on the local, state, provincial, and federal level, and parochial schools are usually overseen by their respective archdiocese or other religious boards, they often experience more pressures related to *external* policies than to traditional mindsets *inside* the community, which we will describe later in this chapter when we explore the challenges connected to policy. Schools can combat some of those pressures by inviting policymakers into the schoolhouse, to see the power of student-centered learning. Bringing key players to student exhibitions of learning, for example, shows policymakers that learning can be more authentic while still meeting the expectations of schools' respective boards and systems of oversight, whether they be from an archdiocese, local district regulations, or even state and federal mandates. Such existing policies don't necessarily keep schools from doing what's right for students, but initiatives that appear unrelated to core academic standards rarely survive, which is why arts programs are often the first to go when public schools have funding problems (Gibson, 2018; Timon, 2021).

In spite of funding being connected to test scores in many parts of the world, and curriculum being government controlled, public schools are filled with dedicated educators and families who believe in the power of education to change one's circumstances. Families whose own educational experiences may not have served them well appreciate and support a school that takes steps to make learning more meaningful for their children. Parochial schools, on the other hand, will find that the landscape model aligns well with the values of inclusion we see across most major religions. We encourage parochial schools, whatever their affiliation, to identify and leverage those value alignments when presenting the goals to stakeholders (see more on aspirational values in chapter 8, page 203).

The Challenges of Understanding and Discussing Identity

Another challenge lies in educators' skills when it comes to managing complex and difficult conversations about socioeconomics, race, and other factors that may be sensitive for students and their families. Research proves that the relationship between students and teachers is key to student success and that conversely students suffer when they don't feel safe, heard, and valued (Ondrasek & Flook, 2020). Being able to communicate in meaningful ways is a foundational skill needed to support genuine relationship building (Ondrasek & Flook, 2020). For example, not every educator feels comfortable talking to students about their gender identities or sexual orientations, if students open up to them, and not every educator has the natural savvy to discuss socioeconomic differences with colleagues, nor to lead discussions of this kind with students. The first step to entering into these conversations is developing trust, an essential precursor to this type of complex and deep relationship building (Bonior, 2018). Quite often, educators who don't interrupt sexist, classist, or racist behavior among students stay quiet out of the fear that comes from a lack of training, not a lack of interest in championing students; they simply don't know how to respond effectively, so they quietly do nothing, which of course only exacerbates the problem.

Following are a few strategies that can help educators prepare for and manage such conversations and interventions.

- **Classroom norms or agreements:** Classroom norms, particularly when they are co-constructed as agreements with students, are a wonderful first step toward inclusive thinking and behavior in the classroom.

Norms such as sharing power, listening with respect, and only speaking from the "I" perspective help students—and teachers—learn how to have difficult conversations in a safe way. Co-constructed agreements are appropriate for all grade levels, and students tend to hold each other accountable when they were involved in creating those agreements.

- **Ouch:** One strategy used in many schools to interrupt non-inclusive language is the simple use of "Ouch" as a reaction when anyone in class makes a comment that could be hurtful, and this strategy is appropriate for all age groups. *Ouch* suggests discomfort and pain, but does not blame or judge, and can quickly become an easy way for anyone in the class to publicly recognize a lack of inclusion, even if they weren't the target of the hurtful comment. Please note that ouch moments should always be followed by a chance for someone in class to explain why the comment hurt, and to agree as a class that we won't use that kind of language in the future.

- **Protocols:** If the topic is particularly sensitive, and the educator can plan in advance how they want to address it with students, consider using a protocol such as brave space to support low-threat, high-honesty conversations (see our explanations of brave space in chapter 3, page 76). When handling conflict, restorative practices offer strategies such as restorative circles for managing difficult dialogue. Such protocols provide a structure that helps students feel safe, as well as providing educators with the language they need to run such discussions and manage what arises.

When educators have concrete strategies and steps they can take when challenging topics arise, they are much more likely to know what to do—and to actually *do* it. While we will explore professional development more deeply in chapter 8 (page 211), we believe that fostering a growth mindset and a willingness to lean into discomfort are more important than anything else leaders do with teachers.

Jennifer has collected a list of norms for work among educators, designed to help them envision how to handle similar experiences with students, most of which come from schools and networks that have embedded them into their culture:

- Share the well
- Begin from questions
- Assume the best intentions
- Fail up and forward (Maxwell, 2000)
- Be present
- Lean into discomfort
- Be open to learning
- Respect confidentiality
- Have fun

One of the core norms, to *lean into discomfort*, is on the list specifically to help educators handle uncomfortable topics, and another, *fail up and forward*, is designed to create space for risk-taking and mistakes—as long as all participants learn from them (see more on building culture in chapter 8, page 221). If leaders can engage teachers just as we hope teachers will engage students, and are thoughtful about building school culture, professional development will have a more direct impact on the classroom because teachers will understand the power of best practices as learners themselves.

The Challenges of Educational Management Technologies

On a strategic systems level, schools that adopt the landscape model may find it necessary to rebuild or at least adapt elements of their gradebooks and learning management systems (LMSs), both to help track growth and to organize student and educator documentation. Most traditional online gradebooks and LMSs aim for more traditional checks and balances in schools. While schools can certainly translate the landscape model into the more traditional checks and balances of achievement, the alignment will be more organic if a school's LMS includes more space for narrative feedback, more space to note the growth of essential skills for our times, and even adjustments to language so that evaluations have less to do with number and letter grades, and more to do with patterns of growth (emerging, developing, and so on). Ideally, an LMS should also include places for student protagonism as we've described it on the landscape (see the following list).

If your school's online gradebook doesn't provide ways to document the growth of essential skills like collaboration and self-management, for example, we recommend that leadership find ways to adjust the *tool*, not the approaches to *learning*, so that what works best for students remains the priority. That might look like adding fields for narrative feedback, shifting from numbers and grades and toward the language of growth, or simply adding grading categories for students' skill development. If the capabilities of your school's LMS end up driving the curriculum more than the institution's ideas about students, this isn't good for students or educators.

An LMS for the landscape model should include the following.

- Tools for organizing and tracking progress along a personalized curriculum, especially those that allow for tracking along a continuum
- Fields for notes on progress and growth, evaluation of essential skills, and so on

- Tools for student documentation, especially those that students can control and input themselves
- Tools for many of the evaluation strategies in chapter 6, such as co-constructed rubrics (page 172)

Such an LMS, and the accompanying gradebook, should reflect the values and beliefs of the educational community and work *with* that vision, not against it. Options that do this from providers focused on serving traditional grading environments are quite slim. However, some LMS providers will work with schools to customize their gradebooks in significant ways. Other schools use open-source systems, such as Moodle, having internal information technology professionals build their own reporting systems in a shared space, based on the school's philosophies and guidance from instructional leaders. However it is accomplished, the tool should support the pedagogy, not hamper it.

The Challenges of Buy-In and Accountability

Another challenge is one noted by several of the thought leaders we spoke with during our investigations: the need to build a deep sense of commitment to and responsibility for using the model across the entire school community. While the model is designed to be implemented in as little as one classroom, our hope is that whole schools or districts adopt it. At a school level, we envision that the academic elements of the landscape model will be implemented by classroom educators, made all the more tenable with the constant support of a robust school advisory program run by advisors or homeroom teachers who know the students and even come from their neighborhoods where possible (see the HSRA model for advisors in this section). However, this work will be most effective, and inclusive prosperity a more realistic goal, if it happens across all aspects of students' experiences in our schools; we will reach greater success the more fully the entire community sees it not as someone else's role, but as *everyone's* role to know students and personalize how far they might go. At a district level, it is feasible that superintendents and school boards support the effort by reducing or eliminating ranking, diversifying measures of achievement to offer grants and additional funding based on more than just standardized high-stakes testing, and increasing capacity building in student-centered pedagogy and instruction.

Kristen Pelletier, former head of student support services at the International School of Brussels and current director of redefining access, notes how challenging it is to support a broad range of students with varied needs, a situation made all the more challenging by the mentality that addressing those needs is someone else's responsibility (personal communication, April 23, 2021). Equally dangerous is the adherence to roles regardless of potential impact (for example, the perception that the office assistant who all students know and love should never be involved in planning students' education because that individual isn't an educator). Such divisive thinking, and the silos we have created in most educational contexts, academic or otherwise, would place all responsibility on the shoulders of classroom teachers, making it a potentially untenable goal.

Part of the solution is to build a deep sense of commitment across the school community through the following (Lee, 2019).

- Inspiring experiences can be shared by current students, teachers, and leaders at back-to-school nights and other school events, through social media campaigns, on the school's website or publications, and even at board meetings
- Alumni stories can be shared at events, by bringing alumni back into the schoolhouse as experts for projects, on the school's website or publications, and through social media campaigns
- Space for educators to reflect on their own experiences through grade-level team meetings, professional development discussions, mentor-mentee meetings, and faculty meetings
- Deep aspirational work around the mission, vision, and values of the school (see more in chapter 8, page 201)
- Other heartstring approaches to transformation that help inspire educators in new directions

In their article on building stakeholder ownership, Ronald Williamson and Barbara Blackburn (2019) assert that there are three core tenets to developing stakeholder buy-in with new or challenging initiatives.

- Find authentic opportunities for participation and shared decision making so initiatives are not simply mandated from above.
- Determine who to involve in different activities, with a focus on those who have a reason to invest in the change.
- Build effective two-way communication so that stakeholders have an actual voice, not a tokenistic one.

But more important will be a systems approach to each of the landscape model's three elements of (1) ecosystem, (2) horizon, and (3) pathway. If you can organize adults and students in ways that leverage the most effective relationships, this can help ensure success and deepen everyone's commitment to the goals of the model. For example, at the High School for the Recording Arts in St. Paul, Minnesota, they find it very difficult to find high-quality core subject teachers who come from the same neighborhoods and cultures as their students (M. Lipset and T. Simmons, personal communication, April 16, 2021). As a result, the school has complemented core academic teachers with full-time advisors who come from the students' neighborhoods and cultures, who can relate to students' experiences more personally, and who guide students throughout their time at the school with a deep understanding of their contexts and identities. The HSRA advisory program is as robust as their academic program because they recognize that educating is about guidance as much as academics. They hold time in the schedule for advisory, and they ensure advisors work alongside academic teachers to address students' challenges and needs during the learning journey. Using these strategies, in combination with structures that ensure the two groups communicate and collaborate consistently, allows the High School for the Recording Arts to provide challenging learning experiences *and* the kind of personal (and personalized) guidance the model requires.

The Challenges in Traditional and Progressive Contexts

More traditional school contexts are likely to have more voices of dissent in response to a student-centered model, and we can expect some parents in these contexts to see the shift as potentially dangerous because their preexisting ideas about achievement resemble the racetrack more than the landscape. This is no surprise; parents know how they were educated, and if they are successful in their professions, they tend to see traditional rigor as the only way into college and beyond. There are many potential solutions to this challenge. On the one hand, it is worth the time to help parents see the value of a more personal (and personalized) approach for *all* students, including theirs, and to help them let go of the belief that the goals must be the same for all students in order for education to be fair. On the other hand, more traditional schools may find they have to take a middle-path approach, weaving in more traditional measures of academic growth to help parents see that their students are being prepared in both ways.

As Jennifer wrote while serving as the head of school at Gimnasio Los Caobos in Colombia, a fairly traditional school before its shift to PBL in 2014:

> Caobos must ensure our students are accepted to the best universities in the country—and that means students must be as successful in traditional, standardized assessments as they are in more authentic evaluations of growth. While we would love to eliminate exams, grades, homework, and academic subjects taught in isolation, using some traditional practices ensures our students can thrive in any context. (Klein, 2020, pp. 104–105)

Particularly traditional schools may find a "choose your own pathway" course model highly challenging, an approach we will explore more in chapter 8 (page 195), but they might create space for more personal (and personalized) experiences through the following.

- **Flex blocks:** These usually happen once or twice per cycle or week, and are a time which can be used for any needs, including passion projects and other types of learning that position students as protagonists—but also including more traditional options like getting extra support from teachers and tutors. If it's too hard for your school to go all in on the landscape model, consider using flex blocks to open up time for more authentic experiences that more fully honor what students bring into the ecosystem.

- **Project blocks:** These are often used as a first step in schools trying to transition toward project-based learning but where instruction is generally more traditional, or in schools where scheduling makes interdisciplinary projects particularly challenging. Like flex blocks, project blocks happen once or twice per cycle or week, and provide the space for teachers and students to collaborate more easily across disciplines on projects that allow students more protagonism.

- **Electives:** While true choice of courses is a better goal, and schools with large populations can often provide a variety of options that meet the same standards (such as language arts course options based on the books to be read, or social studies courses that meet the same conceptual objectives through different periods or themes), electives are a simple way for any school to move the needle when it comes to honoring students' talents and interests. Such courses usually meet once or twice per cycle or week, and they provide a space for special interests such as creative writing, theatre, and other courses not always included as *core* learning in more traditional schools.

- **Selected courses:** Rather than trying to implement deep use of the landscape across the entire school, it may be easier for more traditional schools to start by developing specific courses where more student-centered learning will occur. For example, each grade level might include one interdisciplinary course that uses student-centered learning deeply, such as a humanities course where getting to know what students bring into the ecosystem is easily included through novels or social justice themes. Similarly, many high schools offer global studies or entrepreneurship courses that can easily be adapted to include student-centered experiences. While the authors prefer to imagine use of the landscape across all courses, beginning with a few selected courses can help students, educators, and parents to see the value, which opens doors for more.

- **After-school programming:** Some educational communities may find the academic schedule too inflexible for more landscape-oriented work, in which case after-school programming can be used to build students' skills as protagonists. Ultimately, ensuring inclusive prosperity after school isn't a great way to bring more of the practices into the school day, as it does make such approaches appear *extra* and optional to educators, parents, and students. But as RESCHOOL has discovered, sometimes it's the most direct way to offer students the opportunity for protagonism. (See more on curricular organization in chapter 8, page 215.)

All of these are small steps a school can take if shifting toward the landscape model across all coursework creates controversy. Sadly, all of them have the potential to create a division between what will be perceived as rigorous learning and these more authentic, vigorous experiences, which can actually exacerbate the misimpression that landscape learning isn't academic. If a more traditional school is invested in moving toward true student-centered learning and a robust use of the landscape, it should look more like students-as-protagonists in *most* learning experiences, but with regular but limited use of more traditional measures of learning, such as academic exams, so that students get practice with both.

In more progressive school and community cultures, the challenges lie in ensuring that students *are* still prepared for the expectations of more traditional universities. While the landscape model itself is unlikely to cause challenges in these contexts, high levels of student protagonism must be coupled with systems designed to ensure students develop essential academic skills. There is nothing worse than reaching the end of an engaging project only to discover that students didn't master the standards intended; no matter what the model, educators still have to keep an eye on long-term student success and make sure students are prepared for the still largely traditional expectations of most universities.

Jennifer lived this challenge personally, as her experiences at Bard College unearthed perceived gaps in her education as compared to her peers, after an entire childhood of progressive education—and this at one of the most progressive colleges available to her at the time. While she had written hundreds of pages during high school, Jennifer had almost no experience with the kinds of academic writing expected at Bard. And though she had read tomes and tomes of literature in high school, she had never been taught to analyze what she read in more traditionally academic ways. When Jennifer complained about the shock and challenge, Open School founder Arnie Langberg always pointed out that progressive education had equipped her with the skills she needed to manage the challenges. Still, it was a very hard transition that could have been smoother had Open School also prepared her for these different expectations.

Kapono attended progressive elementary and university programs at Hanahau'oli School and The Evergreen State College respectively, but had a very traditional college preparatory middle and high school experience at Punahou School. While the timing of the challenge was different than what Jennifer experienced, the contrast and adjustment weighed heavily on him.

In the context we find ourselves, the middle path is perhaps the most reasonable solution to these extremes; just as traditional schools need to make space for student protagonism, highly progressive schools need to make space for experiences that help prepare students for the more traditional academic rigor they are likely to encounter in other stages of their education.

The Challenges in International School Settings

International schools, particularly those with a transient community, have a unique set of challenges when it comes to charting progress across time. Standardized benchmarking, such as that provided by the Northwest Evaluation Association (NWEA) Measures of Academic Progress (MAP) Growth Test, can help any school to ensure academic progress and is widely used by international schools in most of the world. As long as schools don't let test results drive all programming—and ensure *students* see, understand, and can communicate about what they learn from those results—such measures can be a helpful tool. However, such testing systems are built on the assumption that all students of a given age are learning the exact same thing at the same time, which can make them problematic in a school dedicated to the landscape model. They are further complicated by the southern hemisphere's opposite school-year calendar, which means schools are often comparing first-semester students with their second-semester counterparts in the United States. However, part of why the NWEA MAP Growth Test has become so popular in international schools is *because* it provides a snapshot of how students in a given school compare to their peers in the United States at that grade level, allowing international schools to stay more or less in sync when it comes to their academic programs, and allowing students to move between schools where, for example, cursive will almost always be taught in second grade and U.S. history in tenth grade (Cordray et al., 2012).

This alignment across international schools is particularly valuable for "Third Culture Kids" (TCKs), students whose families move to a different country as often as every two to three years (Mayberry, 2016). When families move from country to country regularly, schools have to address potential gaps in curriculum, something we hope the personal (and personalized) approach of the landscape model will make much easier because students who have been protagonists will come to their new school knowing themselves as learners. Instead of assuming that moving to a new country and school will create gaps because of curricular differences in each institution, the landscape invites us simply to understand where students are (ecosystem), set goals with them (horizon), and support them to move forward (pathway). However, families also have to make sense of their new context, and the schools that serve them will need to understand how the various places they've lived have shaped who they are today. Having students with varied contextual upbringings requires more intentional systems to ensure teachers and administrators get to know new students and their families quickly and deeply on arrival. The lifelong growth journey may also be harder to capture when a student changes schools five times between preK and twelfth grade, though less so if all the schools they attend position students as protagonists who carry evidence of their journey with them.

Even more challenging, high teacher and administrative turnover in most international schools will require very thorough and effective onboarding systems to maintain continuity. First and foremost, schools hiring educators from outside the dominant culture will need those new hires to understand the local culture they've come to live and work in, so that intercultural relationships are effective from the start, particularly if their student body is predominantly local. If their student body is more international, international schools will also need to understand the varied cultures their students come from or have lived in. This kind of deep understanding of so many varied cultural contexts can take time; it's certainly not something one learns in a month or two on the job, and it takes more than a few hours of professional development to acquire. Educating on the landscape requires deep, sustained, and reflective professional learning to shift practices (see chapter 8, page 211, for our thoughts on the arc of professional learning). Given that most international schools contract teachers for two or three years, and that many international educators move to a new school and country each time a contract ends, onboarding systems will need to be all the more robust and effective to provide continuity for students.

The Challenges and Opportunities of Parents and Other Caregivers

While parents, guardians, and other caregivers can feel like a challenge in any context, and they often do challenge what happens in their children's schools, they can also be educators' greatest resource for understanding students' contexts, defining a horizon that aligns with family aspirations, and supporting students as they chart their course as protagonists. In Jennifer's work as a head of school, she found that a focus on constructive involvement is key, and she modeled project-based learning for parents by running monthly workshops designed to help them become constructive collaborators, allies of the school as much as allies of their children—and to help them understand the power of participant-driven learning. In these project-based experiences, parents became protagonists themselves, solving the challenges of how to coach their children at home toward better collaboration, more autonomy, and a growth mindset, to name a few. The goal of these sessions was to take caregiver concerns and turn them into an exercise in constructive problem solving, just like the Caobos educators were doing with their children inside the classroom (Klein, 2020). Caobos also built a database of parents interested in serving as experts for projects so they could collaborate constructively beyond their children's classrooms. Such practices helped parents and other caregivers to understand the power of participant-centered learning by letting them experience it, and the topics helped shift parents toward a more constructive support role from home because they demonstrated, for example, the negative impact on autonomy that comes from constantly rescuing their children from challenges or doing their schoolwork for them.

Avante Global School in Cartagena, Colombia, has taken caregiver involvement even further, building a Parent Pavilion into their building with the guidance of educational architect Frank Locker. Avante Head of School Amaris Salazar describes its purpose as follows:

> The Parent Pavilion is a purposefully designed space for use by our families during the school day in which they can network with each other, conduct virtual meetings or just hang out. It allows parents to feel a part of the Avante community by giving them a space that is all their own, where they do not feel they are infringing on much needed learning spaces for students. Its other purpose is to give our students opportunities to practice and develop entrepreneurial skills by designing, planning and running the coffee shop within the pavilion. It provides a much needed "safety net" for first-time parents and parents of very young children, who often need as much skill development in separation as do their children. The parents and school become trusting partners from the youngest of grade levels. (personal communication, June 25, 2021)

This approach effectively turns parents into learning partners, and while it may feel like too much parent involvement for some schools, the intentionality around design actually lowers the amount of time and energy educators and leaders need to devote to parent concerns.

Parents can also be helpful allies with each element of the landscape model in particular. Involving parents in the work of understanding the broader experiences and identities students bring into the ecosystem is an easy and natural fit, as home visits and events that bring families to school provide a window into their lives and cultures. As many thought leaders have pointed out to us during our investigations, it is worth taking the time to get to know families well at the beginning of the year, and many schools do home visits each year, some more virtual than presential, particularly with new families (National Center on Safe Supportive Learning Environments, 2011; Valli, Stefanski, & Jacobson, 2016).

Conversations with families also allow educators to drill deeper into the aspirations they have for their children, which allows educators to better understand how to frame students' goals when they define the horizon with them. Defining goals includes much more than just next steps for learning, and family aspirations should be central when we set goals with students. (See chapter 4, page 95, for more on defining goals.)

Finally, families who are involved constructively can be important allies as educators navigate the pathway, helping to support learning at home. This element is perhaps the most complex for many parents, particularly when it comes to not rescuing their child from frustration, not comparing their child's place on the landscape with where their peers are, and not doing their child's work for them. It may also be challenging for parents who did not receive the education necessary to support their children academically. Schools can provide intentional orientation and support for parents with these concerns, however; as long as educators see families as allies and work with them accordingly, we believe that parents can support our work on the landscape.

The Challenge of Policies and Politics

As we mentioned earlier in this chapter, some educational contexts make student protagonism more challenging, and the deep work needed to unpack implicit bias may or may not be embraced in some communities. Given that the political context, as well as laws governing public education, can have a significant impact on a district or school's ability to implement inclusive practices, some schools have championed student protagonism through electives, clubs, extracurriculars, and other flexible spaces, instead of inside their core courses. Similarly, some communities have chosen to work around schools entirely, in those cases where school, district, state, or provincial policies make it difficult to do this work in the schools themselves.

In one such example, the nonprofit RESCHOOL Colorado developed what might be described as parallel programming to complement what schools provide across the state of Colorado. After several years trying to bring change directly into the educational system, the people leading RESCHOOL were inspired by a parallel system of schooling they'd seen in Rio de Janeiro, Brazil, a new school system designed to function alongside the existing one, for kids who were starting school for the first time after leaving the *favelas*. It offered a parallel system that leapfrogged the challenges of the old and created something new, in partnership with students and families who had historically been non-consumers (or under-consumers) of the existing school system. Executive Director Amy Anderson explains:

> We like to design to the margins; we like to work with the kids and families for whom the current system just hasn't worked, and understand why, and lift their ideas and solutions, and then invest in those and co-create a different path forward. (personal communication, April 2, 2021)

With a broad range of success stories and evidence that their programs are building the skills of self-advocacy in families as much as students, RESCHOOL offers strategies, tools, and even funding for learning experiences beyond the school. For example, RESCHOOL supports students and their families through learning advocates who help students connect with enrichment opportunities connected to their passions, such as guitar lessons or an internship at a film studio, as well as funding for such experiences. RESCHOOL also developed the REVOLVE game mentioned on page 136, which takes players through a year in the life of a student. (Visit www.reschoolcolorado.org to learn more about the RESCHOOL model.)

In most parts of the world, educational policy changes every time there is a change in the party holding power in government, and the top-down re-regulation of education every few years is often more dangerous than helpful, undermining effective programs and changing policies that were working for students—and yes, occasionally offering new and better pathways (Lee, 2019). State legislation in many parts of the United States is censoring how U.S. educators teach their own history, for example, limiting educators' right to teach about slavery and systemic racism (Duncan, Zawistowski, & Luibrand, 2020). In fact, we see more and more attempts by government to restrict education across the globe, such as the 2021 Hungarian legislation that outlaws any teaching of LGBTQ+ topics or experiences (Rahman & Gupta, 2021). Similarly, Hong Kong enacted an educational mandate in 2020 that requires teaching national security law and clarifies what the government believes qualifies as government subversion (Aljazeera & Reuters, 2021). These legislative restrictions leave educators with three choices in any given context.

1. Follow the laws regardless of their impact on students.
2. Do what's right for students regardless of the laws.
3. Do more inclusive work outside the school.

The authors are hopeful that the landscape's more student-centered, personalized education will inspire future policymakers who will build a better system altogether, but that will take longer than our current students can wait.

While providing meaningful learning experiences outside the school certainly enriches the lives of students and their families, who come as willing and eager participants, it does little to improve the schools themselves or support those who do not participate. In fact, when implemented in states or provinces that divert funding from public schools to support such extracurricular efforts, such programs may further hinder schools' ability to deliver deeper and more inclusive approaches to education as part of the school day. Just as the voucher model of school choice can end up pulling funding away from public education, it stands to reason that funding experiences outside of school could become a similar monster (Nichols & Dynarski, 2017).

We would like to believe that schools themselves can become steeped in passion- and purpose-based experiences for students, that they can become the places where students learn on a landscape as protagonists, and that educators don't need to circumvent schools to get this right. Jennifer's early experiences at Rotzel's (1971) School in Rose Valley demonstrate that it's been possible in private education since 1929, and her Open School experiences suggests it's been possible in U.S. public education, at least as an alternative school model, since the early 1970s. The Summerhill School in England, perhaps the oldest model of what the authors believe is possible, has been doing student-centered learning since 1921 (Jones, 2020). There are plenty of models to suggest it's already possible anywhere there is a will to rethink education. That said, we believe that every community has to find its own best solution, one which allows them to circumvent counterproductive restrictions and build inclusive prosperity of experience and opportunity for all, whatever that might require. Ideally, that should happen inside the school; when that's not possible, communities will have to find alternatives like RESCHOOL that allow all students to thrive through rich, personal (and personalized) opportunities.

While we will address broader policy changes in chapter 9 (page 235), particularly those we believe would provide space for more Indigenous, place-based approaches to education, we want to make sure policy doesn't impede at least some progress toward the landscape model and the goal of inclusive prosperity. Schools can take small initial steps to engage the landscape model as they advocate for change at the district, diocese, or even state, provincial, or national level, such as implementing the three elements of the landscape without making significant changes to the pacing of academic objectives for individual students.

Or, as in the case of RESCHOOL, they can go around the system and address more student-centered, landscape-oriented learning as an after-school experience if there is no way to ensure it happens inside the school day (A. Anderson, personal communication, April 2, 2021).

Whatever the solution, we need to make sure we are meeting the needs of students in our classrooms, regardless of policy. Kate Robinson (2021), daughter of Sir Ken Robinson, quotes her father as saying often that even when we can't change broader systems, we can always make a difference for the children in the room with us, and it *will* matter to them. And in the meantime, make sure you have at least one policymaker in the building when students are showing off exceptional work; every school carving a less traditional path will be well served to build partnerships with local government, and to at least begin to identify key allies for continued change.

Reflective Questions

Respond to the following questions alone or with your school team.

- Which of the challenges in this chapter are particularly salient for your educational community? Why?
- Have you worked with, visited, or read about schools that have overcome such challenges and managed to offer deeply personalized, student-centered learning experiences? Why do you believe they were successful?
- How were these challenges true in your own education, if they were? Did your school see them as problems? Did you have teachers who made more personalized choices in spite of the broader system? How did such experiences impact you as a learner?
- What are a few small steps you might take in the coming weeks or months, to help address the challenges to implementing the landscape model in your school, even if it's just inside your own classroom?

Takeaways

The following summarizes key ideas from the chapter.

- The unique challenges your school might encounter will depend on the type of school and context you are in, but the landscape model hinges on student-centered strategies that have existed since the early 1920s.
- Educational policies around the world may create obstacles for educators trying to use the landscape model, but even small steps

inside a classroom—or outside of school entirely—will be beneficial for students.

- All challenges have their solutions, generally rooted in student protagonism and the development of deep buy-in among stakeholders and policymakers.

CHAPTER 8

Landscape Model Implementation for Long-Term Success

Many leaders are tempted to lead like a chess master, striving to control every move, when they should be leading like gardeners, creating and maintaining a viable ecosystem in which the organization operates.

—Stanley A. McChrystal

Anyone who works in schools knows that new initiatives can easily become passing fancies, and much in education feels to teachers like a flavor-of-the-month club wherein leadership layers initiatives like one might layer a wedding cake—until it falls under its own weight. We believe that the landscape model can't be allowed to follow the same course; whether or not it is implemented exactly the same way one year as the next, the goal should be to integrate as deeply as possible the elements and accompanying strategies, and the overarching focus on student protagonism and inclusive prosperity. To do so requires educators to frame their use of the model not as a *new* initiative but as an intentional shift in school culture and community mindset that makes existing programming more successful *and will therefore benefit all learners*. This work takes time and commitment, and it will get easier to implement with practice. Each year will bring new students and new challenges; as long as you have clear core principles and keep what's good for students at the heart of everything you do, you can develop an adaptive mindset in all members of the community. Leading this work requires agile leadership, long-term planning, and transformative professional development to reach the levels of success we believe are possible.

This chapter discusses educator profiles and recruitment; aspirational values, school mission, and vision; transformative professional development, curriculum adjustment; course and student reorganization; and a culture of inclusive prosperity. Visit **go.SolutionTree.com/diversityandequity** for the "Three-Year Plan Development" reproducible that can help as well. While the focus of this chapter is on the work school leaders need to do with teachers and other staff, it intentionally mirrors many of the practices educators will use with students, as the goal is to build the landscape model into all aspects of school culture.

Educator Profiles and Recruitment

To be able to educate in the most deeply equitable and inclusive ways, as the landscape asks us to do, school and district leaders will need a core of faculty and staff who, at the very least, don't need to be convinced that student protagonism and inclusive prosperity are important, and who, in the best of cases, already embody what we are looking for in our teams. This section will explore the development of an educator profile that allows us to identify what we're looking for in candidates, as well as recruitment strategies that can help us find educators who meet that profile—or who demonstrate core tendencies that signal alignment with our goals and a willingness to learn.

Educator Profiles

As your leadership team develops your school's educator profile, you need to consider not just an individual's ability to teach the given subject or age group you hire them for, but their ability to build deep relationships with students and to see them through an asset lens, leveraging their strengths, talents, and passions to foster growth in areas needing improvement. Prior training in culturally responsive pedagogy and the recognition and deconstruction of implicit bias is obviously a plus, as is experience with student-centered strategies. In many contexts, however, it will be the school's responsibility to teach and coach faculty in these topics, which may not be part of local educator-preparation programs but which do make up the heart of the landscape model; the model's successful implementation depends on it.

According to Rohit Kumar, CEO of the Apni Shala Foundation in India, it is the work of administrators to help teachers learn to unpack the complexities of identity and culture in educational communities, but a clear belief in students, *all* students, is what should lie at the heart of a school's recruitment strategies (personal communication, May 4, 2021). Such belief may exist even where leaders don't see an understanding of implicit bias, nor a recognition of how easily teachers from different backgrounds than their students can fall into the trap of charity-based, savior-oriented teaching and learning. He finds that as long as educators believe deeply and implicitly in all students, he can train them in the specific inclusive strategies he wants to see.

Roberto d'Erizans looks for educators who are learners to the core, who exemplify the open-minded, flexible learning attitudes and relational mindsets he wants to see them cultivate in their students (personal communication, June 1, 2021). And as we've noted before, the High School for the Recording Arts recruits core teachers for their ability to teach their subject to teenagers, regardless of whether they come from the neighborhoods the students do, complementing that staff with a core of full-time advisors who *do* come from the same cultural contexts as the students and can offer more culturally aligned guidance. The magic of the High School for the Recording Arts model is in how it *organizes* people as much as in the profile its leaders hire for, leveraging strengths in a variety of ways to ensure all students can reach their horizon.

Once we define what we are looking for in educators, and have established a concrete profile that captures our priorities, we can begin the recruitment and hiring process. We do need to value dissent and diversity, however, so we should never be so tied to our educator profile that we hire only those who "fit" the model; doing so can undermine diversity and eliminate critical conversations in the long run, and can be just as dangerous as only accepting students who "fit" our school. Any good faculty should have that magical mix of styles and experience because those differences allow us to offer students more diverse experiences across the course of their education. There's a difference between someone who struggles with change, and someone who openly resists and even sabotages the vision, however. We hope that deep work on values and vision, combined with transformative professional learning, can help inspire everyone toward this work, as we explain later in this chapter.

Recruitment

Most schools depend on administrators to manage all aspects of recruitment and hiring, but the landscape model suggests that classroom teachers and even students should likely be involved. A hiring committee that includes stakeholders from a variety of groups is more likely to notice nuances of personality, knowledge, and skills from more varied perspectives—and involving students is just one more way of ensuring student ownership and protagonism at school. It may be very challenging to find local educators who already know how to teach through more student-centered approaches, depending on the local teacher-preparation programs and the norms of culture that govern them. In Colombia, for example,

Jennifer found it nearly impossible to find teachers with actual project-based learning training or experience, but significantly easier to find educators who were inherently predisposed to think about education through the lens of equity and protagonism, even if their specific vocabulary for it didn't yet resemble the school's. In addition to defining the educator dispositions we are looking for, constructing a teacher profile to define the mindsets, attributes, and experiences leaders want in their team, school leaders must also consider their approach to shifting culture among existing faculty, not all of whom may have such attributes. Returning faculty and their new colleagues will need transformative professional development, which we will explore later in this chapter.

RESCHOOL uses a process called *responsive recruiting* to ensure that students see people who look like them and have similar backgrounds to them (A. Anderson, personal communication, April 2, 2021). Sometimes described as *culturally responsive recruiting*, this is a system of first vetting the most qualified candidates and then exploring how a professional community can be purposefully built to ensure it is diverse as well as representative of those it serves (Johnson, 2006). Kumar describes the goal of responsive recruiting as ensuring some level of natural understanding of the students being served by educators (personal communication, May 4, 2021). For example, responsive recruiting might look like ensuring a student body with a number of Latinx students has Latinx educators they can see themselves in (while acknowledging variation across Latin American cultures). This facilitates cultural context building and understanding. For example, it's essential in recruiting that female students see female teachers of science and mathematics, again an opportunity to not only break stereotypes but also to start from a place of context bridging (Lynch, 2016). Research demonstrates that students need to see teachers with identities similar to their own in order to envision themselves as successful in fields that traditionally did not include them (Gershenson, Hart, Hyman, Lindsay, & Papageorge, 2018), as in the example of girls in science and mathematics.

The opposite is also true. While students need to see educators like them, they benefit from being around teachers unlike them as well. Students of color *and* White students benefit from having educators of color (Anderson, 2015). This allows a richer context to form. If not, the school won't leverage the power of diversity of context.

Kumar gives us a powerful analogy of windows and mirrors. He asks: "Are there opportunities for me to reflect on my own socio-culture/ideas (mirrors), and are there opportunities for me to learn from how others live (windows)" (personal communication, May 4, 2021)? This metaphor of windows and mirrors comes originally from the work of Rudine Sims Bishop (1990), who developed it as a way to think about how diverse reading choices allow students to see themselves and others more clearly. When we apply this analogy to education as Kumar has, it becomes central to understanding context and responsive recruiting. Consider the following (Style, 1988).

- **Windows:** These can mean many things in this paradigm. A window can be any process, protocol, or strategy that allows one to see beyond themselves. A great example of a window is a home visit (page 84), which is a window directly into the home lives of students. Another window might be having educators do summer reading that comes from a different cultural context, but which has important implications for their own school context.

- **Mirrors:** These can be any process, protocol, or strategy that allows one to look inward and learn more about themselves. A great example of a mirror is a personal journey map: ask educators to use a map as a metaphor to share their personal-professional journey with peers. In professional journey maps, teachers use the metaphor of a map to share the steps they took to get to where they are. Teacher journals and portfolios are also a mirror, where teachers are able to reflect on their practice in very personal ways. Similarly, affinity groups for educators can be used a powerful group-reflection tool.

School leaders must ensure that recruitment strategies intentionally create mirrors and windows for students, which allows them to build their understanding of themselves *and* their understanding of others. And when educators can see their students as mirrors and windows as well, they are more likely to understand what each brings into the learning ecosystem, and to work intentionally toward ensuring all students participate in class with equal voice, for example, especially when that voice is from a student who does not come from privilege.

Geoff Smart and Randy Street have developed a protocol for recruiting, interviewing, and hiring that leverages what they call a *scorecard* (as cited in Vitaud, 2018). The goal of the scorecard and who interview is to identify the right person with the right skill set for your goals, clearly identifying who you should be hiring. It starts with identifying the outcomes of a position—what SMART goals are you currently hiring for? (Refer to page 101 for more SMART goals.) For example, are you hiring for a department chair, someone with leadership skills? Are you hiring for a first-grade reading specialist who will be tasked with improving reading outcomes? Or are you hiring for a PBL innovator who will change the learning culture of your school? Similarly, are you hiring so students see themselves in the teacher? Or is increasing the diversity of educator backgrounds your goal? No matter the goal, the scorecard asks us to be explicit, measurable, and tangible about the skill set this position demands and what their outcome will be (Vitaud, 2018).

See figure 8.1 for a sample scorecard for a school leader.

Objective	Notes and Assessment
Lead the development and implementation of a progress-based reporting system in the middle school that incorporates best practice and constituent feedback by the start of the following school year.	
Maintain and advance current communication channels to ensure continued and improved school-home relationships as measured by teacher and parent survey feedback.	
Evaluate and implement potential improvement to the schoolwide social-emotional learning program by the end of the school year.	

Figure 8.1: Sample scorecard for a school leader.

The who interview then holds those cards close, in a manner of speaking. The questions ask the person being interviewed to recount their accomplishments and failures in their previous positions, while interviewers listen for indications that the person has had success or has learned the lessons from failure to successfully accomplish the outcomes. The person being interviewed does not know the outcomes until later stages in the process.

As a school leader, Kapono has followed this protocol for years, and he has found that the results it yields are unmatched. The process works only when leaders are explicit about what they want in a hire, and when the entire organization commits to making implicit biases explicit so those biases can be addressed overtly by the hiring committee. For example, the protocol demands the hiring committee talk about what finding someone who looks like the students actually means. What does it mean to be Latinx? Who is? Who isn't? How do we know? Do we ask a candidate how they identify? Is that legal? The process itself is not perfect, as no process is, but it demands that we work toward our ideals and gives us the tools to do so.

A Shared Vision of What's Possible

Once school leaders have a mix of returning and new faculty, leaders need to take the time to offer their faculty a deep values orientation around the things that matter in the educational community, those deep elements of school culture they hope all educators will embody. These are the values leaders and the hiring committee should clarify and work toward during the recruitment process as well, as noted in the previous section. This is more than just sharing a guiding document on the first day of the school year and never referencing it again, or showing a video about the history of the school. The goal is to encourage all members of the community to live by a shared vision of the school culture they are building. We will explore how to build such culture through the school's mission, vision, and values statements, by establishing community norms, and by leading from aspirational values through tools such as the SOAR model inquiry, this time for use with teachers.

Mission, Vision, and Values Statements

These three elements of school identity, which are usually defined by school leaders and boards, and are often deeply ingrained in a school's history and culture. While most schools develop such statements, including them in school documents and even positioning them visibly around the school, that doesn't necessarily mean that they are always lived elements of culture. The authors have been in schools where teachers can cite the mission statement perfectly, for example, but their classroom practices don't align to what they're reciting. For the landscape model to become deeply ingrained in school culture, elements of inclusive prosperity and student protagonism should appear in their vision, at the very least, and leaders should strive to ensure they become lived elements of school culture.

- **Vision:** A school's vision statement looks forward and creates a mental image of the ideal state that the school wishes to achieve, as well as its potential impact on the world. It is inspirational and aspirational, expressing where the school *wants* to be in the future, as well as the impact it hopes to have (A-M. Balzano, personal communication, January 24, 2022).

- **Mission:** A school's mission is a concise explanation of the school's reason for existence. It describes the school's purpose and overall intention, and it explains *how* the school works toward its vision. The mission statement supports the vision and serves to communicate purpose and priorities to faculty, staff, students, and their families (A-M. Balzano, personal communication, January 24, 2022).

- **Values:** A school's values statement lists the core principles that guide and direct the school and its culture. A school's values create a moral compass which helps guide decision making and establishes a standard against which actions can be assessed. In schools, these core values are an internalized framework that is shared and acted on by leadership, faculty, students and their families (A-M. Balzano, personal communication, January 24, 2022).

The vision, mission, and values of a school should be lived in everyday practice across the community, which means leaders need to build in time at the beginning of each school year, and at checkpoints throughout the year, for deep understanding of and reflection about the ideas they contain.

Community Norms

Connected to the mission, vision, and values statements of a given school are the explicit community norms that establish the day-to-day agreements all members of the community should live by. Every school should create its own community norms, just as students should establish their own agreements for behavior in the classroom. Community norms are most effective if they are developed with input from the school community initially, including stakeholders such as students, teachers, and leaders, but once created, such norms usually become a permanent mainstay of school culture that do not change significantly from year to year, as they help school leaders maintain certain elements of school culture over the long term.

We believe the High School for the Recording Arts offers an outstanding example of community norms with equity at their core, as their ten equity commandments (Lipset & Simmons, 2021) provide a clear framework of non-negotiable values for the entire community. The ten equity commandments offer a road map for the HSRA community, allowing them to continually align themselves in their efforts, without it feeling like a list of rules (even under a title like *commandments*). Please note that this particular set of norms is designed by and for the HSRA community; each educational community should develop its own community norms, around the values it most want students and educators to live by—and ideally, students should participate in crafting them.

Following are the ten commandments at HSRA from *Education Reimagined* (Lipset & Simmons, 2021).

1. Issue no commandments.
2. Know who impacts what and how.
3. Accept you were not in the plan.

4. Find your truth, and never stop exploring it.
5. We are problematic; this is our gift.
6. Co-design space for truth and freedom; accept all, and then believe what you see.
7. The work is never finished and spans both space and time.
8. Dynamics always shift, so we must always learn.
9. Don't sleep on nothin'!
10. Love the journey.

In our conversations with Tony Simmons, executive director of HSRA, and Michael Lipset, director of social impact (personal communication, April 16, 2021), all roads lead back to these commandments, particularly numbers eight and nine, when it comes to ensuring their faculty can do what the school believes is possible. We note an important connection between the High School for the Recording Arts's *Don't sleep on nothin'* and Glenn E. Singleton's (2015) ideas about persistence as a core element of educational equity. Building a school culture of constant reflection and flexibility, based on student needs and a sort of diligent awakeness when it comes to their goals, the High School for the Recording Arts recognizes that educating this way requires a significant shift for many educators, and they work hard to avoid teachers backsliding in their practice.

Aspirational Values

If you want all members of your community to develop a deep commitment to the goals we've outlined in this book, as addressed in chapter 7 (page 182), Ackers-Clayton (personal communication, May 12, 2021) suggests you do so by leading from aspirational values at all levels of the school, which parallels nicely with Singleton's (2015) ideas about passion being core to equitable learning. Working from an aspirational point of view, and being able to articulate those goals, is key to building relevance as much as opening limitless possibility for all members of the community. Further, it supports the aspirational work educators will do in the classroom with students, as they work to define their horizons, and it supports an asset mindset across the school's culture.

Ackers-Clayton recommends beginning not just with the aspirations of leaders but with those of *teachers*, working to define and chart out their own aspirational values and goals as educators so that they can do the same with students (personal communication, May 12, 2021). Where our purpose is visible from the start, and where educators and students can define next steps and "climb the stairs together," building the safety to talk about these aspirations together as a community, Ackers-Clayton feels we can reach a level of cognitive and situational relevance that will bring out the best in all members of the community (personal communication, May 12, 2021). One of the best tools for such aspirational work is the SOAR model analysis, often referred to as a tool for appreciative inquiry.

Appreciative Inquiry With SOAR Model Analysis

The SOAR model, which we introduced in chapter 4 (page 112) as a tool for students, comes in various forms and is easily adaptable to work with adults and students, whether in relation to strategic planning, a schoolwide initiative, or a classroom project. When it comes to leading the landscape, SOAR provides an excellent framework for deep conversations about strengths, opportunities, aspirations, and results in concert, which is useful in any opportunity for reflection and consensus building around the school's vision—and a perfect way to involve the whole adult community in establishing shared aspirations.

Please note that the following example, which is adapted for this purpose relative to the version we present for use with students in chapter 4 (page 112), includes questions that may be irrelevant to some communities. Leaders can and should adapt SOAR questions to suit the realities of their community as needed. We recommend using small-group discussions, such as grouping faculty in grade-level teams, and full-group shares to the whole faculty, to ensure equitable participation and collaboration, ideally including opportunities to identify intersections and address divergences in teams' ideas.

Strengths: *What can we build on?* (Colorado State University Extension, n.d.; Otte, 2015; Peregrine Global Services, 2020)

- What are we most proud of as an organization?
- What makes us unique?
- What is our proudest achievement in the last year or two? (Otte, 2015)
- How do we use our strengths to get results?
- How do our strengths fit with the realities of the marketplace (if relevant)?
- What do we do or provide that is world class for [our students], our industry, and other potential stakeholders?

Opportunities: *What are our stakeholders asking for?* (Otte, 2015)

- How do we make sense of opportunities provided by external forces and trends?

- What are the top three opportunities on which we should focus our efforts?
- How can we best meet the needs of our stakeholders?
- Who are possible new [partners and allies]?
- How can we distinctively differentiate ourselves from existing or potential competitors (if relevant)?
- What are possible new markets, products, services, or processes?
- How can we reframe challenges to be seen as exciting opportunities?
- What new skills do we need to move forward?

Aspirations: *What do we care deeply about?*

- When we explore our values and aspirations, what are we deeply passionate about?
- Reflecting on our strengths and opportunities conversations, who are we, who should we become, and where should we go in the future?
- What is our most compelling aspiration?
- What strategic initiatives (projects, programs, and processes) would support our aspirations?

Results: *How do we know we are succeeding?* (Peregrine Global Services, 2020)

- Considering our strengths, opportunities, and aspirations, what meaningful measures would indicate that we are on track to achieving our goals?
- What are three to five indicators that would create a scorecard that addresses a triple bottom line of . . . ? (Note: Leaders should decide on the three core terms that come from strategic planning priorities—such as belonging, challenge, and agency—or have teams use the top three opportunities they identified earlier.)
- What resources are needed to implement vital projects?
- What are the best rewards to support those who achieve our goals?

What makes the SOAR model unique and powerful is its use of appreciative inquiry, which frames all questions in language that invites asset-based thinking. Its ugly cousin SWOT planning, which asks us to identify strengths, weaknesses, opportunities, and threats, is much more negative in its framing, and as such is not as appropriate for use on the landscape (NMBL Strategies, 2021).

Strategies for Tapping Into the Community

The work of equity and inclusive prosperity doesn't happen because just one teacher shifts practices in his or her classroom, though it's certainly a step in the right direction. In order to ensure that equitable, inclusive practices happen throughout our students' education, we have to ensure that the entire community assumes a role in the work. This doesn't mean that all adults will do exactly the same things to support students on the landscape, however; as Zhao's (2021) jagged profile suggests, we have varied talents and assets across any educational community, and we need to find ways to leverage individual and collective strengths to provide an effective network of support. The following strategies, asset mapping and role organization, and community-based learning—concentric circles for educators, can help leaders identify where we have strengths we might leverage, both inside and outside the school, and can help us organize people and partners in ways that best serve the needs of students.

Asset Mapping and Role Organization

Creative organization of roles and responsibilities will help ensure success with the landscape model in any context, whether in terms of when and how we teach content and discipline-specific skills, as noted in chapter 5 (page 130), or in terms of who steps up to support students' social-emotional needs along the journey. Some of the most creative, impactful work we've seen in schools has been done by leaders who think outside the box when it comes to roles and responsibilities, leveraging strengths and relationships in ways that best meet the needs of students. Ackers-Clayton recommends that schools undertake a process of asset mapping the internal and external community, to understand the assets adults each bring to their work (personal communication, May 12, 2021). Unlike affinity mapping, the goal of such asset mapping is not to group people, but to understand already existing assets both inside and outside the school community, so that those strengths can be leveraged to support all students. Please note that the following process can also be adapted for use by students in project-based learning experiences connected to the internal and external community, as described in place-based learning concentric circles for students in chapter 3 (page 81).

It is important to distinguish between internal and external asset mapping, as the goals are slightly different.

- *Internal* asset mapping allows educators to see which individuals in the school community have which talents and skills to offer, so that they can organize people appropriately and can effectively leverage those talents for the good of students and their education. When mapping internal assets on the landscape, we should be watching for the assets of people above all, such as additional languages spoken, intercultural experience, connections to key strategic partners for learning, comfort with particular topics, identities that match those of the students and teachers they might support, and so on.

- *External* asset mapping allows educators to identify key strategic partners beyond the schoolhouse who can support the learning journey. When mapping external assets on the landscape, we should be watching for the assets of people above all, so that all students make connections with people who can support their growth, even if those individuals are outside of the school. However, we might also consider local sites or organizations which could play a role in supporting educators and students, such as cultural sites that might help orient faculty to students' cultural needs or provide professional learning opportunities, public services that our students and their families might benefit from, or organizations that might be appropriate for student internships.

In more traditional asset mapping, the process usually includes identifying tangible assets, including natural; structural; infrastructural; social, community, or cultural; public services; and more.

Similar to understanding context with students, the asset-mapping process helps school leaders to identify core strengths and relationships for the sake of organizing people creatively. It also allows them to honor differences among staff, rather than working toward homogeneity in the faculty. The point is *not* that all educators do exactly the same thing, says Ackers-Clayton, or even that an entire faculty learns exactly the same strategies, but that they build a team with strengths to bear in a wide diversity of situations (personal communication, May 12, 2021). This includes thinking differently about professional learning as well; if educators recognize that students are at different points on a landscape and have different needs and strengths, it follows that leaders should see educators this way as well. Thus, educators will also benefit from a personal (and personalized) pathway for growth, such as choice from a selection of different professional learning experiences, or even personally built pathways for their individual learning, based on their needs and interests as educators.

While schools sometimes isolate themselves from the communities around them, whether intentionally or not, external community partners can be an incredible support for schools implementing the landscape model, so asset mapping potential community partners will also be important. Great project-based schools don't hire experts in everything the students might want to learn; instead, they build relationships with local and global organizations and individuals who can step in to offer what their community members might not be able to. And the best project-based schools teach students to network for themselves, recognizing that self-advocacy and resourcefulness set students up for lifelong learning that's not isolated (picture a scholar with piles of books, alone at the library), but instead is interconnected and interdependent (picture students working collaboratively with partners across the online social networks they already use).

Asset mapping the community around the school, locally and globally (*glocally*), can help support deep and meaningful learning. This is particularly important on the landscape when it comes to culturally responsive teaching and learning, as making use of glocal partners means educators never have to answer for a given cultural group outside of their own experience. When in doubt in the classroom, or when working with a new family from a culture they don't know, teachers can draw in partners from the community to support learning and relationship building. Such partners help expand everyone's definition of community, teaching adults and students alike about interdependence and what it might mean to be a global *and* local citizen. Furthermore, such partners can be of great benefit during projects and other student experiences, either because they are working on the same problems the students are studying or because they are *living* the problems personally. For example, the Denver Center for International Studies makes use of an extensive network of local community partnerships for student internships, expert classroom visits during project and field trips, and even career mentors, in addition to the global partners who offer international perspectives and experiences (K. Farmer, personal communication, January 15, 2016). Their partnerships include organizations that can help support families' needs as well, such as job training, language services, and financial support, as the three schools in the Denver Center for International Studies network recognize that supporting families is essential to the success of their children.

We encourage leaders to run asset-mapping protocols with teachers, and teachers with students, so that the school can develop a broad network of community partners who can step in to support learning more authentically. In tandem, we encourage work with faculty and students around becoming comfortable with areas of inexperience, or *leaning into discomfort* when they don't have answers, a tough thing to do in a profession *based* on expertise. This means accepting that we, as educators, don't have to be able to know, do, or teach it all personally, and it means modeling transparency when we encounter something we don't know or know how to handle. Instead of tightly controlling every move to ensure we stay in our comfort zones, educators can build communities where we become *comfortable with the uncomfortable,* an incredible asset for any school interested in more authentic teaching and learning.

There are many different strategies for mapping assets both inside and outside of a community. Many protocols suggest the use of literal maps to help visualize where the assets exist, while others simply encourage bubble charting or other approaches. Many project-based educators use the asset-mapping process as developed by the Local Initiatives Support Corporation in their local leaders' Creative Placemaking Toolkit (https://bit.ly/36BgrPI) for external community asset mapping. For more internal mapping of people and their connections, we encourage schools to design a simple visualization tool that suits their community and needs. The following protocol, concentric circles for educators, offers another useful way of framing and running such mapping, specifically focused on identifying partners to support the learning journey. Whatever the approach your school chooses, the goal is to bring to light strengths, talents, and resources across the community, people who can help to support and strengthen your work on the landscape.

Community-Based Learning—Concentric Circles for Educators

Concentric circles is a quick protocol Kapono designed as an exercise for educators to ground their units or projects in a sense of place while firmly starting from an asset lens. This protocol, as described in this section, is the original version, with a version adapted for students included in chapter 3 (page 81). The goal of this particular protocol is to allow you to see resources in your community (and beyond) that can support learning. Viewing your community and the people in it as assets is the starting place. Becoming grounded in a sense of place and exploring the importance of that grounding in learning is a benefit of this exercise.

The concentric circles protocol is best conducted in groups of three or four educators, with one person facilitating (ideally a member of the same team). The goal is to map resources in the community, near and far, that can serve as context to enrich learning.

1. Educators start with a large piece of chart paper and one marker per person.

2. The facilitator draws three concentric circles on the chart paper and prompts the group three times.

    a. In the innermost circle, brainstorm and write any and all community resources you can think of *on your campus* that might support students' learning in this unit (*this unit* is a placeholder for whatever topic you choose). For example, is there a historic or cultural site that is part of your campus? Are there people, like potentially a teacher or staff member who personally experienced a war? Are there natural features on campus like gardens, streams, and so on? Are there historic items on campus that can serve as context for learning?

Reflect as a group on the following questions: How can these assets support who students are as learners? How can they help our students to see themselves in their community? See themselves as protagonists of their education? See themselves as successful in the future?

b. In the next circle, brainstorm and write all community resources within walking distance (or easy transit, if you live in a more rural community) from your campus. Are there businesses that you know will partner with schools? Are there community parks that can be used as learning sites? Are there museums, historical sites, religious buildings, or sites to visit? Are there natural phenomena nearby that can facilitate learning, such as streams, lakes, or grasslands?

Reflect as a group on the following questions: How can these assets support who students are as learners? How can they help our students to see themselves in their community? See themselves as protagonists of their education? See themselves as successful in the future?

c. In the outermost circle, brainstorm and write all resources that are too far for you to imagine visiting with your students. Once listed, consider if there are ways to engage with these resources virtually. Are there businesses that can be reached out to? Are there virtual museum tours that can be done? Are there Indigenous groups or elders, cultural leaders, or thought leaders that can be engaged?

Reflect as a group on the following questions: How can these assets support who students are as learners? How can they help our students to see themselves in their community? See themselves as protagonists of their education? See themselves as successful in the future?

3. Once the map is complete, take a step back and observe. What's missing? What is most exciting? What connections do you have already? What units might connect to these resources? How do the community assets help students see themselves as assets?

Transformative Professional Learning

School leaders everywhere agree that deep, continual professional learning, experiences that strive to inspire and transform as much as to teach and inform, are necessary to ensure success with any initiative they want to stick, and this is certainly true for the landscape model of learning. This work requires much more than *drive-by PD*, or what educational consultants often call the *spray-and-pray method*, because it constitutes a type of professional development done quickly and without lasting impact, in which leaders and consultants "pray" for any level of impact they can get. Success with the landscape model hinges on the deep transformation of our thinking about equity and success; because of that, effective and sustained professional development must focus on student-centered teaching practices and how educators can build relationships with students. Professional learning will be most successful if internal capacity can be built to manage regular coaching, classroom observations, and feedback cycles, so that we reach Singleton's (2015) equity goal of establishing the use of the best instructional practices possible across the community. Not all of this professional development needs to be given by outside experts, but the authors note the sometimes myopic internal cultures that can develop if we don't bring outsiders in occasionally to stir things up and integrate new ideas or practices. Similarly, any practices related to implicit bias or culturally responsive teaching should include at least some interventions from external experts, unless you are fortunate enough to have such expertise on your campus.

The following sections discuss the arc of professional development for the landscape, self-reflection and self-discovery, and modeling as professional development.

The Arc of Professional Learning for the Landscape

We believe that the arc of professional learning should include the eight topics in figure 8.2 (page 212), more or less in the following order of priority, depending on the particular characteristics of your school community. We have put an asterisk by those we believe require expert facilitation.

Self-Reflection and Self-Discovery

One of the most important facets of professional learning for the landscape model is a process of self-reflection and self-discovery which every educator should go through early in their learning process. Before educators can authentically understand students in all their complexities, they need to know themselves. Author bell hooks (1994) describes her theory of *engaged pedagogy* as emphasizing such personal well-being for educators, writing, "Teachers must be actively committed

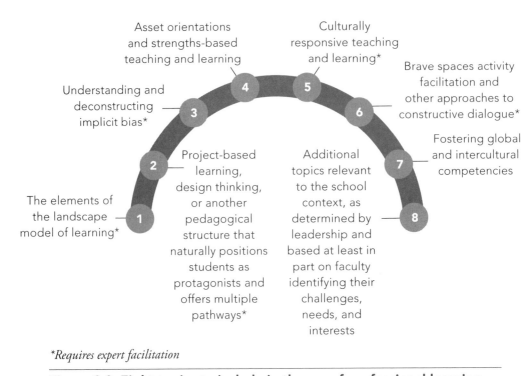

*Requires expert facilitation

Figure 8.2: Eight topics to include in the arc of professional learning.

*Visit **go.SolutionTree.com/diversityandequity** for a free reproducible version of this figure.*

to a process of self-actualization that promotes their own wellbeing if they are to teach in a manner that empowers students" (p. 15). While professional learning rarely takes the human being into account to this degree, the landscape definitely requires that leaders honor the complexities of educators' lives and careers as much as we do so with students. Leaders must create the conditions for educators to do—and continue doing—deep work around who they are and what *they* bring into the learning ecosystem with them.

For example, Jennifer has been on a lifelong journey around her Jewish identity, which includes unpacking her privilege as someone who looks more White than Semitic, grew up in a middle-income household, comes from a lineage of artists and intellectuals, and carries advanced degrees from good schools. But her work has also included deep affinity work in international spaces, which has allowed her to recognize how elements of her upbringing in secular schools "othered" her and impacted her identity dramatically. She has worked through the early trauma of a peer in second grade telling her Hitler was coming for her family, and she has learned to respond with more patience when people tell her they "knew someone Jewish once." She no longer struggles with what to put on forms when asked for her identity (although *other* is usually her only choice), nor with the fact that one boss called her "my Jewish teacher" for eleven years in spite of her lack of religious practice or political alignment. And all this is because Jennifer has taken the time to understand what it means to be ethnically, religiously, culturally, and politically Jewish, and she has been intentional about which elements of that identity are central to her life, and which are not. While her roles have rarely included counseling Jewish students in particular, Jennifer would not be able to work with educators, parents, or students on topics of self and identity without having done this work herself.

To ensure that professional learning is deeply transformative, leaders have to make it personal and keep it personal by making sure educators have opportunities to reflect on their own educational experiences growing up, on the moments when they've successfully brought out the best in their students, and on the *ouch* moments when they may not have handled a challenge well. They need chances to dig into their own identities, and to understand what they carry into the ecosystem from their broader lives. As educators, we can't explore implicit bias, for example, without looking at ourselves; we can't understand privilege—or the lack of privilege—until we unpack how we were raised, where and who we come from. This means creating the space for teachers and leaders to get real with each other, to dig deep and engage in hard conversations, and to learn how to do the same with students. Making professional development transformative means inspiring as much as teaching, moving educators' heartstrings in new directions, and motivating a shift that starts from a deep commitment that has little to do with how we make our living and everything to do with believing in students. And it means focusing on the *why* as much as the *how*, providing the deep motivation that comes from shared purpose and vision, as much as the strategies we will use to reach them.

Modeling as Professional Development

The other powerful form of professional development, which is just as important as self-reflection and self-discovery, yet rarely formalized, is the constant modeling of what educators want to see in the classroom. We are not talking about modeling in the more traditional "I do, you do, we do" model, which runs counter to the tenets of project-based learning and design thinking, but about modeling the practices of inquiry, transparency, student protagonism, and inclusion (Frey & Fisher, 2013). Simply put, we suggest that leaders consistently do with teachers what they want to see teachers do with students. Modeling consistently helps teachers not just envision *how* to do this work with students but reminds them continually of *why* it's so powerful through the impacts they'll feel personally. This might look like faculty meetings that begin with activities connected to the three elements of the landscape model, faculty workshops designed as PBL experiences, brave spaces where leaders share their truths first, and other participant-centered practices where teacher voice is heard and elevated.

Leaders should also encourage teachers to visit each other's classrooms, not to evaluate each other but to learn from the best practices and strategies they encounter in their colleagues' spaces, all with an eye to doing the best they can for every student. The School for Examining Essential Questions of Sustainability, led by Buffy Cushman-Patz, has adapted and adopted Harvard's instructional rounds protocol, which guides educators in deprivatizing their classroom practice by making the presence of teachers in each other's classrooms normal, helpful, and safe (B. Cushman-Patz, personal communication, August 2017; City et al., 2018). At the School for Examining Essential Questions of Sustainability, as at many other schools, adopting protocols such as instructional rounds has paid huge dividends in building a culture of learning and improving student outcomes. City and colleagues (2018) attest to the efficacy of this protocol in transforming education in schools, especially when agency is handed over to the faculty.

Similarly, we encourage the use of educator portfolios to demonstrate growth over the course of each school year (see figure 8.3). This is a valuable practice for any educator, as portfolio development allows them to reflect on their best moments and collect their best work, as well as to reflect on their areas for growth in the coming year.

Portfolios give educators practice with how to design and support their *students'* portfolio work, which can have a positive impact on how they manage the process in the classroom. Most importantly, portfolios allow leaders to read for core attributes like growth mindset, understanding of the elements of the landscape model, inclusive thinking, positive relationships with students, flexibility, and any other tendencies that school leadership values (Redd, 2021).

As part of each teacher's plan for professional growth, portfolios become an articulation of that growth, just as they do for students. Encourage educators to use any format they want for their portfolio, including video, visual arts, writing, and so on. As long as the portfolio includes honest reflections on educators' learning during the year, all forms should be acceptable—after all, we want teachers to feel that same freedom to express themselves through their talents that we try to offer students. Jennifer has found teacher portfolios incredibly valuable, if rather time-consuming to read, because they taught her what each educator needed most the following year, and helped her build spaces and systems that allowed for individual and collective learning based on those needs.

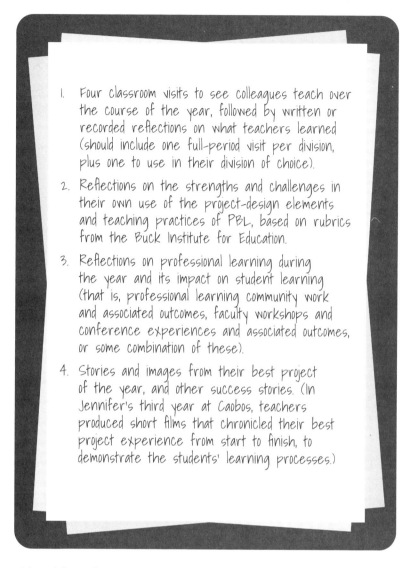

Source: Adapted from Klein, 2017.

Figure 8.3: Sketch of an educator portfolio—final artifact of teachers' professional growth plan.

Curriculum Adjustment

The authors recommend a deep analysis of the current curriculum as schools begin to work with the landscape model. This usually takes the form of an internal curriculum audit leveraging a curriculum coordinator or curriculum team. However, in the authors' experiences, external consultation can also be helpful for two reasons.

1. It is hard to see the forest through the trees, and therefore it may be more difficult for educators *in* a system to see needed changes clearly.
2. Individuals often feel emotionally tied to existing curriculum because of the time they put into its development, or the enjoyment they experience in facilitating it. This emotional attachment makes removing elements of a curriculum difficult.

The audit most often includes looking at what is taught as well as how much time is spent on each subject. This gives a picture of where resources are going, especially the most valuable resource: time. The result of these curricular analyses is typically the prioritization of some concepts and knowledge over others, and ideally, the removal of some breadth for the sake of increased depth. A tool to support curriculum adjustment is the collaborative protocol for defining outcomes in chapter 5 (page 147).

Generally speaking, schools tend to add curricular layers and expectations annually, but rarely do they remove any of them. This leads to overloaded educators and students, teacher burnout, and the pervasive sensation that there isn't enough time for anything beyond that curriculum, such as authentic work, flexible time, or deep relationships. The authors continue to question whether everything we *think* we need to teach actually *needs* to be taught, a challenge to standards and university entrance expectations in general. But while the system continues to work as it does, leaders need to find ways to trim back, condense, or better organize the curricular load—at the very least opening up more space for personalized support, reflection, identity development, passion projects, and other meaningful experiences not always included in the scope and sequence of the formal curriculum.

In our conversations with leaders, several noted that a conceptual curriculum is much more effective than a content-oriented one. For example, a content-oriented social studies course would have learning objectives about specific historical events, and might ask that students learn about specific people involved in crafting their country's constitution, for example, both of which are easily searchable online. A conceptual curriculum, on the other hand, would have learning objectives around understanding how and why societies define their own constitutions and laws; students might still learn about people and events along the way, but the primary goal would be conceptual. Like the earlier example of the unit on interdependence, a more conceptual approach allows for more flexibility to adapt to the local context (the study of interdependence among bees). Kristen Pelletier described an extremely talented violinist at the International School of Brussels for whom it condensed the curriculum significantly, so she could participate in events and a rigorous practice schedule (personal communication, April 23, 2021). If she, as a leader, can do that for the virtuoso, all of us, as educators, can do the same for *all* student in our schools.

A strict focus on Common Core State Standards (National Governors Association Center for Best Practices & Council of Chief State School Officers, n.d.a, n.d.b) in English language arts and mathematics, if taught in their entirety, for example, would leave no room in the school day for art, music, physical education, or drama. Educators already make the choice to rush over topics and move on before students understand so they can teach to core subject areas, but the goal isn't to *teach* a subject; it is that students *learn* it. The choice educators already make is to sacrifice learning for coverage. As a result, it's commonplace to find schools claiming that educators "did their job" and that it was students who fell short. We don't believe this at all. As educators, we all fall short when students don't learn; therefore, time must be a factor in planning learning. Strategies such as student-centered iterative unit planning (page 137) can help us focus the curriculum around what really matters. It is essential we lead our schools toward learning more than teaching.

What happens to this feeling of not having enough time for instruction when educators trim back curricular standards or remove facts that are easily searchable online in thirty seconds or less? For most educators, it disappears. In fact, when educators adjust the curriculum this way, focusing on discipline-specific skills, essential competencies, and overarching concepts, they might even have time for practices they often feel they can't prioritize because of the curricular load. That might mean igniting students' souls, hearts, and sense of beauty through deeper experiences with the arts, expanding their comfort zones through outdoor education and nature-based experiences that will deeply enrich their lives, or developing deeper global collaborations and co-creations with peers and experts around the world.

If words like *trim* or *condense* are too scary for your educational community at the moment, consider starting by flipping classrooms so that content and discipline-specific skills are learned online as personal homework for those who need it (Låg & Sæle, 2019). There are many ways to deliver content learning, as noted in chapter 5 (page 117). Within a structure like PBL, there are also many ways to ensure students learn what a project's scope and sequence identify as important while still providing significant student agency.

In an ideal situation, PBL becomes the vehicle for *all* content and skills, while remediations and accelerations of learning happen both inside and outside of that project. On the landscape, every moment of class time is precious because it allows us to work with students in different groupings, and it allows students to work collaboratively with our scaffolding and support. Whatever the post-pandemic landscape brings, there is no question that all educators will need to be flexible and agile with the curriculum, making sure they prioritize the kinds of learning and growth they consider most valuable.

Student and Course Reorganization

School leaders also need to consider how their school organizes curriculum—and students. Even with the strategies addressed in this book, we know that it will be more complex to manage a classroom that contains students at vastly different points on the landscape. But that problem stems from an adherence to grade-level, age-based groupings that move through the curriculum together. When schools stick to a move-together model based on age, they ignore opportunities to group students based not only on their interests but also on their talents and needs. While there can be challenges associated with groupings based on needs and academic level (Barro, 2018), the authors do not mean to suggest that *all* learning happen in homogenous groups. For example, many schools are currently pulling students into different level groups as needed to accelerate learning as a response to the COVID-19 pandemic. This allows educators to offer level-appropriate instruction and support to the students who need it, while also offering level-appropriate experiences for students who are ready for more complexity and challenge.

The other side of this strategy is to offer different pathways through learning based on students' *interests*, while still meeting the same learning objectives. This approach can create more variance in ability across a given class, or it can create less, depending on how the choices are structured. What is clear from research is that students will need the support of adults to make good choices, but that their intrinsic motivation will skyrocket if we can offer this kind of choice (Barro, 2018).

In an ideal situation, the landscape asks us to consider groupings that accomplish a bit of both. These less age-based, flexible groupings, such as those created by varied course options students can choose from, allow educators to meet standards without moving students through learning in such a standardized way. Flexible groupings can make classroom management and progress tracking much easier for educators because students will be appropriately challenged and have an interest in the content being taught. For example, students might choose from a variety of language arts classes based on different novels, with opportunities to choose from different levels of complexity and different themes, but which meet the same ELA standards; or some students in a given grade level might need a more remedial chemistry class but a more advanced biology option than what more traditional grade-level courses would offer. However we structure courses and organize students, the goal is to make sure that we have engaged, curious students working in their Zone of Proximal Development (Vygotsky, 1978). Such groupings can also lower boredom for highly proficient students and frustration for students who struggle, ensuring educators are almost always working with students who *want* to be where they are. Organizing students this way may even lower the stigma connected to skipping or repeating a grade level, as it would become largely unnecessary—and mixed-age classrooms would become more normal. The more such reorganization of learners can be based on student agency, with support from adults, the more students learn to reorganize themselves as protagonists on the landscape.

The High School for the Recording Arts offers an interesting example of the intersection between reorganizing students and reorganizing courses, as well as opening opportunities for students to make both need- and interest-based choices. Students at the school are offered a variety of ways they might meet any given set of standards, an entire catalogue of options, from expeditions to workshops to projects and more structured courses, open to students of all ages (T. Lipset and M. Simmons, personal communication, April 16, 2021). Each learning experience carries a certain number of credits in a particular academic area, and students are able to make choices with the support of their advisors about which experiences they want to have to fulfill those credits. When students have a significant experience outside of school, such as a student at High School for the Recording Arts who sued the city of Saint Paul, Minnesota, for unemployment benefits for teenagers during COVID-19, advisors work with the student to support the process, identify which standards have been addressed, and decide on credits earned (T. Lipset and M. Simmons, personal communication, April 16, 2021). And yes, this did happen, and yes, the student *won* his lawsuit, which is why teenagers in St. Paul now have a legal right to collect unemployment if they are central breadwinners.

At the Open School in Colorado, students have similar options, including a wide array of expeditionary learning experiences and classes that fulfill a variety of competencies for graduation (Jefferson County Open School, n.d.). The most important learning experiences are independent projects called *passages*, in which students work with an advisor to define their own goals, identify the competencies they'll master, manage the entire project process, and evaluate their success, all in collaboration with peers and educators. In addition to demonstrating mastery in over fifty core competencies through expeditions, workshops, and classes,

Jennifer completed six passages during her three years of high school, including three which she completed during eight months living and traveling in the Middle East and Europe. In her career-awareness passage, she interviewed professional authors, wrote a piece of short fiction of her own, and revised it over several months using professional creative writing processes, ultimately submitting the story for publication in a magazine. In her global-awareness passage, she investigated the communities of Ethiopian Jews who were relocating to Israel, ran awareness campaigns and clothing drives across several Denver-area schools, and then coordinated getting those donations to Israel to support Ethiopian refugees there.

As former principal (and Jennifer's high school advisor), Rick Posner (2009) explains in the first longitudinal study of the Open School, passage experiences are designed for:

> Exploration, experimentation, and skill building. Students are consistently asked to design, modify, and evaluate the learning that takes place. . . . By making life skills and the love of learning part of their school curriculum, most alumni felt that the school made it easier for them to transition to adulthood. For some alumni, the continual pursuit of inspiration was shaped by a belief that anything related to their interests was valid and important, something to be taken seriously. (p. 124)

In fact, Posner (2009) finds that the impact of passage work lasted well into adulthood, writing:

> Students who have had opportunities to discover and nurture enthusiastic pursuits in a project-based curriculum find that their familiarity with the experiential process serves them well as adults. They look at their lives as a series of never ending projects and adventures. As a result, many former students have had the courage to take the road less traveled. (p. 128)

While such choice-based approaches have their complexities, they can provide a much higher level of student agency than trying to move a grade-level group through the same standards together, regardless of students' individual strengths and needs—and both the learning experience and evaluation processes will be more meaningful for students. In both the High School for the Recording Arts and the Open School, there is much more reliance on students to define their own horizon and chart their own pathways, with the support of educators, and evaluation relies much more heavily on students' self-evaluation than it would in a more traditional school context (T. Lipset and M. Simmons, personal communication,

April 16, 2021). The Open School does this successfully starting in preschool, and without grades (Posner, 2009).

For those raised in traditional schools and schedules, the design can look pretty chaotic, with students working on very different tasks, alone or in combination with different-sized groups of peers who might come from different grade levels, and educators become facilitators who help guide both learning and evaluation processes. But the magic of this design lies in several concrete strategies (Olsen, 2020; Wheaton et al., 2016).

- **Scaffolding:** Adults constantly scaffold the skills students need in order that students might be able to better manage their own learning plans. Skills are introduced and practiced and feedback is provided.

- **Advising:** Advisors play a key role in helping students make good choices, which fulfill their credit or competency needs. Systems that support the advisor-advisee relationships are implemented and progress based on advising is tracked and recorded.

- **Building trust:** Successful student-centered schools build cultures of trust, recognizing that most undesirable student behavior comes from disengagement and systemic disenfranchisement. These schools combat such behavior not through military-style discipline and grades but through real, thoughtful learning experiences and brave, honest conversations that help students become self-motivated, self-managed learners who enjoy school.

We recognize that significant reorganization may be challenging in many contexts, but the authors have seen proof of how this kind of organization changes school for students—and for the better. As we see it, this isn't about *more* work for schools; it's about putting more energy into making sure students are where they need and want to be, and a whole lot less energy into disciplining and controlling students who are bored or frustrated because their needs or interests are not being engaged by the school.

Student Protagonism in Building School Culture

Reshaping school culture will be essential not just for ensuring the buy-in of all community members but also for building and maintaining norms around inclusive prosperity, including a deep shift toward student agency and protagonism. But shifting school culture is often harder than the work of teaching and learning, as students and adults have to unlearn deeply ingrained habits and embrace new ways of learning, teaching, and interacting to ensure the changes stick. Without an authentic shift in school culture that goes to the heart, educators will only end up policing and controlling behavior, which is the opposite of the goal.

Unfortunately, for all the great ideas educators bring to the table when it comes to school culture, making significant shifts based on their thinking may not be as easily accepted by parents or students. Particularly if educators' ideas can be interpreted as politically motivated or controversial by parents or policymakers, enacting teachers' most transformative ideas can easily end careers if staff are not careful (Klein, 2020). Take, for example, the teacher who starts a Gay-Straight Alliance at her school, only to be accused by parents of having an agenda and trying to "turn her students gay."

For this reason, for any shift in school culture that might be viewed as controversial, leaders should involve students as early in the process as possible, and building a culture of inclusive prosperity is no exception. Ideally, culture-building should be a collaborative process in which school leaders include all stakeholder groups, but keeping students' ideas at the heart is key to building a sustainable, student-centered culture where students-as-protagonists shape the society they want to live in, right there in the school and, eventually, beyond it. Further, when school culture depends on students' ideas, educators and parents are more likely to fully accept the initiatives students undertake; this makes the initiatives much more likely to last (Klein, 2020).

The core of a culture of inclusive prosperity lies in a deep understanding of community interdependence, in our opinion. Culture needs to become a daily lived experience, not just a mission statement posted on a wall. When community members understand themselves and each other, and they share a common goal and understand it will take everyone to get there, it becomes achievable. Too often, student leadership frameworks like student council are just a tokenistic approach, where student council members are elected but never heard, and students spend much more time and energy on elections than on any significant leadership once final candidates are chosen. A culture of student protagonism requires intentionally trusting students, bringing them to the table any time decisions are made, and *listening* to the ideas they share—with the intention to *enact* the best ideas they have, in partnership with them. This means shifting the power balance between adults and students and creating the space for students to lead constructive change in their school community.

At Gimnasio Los Caobos, Jennifer worked toward a student-centered culture in every way possible. Each time a significant complaint arrived at her office as head, she tried to take that concern to students and see how they might solve it. One example was the student uniforms, which students generally disliked, particularly the teenagers, which meant that dress-code violations were a constant headache for educators. The leadership team brought together student representatives from every grade level, posed the challenge of a uniform redesign, and then simply provided the structure for students to create possible designs and get feedback from their respective peer groups. This process took several months, with student artists drawing designs, receiving feedback, and redesigning based on the opinions of their peers. Once the student body chose the best designs, a design and production company joined in the work, dealing directly with student leaders to understand their designs, tweak them where necessary for practical reasons, and produce prototypes for student feedback. This process ended in new, student-designed uniforms for use across the community—and a lot of very important skill building for students in the process. The final products were so successful that many parents, teachers, leaders, and staff bought and wore elements of the uniform as well, completely voluntarily.

When it comes to adult culture and the goals of the model itself, the shift requires an adaptive lens that always puts students first. Pelletier shared the heart of the inclusion model at the International School of Brussels:

> We serve the *needs*, not the *model*. Whatever is in front of you this year is what you need to figure out. So you want to go into it accepting and expecting that things are going to change as they need to, to meet the needs of the kids who are at the center. (personal communication, April 23, 2021)

We agree that the most important part of any educational improvement needs to center on meeting the needs of the students in front of us each year, and we believe that intentional messaging with the adult community can help keep the focus on them. Fill your leadership and faculty teams with people who will ask, "What's best for students?" first and foremost, and who will always bring discussions back to the students. Even if the discussion is about what brand of cups to buy for the cafeteria, an inclusive student-centered decision mindset will result.

One of the more polemic areas of school culture is what gets measured as part of an educator's job-evaluation process. We recognize that establishing a goal as part of teachers' key performance indicators (KPIs) in their contracts is *not* the same as shifting school culture; in fact, formalized expectations can often work directly against an authentic shift in culture, producing only compliance, just like we see with the impact grades can have on students. That said, our formalized KPIs and other written goals or expectations do help establish what we want to see, as well as providing the opportunity to think about and embark on pathways for growth, as do more informal opportunities for educators to set personal and professional goals—to establish their own horizons, just as they do with students. Authors Chris McChesney, Sean Covey, and Jim Huling (2016) assert and illustrate that goal setting, tracking progress, and reporting on celebrations and setbacks is not only powerful but also essential to accomplishing lasting system-wide change.

Kumar feels that educators tend to teach what we know will be assessed; he feels the same is true of success metrics when educators make them intentional and are transparent about establishing them from day one (personal communication, May 4, 2021). Using the example of a male mathematics teacher who may be excluding girls in the classroom and not even realize it, Kumar points out that many educators may not see the relevance of diversity, equity, and inclusion metrics until they're actually applied to practice in ways that force a change in approach (personal communication, May 4, 2021). Ultimately, if a school is serious about doing this work—and doing it well—the commitment needs to be visible and actionable in all aspects of adult and student life.

Classroom observations will be an important way to gather evidence of how well teachers are implementing the landscape, as will deep analysis of student outcomes that considers how well all students are progressing toward their individual goals. With an eye to evidence of equitable practices, appropriately challenging work, and personal (and personalized) support, leaders can easily develop rubrics that help them identify gaps in practice as much as strengths. In her workshops with leaders and teachers, Jennifer often supports the process of rubric development for classroom observations through the use of a Y chart like the one in figure 8.4.

When students are agile intercultural learners, what do we hope to see, hear, and feel in the classroom and school?

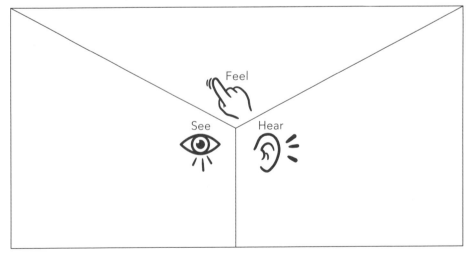

Source: Klein, 2022a.

Figure 8.4: Y-chart.

In this approach, educators are asked to identify what they will *see, hear* and *feel* when they enter a classroom where a given approach is happening at its highest level of quality. For example, what might we see, hear, and feel if we enter a classroom where deep student protagonism is occurring? We might *see* students up and moving, but not off task, actively engaged with their own work and supporting each other; we might *hear* students encouraging and challenging each other, asking each other questions that help deepen the lines of inquiry; and we might *feel* a sense of ownership, empowerment, safety, challenge, and even joy. Once a team has developed a Y-chart for a particular goal in the classroom, it is simply a matter of building those terms into a rubric that helps capture the various levels of quality we might encounter.

Ideally, educators should have opportunities to look at student work and consider, critically, whether they see evidence of growth and challenge, and whether all students are working toward their personal best. Similarly, educators should include student voice in evaluations of everyone's collective work on the landscape, to ensure *they* (students) feel it is working to build belonging, to challenge them appropriately, to support them appropriately, and to meet their individual needs as learners and as humans.

The reproducible "Reflection and Discussion Tool for Teachers on the Landscape" (page 232) is a basic sketch of a reflection-and-discussion tool based on KPIs connected to the landscape model, which could be used and adapted as needed for self-evaluation and reflection with teachers. Please note that this reflection and discussion tool is oriented toward the classroom teacher. We have also provided a "Reflection and Discussion Tool for School Leaders on the Landscape" (page 233), based on the same indicators, to support continual growth and evaluation. Schools may find it appropriate to develop additional tools to ensure that broader systems are also working effectively to ensure inclusive prosperity.

Three-Year Plan Development

We assume that every school will implement the landscape model in unique ways, based on their understanding of their educational context. Just like all students should receive what they need from education, every school will have different needs as well. However, very few of those needs will necessarily incur financial commitments, beyond a deep commitment to professional learning for teachers and every adult in the school who works directly with students. Deconstructing implicit bias and building a toolkit for brave conversations, for example, needs to be taught, modeled, and coached, deeply and over time, by experts in diversity, equity, and inclusion work. A network of strategic community partners, built over time, will also be an essential support for this work, particularly those who might know the neighborhoods, communities, and students in ways educators may not.

As educators begin envisioning implementation of the landscape on the classroom, school, and district level, we offer the following three-year planning framework for such implementation, recognizing that schools will be at very different starting points for what we identify as core priorities. After all, schools, too, are on a landscape of sorts. The asterisks you see in the lists in the following sections indicate topics we believe should be facilitated by external experts. Visit **go.SolutionTree.com/diversityandequity** for a free reproducible version of this content.

Year One: Laying the Groundwork for Change in the Ecosystem

In year one, schools should address the priorities outlined here to most effectively lay the groundwork for change in the learning ecosystem. The following topics we suggest are aimed at creating shared priorities within your community and will help in building a strong *why* at the core of your school-change initiative. Expect planning for systems and professional learning changes to take time. Depending on the level of commitment and resources, particularly time allotted for this work, this may take longer than a single year.

- Systems priorities
    - Connect school transformation work to the mission of the school.
    - Develop a portrait of a graduate or other tool to define (or redefine) educational outcomes.
    - Conduct a curricular audit to understand where and when students are given the opportunity to practice the skills and traits embedded in the portrait of a graduate.
    - Adjust curricular planning forms to support the landscape model.
    - Design a recruiting and onboarding strategy and tools.
    - Run an impact evaluation of all strategies implemented in year one.
- Professional development priorities
    - Train and coach educators in the elements of the landscape model*.
    - Train and coach educators in project-based learning, design thinking, or other personal (and personalized) pedagogical structures which position students as protagonists*.

- Provide formal training and informal opportunities for educators to understand and unpack implicit bias.

Year Two: Shifting the Horizon of the School

In year two, clear, consistent, and bold moves are grounded in transformative professional learning, and narrowed by prioritizing based on resources available. Year-two system and professional development priorities happen simultaneously and span the entire year. Holding a focus on these priorities, making time, and providing resources is key to ensuring success.

- Systems priorities
  - Adjust gradebook systems and learning management systems to support the landscape model.
  - Change the physical learning spaces to support the new vision for learning.
  - Update school policies to support the new vision for learning.
  - Develop and implement parent education.
  - Run an impact evaluation of all strategies implemented in years one and two.
- Professional development priorities
  - Continue year-one professional development topics.
  - Train and coach in asset orientations and strengths-based teaching and learning.

Year Three: Sustaining the Journey and Assessing Progress on the Pathway

In year three, a change narrative emerges, illuminating successes and providing data for areas that still require work. Honest, data-informed, and consistent tracking of progress supports year three. Celebrating successes publicly and making agile adaptations will support success.

- Systems priorities
  - Develop and implement a reporting system to report to the broader community on the school's key performance indicators.
  - Develop a plan for technology to support learning on the landscape. Continue to implement year-one and year-two priorities.
  - Run an impact evaluation of all strategies implemented in years one, two, and three.

- Professional development priorities
  ◆ Train and coach educators in culturally responsive teaching and learning*.
  ◆ Train and coach educators to facilitate brave spaces (page 76) and other approaches to constructive dialogue*.
  ◆ Provide immersive experiences for educators that foster their intercultural competencies, such as global travel or local Indigenous immersion experiences.

Impact Evaluation of the Landscape Model

It will be important in any context to regularly evaluate the impact and effectiveness of the landscape model in schools, particularly given the challenges outlined in this chapter. Educators used the *School Voice Report 2016* (Quaglia Institute for School Voice and Aspirations, 2016) to successfully evaluate the impact of student-centered practices that the landscape model aspires to. Data points as valuable and complex as student perception of choice and agency in schools may be complicated to measure, but using tools such as those implemented in the report make it possible.

We recommend that schools develop checkpoints at various intervals, at least at the beginning, middle, and end of the school year, to ensure that students' individual progress is being stimulated and documented effectively, and to make sure that students feel increasingly heard and valued.

The most important measure of success will come from the students themselves and should rely on regular opportunities for feedback and reflection around social-emotional benchmarks like feeling seen, understood, respected, and challenged. For example, student agency perception, as the *Student Voice Report 2016* measures, has a powerful impact on school design. Similarly, other tools that encourage reflection, synthesis, and action, like those provided in the design-thinking model, can provide traction as a school embarks on transformation (Auernhammer & Roth, 2021). Following, we offer a series of questions appropriate for surveys or discussions designed to gather feedback from students about their experiences as the school—or individual teachers—begin to implement the landscape model.

Questions for students entail asking students to rate their level of agreement with each statement using the Likert scale, from 1 (strong disagreement) to 5 (strong agreement). Provide a space for comments for each if possible. The last three questions are designed to be answered in narrative form. The questions in figure 8.5 are appropriate for students from approximately third grade and higher, with language modifications for third- through sixth-grade students.

> Questions about the ecosystem follow.
> - Do my teachers understand my background and life outside of school?
> - Do my teachers know my assets and highlight them in our work?
> - Do my teachers keep my strengths and needs in mind when they teach?
> - Do my teachers treat me like I'm important?
>
> Questions about the horizon follow.
> - Do my teachers believe in my aspirations?
> - Do my teachers help me set challenging goals that help me grow?
> - Do my teachers involve me in decision making about my next steps?
>
> Questions about the pathway follow.
> - Do my teachers involve me in tracking my growth?
> - Do my teachers help me learn to talk about my learning needs and strengths?
> - Do my teachers make sure our learning experiences work for me as much as possible?
> - Are my teachers there to help when I get stuck or want more of a challenge?
>
> Narrative responses follow.
> - What is one thing I wish my teachers understood about my home life?
> - What is one thing I wish my teachers understood about my life goals?
> - What is one thing I wish my teachers understood about how I learn and how to support me well?

Figure 8.5: Impact evaluation for students in grades 3–12.

*Visit **go.SolutionTree.com/diversityandequity** for a free reproducible version of this figure.*

Educators should also monitor academic progress to ensure that all students are appropriately challenged and motivated. The goals of the landscape model may become KPIs for faculty and leadership wherever this model is used, to ensure it is taken as seriously as any academic initiative, and to help build the accountability needed to make sure no students fall off the radar. Leveraging questions such as those in the *School Voice Report 2016* (Quaglia Institute for School Voice and Aspirations, 2016) can help to create these KPIs in more tangible ways. (See more on KPIs and a reflection and discussion tool for improving teacher performance in this chapter, page 225.) We also believe that asset mapping will be essential every year to ensure that every student has a deep, trusting relationship with at least one adult in the community, so the school can leverage those relationships to support students—and to help other adults understand students' needs.

Ultimately, given that student protagonism is the core of the landscape model, one of the most powerful shifts educators can make is simply to take the challenges that emerge *to their students* to solve. The student-as-protagonist model invites such a shift, so that obstacles educators normally solve before even taking an idea to the classroom become a rich opportunity for collaborative problem solving *with* students. For example, do you think it's impossible to have celebrations of learning in the COVID era? Ask your students how you might pull it off, and they'll come up with actionable ideas no educator would even think of. Do you find it challenging to monitor where every student is on the landscape? Ask students to help come up with classroom systems to make it work. Educators might find this counterintuitive, as we are so accustomed to managing all aspects of learning and to figuring everything out for students before we even walk through the classroom door. But we believe that building students-as-protagonists and fostering students' skills of self-management and self-advocacy require that educators involve students in *real* challenges in the course of their education, not just the project-oriented challenges educators design for them. We can think of no more relevant, authentic real-world challenge than asking students to co-create the systems educators use to support them.

Reflective Questions

Respond to the following questions alone or with your school team.

- How *lived* are your school's mission, vision, and values across your educational community now? Where do you see opportunities to leverage them to impulse change?
- What are the aspirational values of your educational community? What are your own aspirational values as an educator?
- To what degree does your school or course curriculum support more flexible groupings and adjustments to meet students where they are? Where do you see opportunities to create more flexibility, even in small ways?
- How well did the systems of education you experienced as a student meet your needs as a learner at different ages? Were there teachers who seemed to know how to challenge and support you particularly well? How did they impact you as a learner? How did they impact you as a leader?

Takeaways

The following summarizes key ideas from the chapter.

- Deep school change requires that educators feel connected to the purpose and identity of the school and experience the landscape as learners themselves.

- Leaders have a pivotal role in building school culture through professional learning, in evaluating our success, and in reimagining how we might best organize people and curriculum for greatest benefit.

- Students have a vital role to play in school change, and their protagonism will be essential for change to last and meet their needs.

Reflection and Discussion Tool for Teachers on the Landscape

Complete the following as an individual or with your school or district leader.

Goal	Reflections on My Current Strengths	Opportunities for Improvement
I engage every student with an asset mindset.		
I know my students well enough to challenge each of them appropriately.		
I know my students well enough to support their individual growth in areas of weakness.		
I define the horizon with every student and their family in ways that leverage their talents.		
I define the horizon with every student and their family in ways that honor their values.		
I work with students to build a classroom culture of trust and agency.		
I chart a personal (and personalized) pathway in collaboration with every student.		
My students are protagonists who document their own learning journeys.		
I use a variety of formative evaluation strategies to foster reflection and growth.		
I support all students' ability to leverage their talents and grow in areas of weakness.		
I bring out the best in every student I work with.		

The Landscape Model of Learning © 2022 Solution Tree Press • SolutionTree.com
Visit **go.SolutionTree.com/diversityandequity** to download this free reproducible.

Reflection and Discussion Tool for School Leaders on the Landscape

Complete the following as an individual or with your school or district team.

Goal	Score and Evidence 0 = Not at all 5 = Consistently	Reflections on the School's Current Strengths	Opportunities for Improvement
Educators at our school regularly engage with every student with an asset mindset.	Score: Evidence:		
Educators at our school know all students well enough to challenge each of them appropriately.	Score: Evidence:		
Educators at our school know students well enough to support their individual growth in areas of weakness.	Score: Evidence:		
Educators at our school define the horizon with every student and their family in ways that leverage their talents.	Score: Evidence:		
Educators at our school define the horizon with every student and their family in ways that honor their values.	Score: Evidence:		

page 1 of 2

The Landscape Model of Learning © 2022 Solution Tree Press • SolutionTree.com
Visit **go.SolutionTree.com/diversityandequity** to download this free reproducible.

Goal	Score and Evidence 0 = Not at all 5 = Consistently	Reflections on the School's Current Strengths	Opportunities for Improvement
Educators at our school work with students to build a classroom culture of trust and agency.	Score: Evidence:		
Educators at our school chart a personal (and personalized) pathway in collaboration with every student.	Score: Evidence:		
Our students are protagonists who document their own learning journeys.	Score: Evidence:		
Educators at our school use a variety of formative evaluation strategies to foster reflection and growth.	Score: Evidence:		
Educators at our school support all students' ability to leverage their talents and grow in areas of weakness.	Score: Evidence:		
Educators at our school bring out the best in every student they work with.	Score: Evidence:		

CHAPTER 9

Opportunities for the Future

Education is not preparation for life; education is life itself.
—John Dewey

When we authors think about the future of education, we imagine more than small tweaks to an existing system. Ackers-Clayton says that educators use that word *ecosystem* in education without actually understanding this true interconnectedness—or at least not building education based on that interconnectedness. She asks the question, "What would the new forest ecosystem look like if we were to start from scratch?" (J. Ackers-Clayton, personal communication, May 12, 2021). What if we decided to raze the forest and recreate the ecosystem of education, instead of just doing occasional pruning? It sounds sacrilegious to think about destroying all that is. Certainly, tearing up or burning down a forest is not something easy to think about, and neither is tearing down the current structure of school. As much as the authors love to think and talk about huge changes in education, it's difficult and unpopular to talk about truly razing the current education system. People have worked hard to make what was, better. People—our friends, neighbors, and coworkers—*are* the system. Yet, there are times when the ecosystem needs a reset. And like fire can bring new life to a forest, major sweeping change can sometimes be the best way to allow new ideas to grow and take root, bringing about real change.

The future holds something bold. It must. The simple truth is that the majority of our current efforts in educational transformation are bound tightly by two things: economics and childcare. Throughout the 20th century and beyond, the formula of school has remained basically the same, based on these constraints: (4 walls + 1 teacher) × (25 students × 9 months) = school. Regardless of which months of the year make up a school year, which varies in the northern and southern hemispheres, the formula is basically the same—sometimes without walls, sometimes with larger or smaller groups of students, sometimes for more than nine months of the year. But ultimately, this formula is a global reality on which our societies and economies rely. Of course, this formula is just a metaphor for the inputs of the education system. In the end, school has been constrained by not acknowledging the fact that school is also childcare. The COVID-19 pandemic that impacted the world of education shone a light on this fact: *school is also childcare*. That's nothing to be ashamed of, but if we don't acknowledge it, we spin our wheels trying to fix education while we also have on our backs the burden of supervising a generation of students while their parents are at work. We've tried many ways to tweak this formula of school while keeping it balanced: year-round school, staggering start and end times, small classes, big classes, new textbooks, technology . . . . We've tried it all, but always within the boundaries of ensuring that education happens at the same time as childcare at a price-per-student we can afford. The future holds a bold new vision for education. What is it? That is for us to decide.

There are several frontiers that need to be explored as we talk about opportunities for the future and this bold new vision. These are all big-picture areas that demand work outside of the classroom to see real change happen, particularly in the realm of educational policy, but they are areas that will be of high value to truly change how we do school.

Education Evolution to Follow Human Development

It is important that we start back at the beginning, but with a slightly different lens on our collective history. Now that we've established what we believe is possible, the landscape model of learning, what else might the history of human development teach us about what should come next? We believe that, at the very least, the future of education must follow the evolution of humans.

When Horace Mann sailed to Prussia and observed their novel system of education nearly a century and a half ago, the human race was firmly in the throes of a labor economy (Rose, 2012). The power of the human body to perform tasks in an industrial setting propelled the development of what we now call school. Schools were set up to give each laborer a similar and minimal level of education, to allow them to perform similar tasks in a factory. The how of school has remained the same, even as the world has evolved from a labor economy to a knowledge economy, and now, some say, a data economy.

The world that Horace Mann and colleagues designed education for was dominated by oil, steel, and mining. These three industries demanded only a basic education for their workers. Yes, there were management roles to be filled, but ultimately, the mainstay of the economy in all industrialized countries was the factory and the massive workforce that it demanded. Generations of people across the industrialized world grew up aspiring to graduate from high school, get the trade jobs their parents had, and hope for a happy retirement with a company-provided pension.

By 1967, however, IBM, AT&T, and Kodak topped the list of the U.S.'s largest companies (Kauflin, 2017). A shift had occurred: it was no longer the industrial oil and steel industries that drove the U.S. economy. The era of the knowledge economy had arrived, and it was no longer the force of one's body that secured employment. It was now what one *knew* that mattered.

Business management consultant Peter Drucker first coined the term *knowledge economy* in the 1960s to describe the shift he saw happening (as cited in Kauflin, 2017). As the power of the human body was no longer the driver of the economy, knowledge became the commodity of the employee of the 1960s and beyond. This shift was reflected in a massive growth in university attendance. The United States saw college enrollment double from the 1940s to the 1970s in response to the new skill set needed to succeed in business. And it was business that was now the new metric of success.

In the 1960s and 1970s, schools had not yet caught up. With few exceptions, public education was still being designed to get all students to a similar and minimal standard. But it was in the 1980s that new educational philosophers, such as Ted Sizer, former Harvard Graduate School of Education and Brown University professor, began to challenge the accepted formula of education. Sizer, like other educational thinkers of his time, saw the change that people like John Dewey had been writing about for decades already (Anderson, 2009). This new group of educational reformists knew that schools needed to teach students how to *think*, not just the basics of reading, writing, and arithmetic. This trend of educational reform sparked the U.S. charter school movement, and many of today's most well-known educational reform initiatives, including unique university models such as The Evergreen State College, Bard College, Reed College, Hampshire College, and others. Some of these initiatives have thrived, while others have come and gone, like educational fads.

By the 1990s, another change was underway, and it continues to accelerate in the 21st century: technology. Technology is not just driving a knowledge economy; it is commoditizing data. Companies such as Facebook pioneered the model of providing their services free to the customer. But we all know there is no such thing as *free* in the world of business. Facebook has not grown to the top of the tech industry by giving away its product. In fact, Facebook has been the quintessential example of the emerging new economy: the data economy.

In this economy, data are gathered, analyzed, and exchanged to derive value. Companies can now target their advertisements to specific markets, customizing them just for you. Keywords in our emails allow big data companies to know if we're looking to go on a trip soon, maybe a vacation, or if we are on the road already, seeing if we access our computers from a different location than we usually do.

What does this shift from a labor to a knowledge and now data economy mean for the future of education? Rohit Kumar of the Apni Shala Foundation hypothesizes that education will shift, following the journey of human development (personal communication, May 4, 2021). Kumar doesn't see a flaw in how education was designed long ago, but rather a lag in how we respond to sociological shifts. Kumar asserts that these social and economic shifts are part of the journey of human development and asks the question, "How can education change in response to this human journey" (personal communication, May 4, 2021)? This is a key question. How will education need to evolve as we move from a knowledge economy to a data economy?

One example lies in teaching students coding. As recently as 2016, coding was a complex skill set that demanded the user understand one or more of several computer languages (Sterling, 2016). Starting students off early to understand how coding works, and getting them fluent in several coding languages, is a trend that has gone as quickly as it arrived. Now, coding is drag and drop. A coder doesn't necessarily need to know any computer language to code an app or a website. Coders are now coding software that codes, and artificial intelligence (AI) is fast taking over the low end of computer programmers' jobs (Ramel, 2021). In fact, the new frontier has shifted to AI and machine learning. Changes such as these will come at educators faster and faster. How might school respond to the demands of industries that have not yet been invented?

Perhaps even more startling is what some futurists, such as Scott Klososky (2018), are calling our next phase in human development: the age of entanglement. According to Klososky (2018), our next challenge as a species will be to determine how humans will coexist with technology. Given that hackers can stop a person's pacemaker, virtual currency is at a premium, and AI systems are built to learn, it is no longer science fiction—our lives are entwined with the evolution of technology. Does that mean all of the work of education will be passed over to robots and AI? We certainly hope not. But it does mean that education will need to grow with these trends or it will become increasingly irrelevant.

The Next Frontier for Education

We would ask, rather than reforming education in response to a changing world, how might we reform education to help *change* that world? Are schools meant to be a reflection of our past, grounded in the reality of today, or a preparation for our students' future? Probably all three. But in all cases, rather than responding to the shifts in economy with a multi-decade lag, we must see our schools as institutions of change, institutions that empower our students to make the world a better place. We must not let educational policy lag behind a changing society but rather look to education to reshape it. As Zhao (2012) asserts in his seminal book, *World Class Learners*, those who will be successful in the future will be those who create their own opportunity and enterprise, rather than try to fit into existing job niches. Our students will not just inherit a new economy—they will create it. Do we want the next era to be one of competition or empathy? Do we want a world of hierarchy or equity? These are the questions educators must tackle, embracing our agency and leveraging the agency of our students to *shift* the world, not just react to it.

A'ole pau ka 'ike i ka halau ho'okahi is a Native Hawaiian proverb that states that all knowledge is not learned in one place (University of Hawai'i at Hilo, n.d.). School can happen anywhere. But in most cases, it happens in a classroom. Why do most schools relegate learning to a four-walled box? And why is the content of what is taught in that box determined far from the classroom, and usually by non-educators? From local school boards to elite private schools, to state and federal government, the where, what, and how of educational policy are governed by entities that are often far removed from students and learning. Therefore, to truly see educational reform happen, we must impact educational policy and policymakers.

Tara O'Neill, a professor at the University of Hawai'i at Mānoa, has spent her career teaching educators to teach. She wouldn't quite put it that way, as she sees her path differently than most professors in most colleges of education (T. O'Neill, personal communication, May 3, 2021). O'Neill weaves a strand of advocacy into her courses, impressing on all up-and-coming faculty that advocating for their students, their schools, and for meaningful educational change is part of what being an educator today should be about. By this, O'Neill doesn't mean that educators should spend their day lobbying at the capitol. But she does mean that all educators should stay informed about education policy and make their voices heard (T. O'Neill, personal communication, May 3, 2021). Just as we aspire to the student-as-protagonist, we must also aspire to the educator-as-protagonist, central to the decision making of the where, what, and how of school. The advocacy projects of O'Neill's students each look different. Some work at their school level, using data and rhetoric to persuade school-level decision makers. Other projects have aimed at state-level policymakers in the legislature. But one project that stood out aspired to change how a community looked at learning.

The small outer islands in Hawai'i are home to a higher percentage of Native Hawaiian students, a higher percentage of economically disenfranchised students, and can be considered rural, as they lack the infrastructure of the "big city" of Honolulu. Yet *A'ole pau ka 'ike i ka halau ho'okahi*: all knowledge is not learned in one place (University of Hawai'i at Hilo, n.d.). By creating networks between the schools, families, Indigenous cultural sites, community centers, and even community elders as resources for learning, one teacher candidate didn't wait for policymakers to change the rules. She inspired a community to change their paradigm of where, what, and how learning could happen by creating networks and engaging schools to see and experience learning beyond the walls of the classroom. Her story is a perfect example of why local control over educational decision making is so vital, not just for Indigenous communities, but for all communities; we simply can't wait for educational policy to catch up with what we know will be better for students.

While educational policy and change can become very political, we believe education needs certain policy concerns to become priorities everywhere, regardless of who is in governmental power. Most important is the need to localize conversations—and decisions—about what students and educators need to reach their highest levels of success. As noted earlier, we have a long history of top-down governance in public education across the globe, and even private schools fall under state governance in most parts of the world. This approach generally puts non-educators in charge of educational decision making, which rarely leads to relevant mandates on the local level—and which can damage the creativity and passion of good educators who are listening to what their students want and need. At their worst, such policies force schools to follow expectations and policies that simply don't make sense for their particular populations.

At its heart, the policy challenge comes from a lack of trust in educators to do what's right for our students *without* that governmental control, the root source of which lies in the early history of education as a trade more than a profession. At its infancy as a profession, women dominated the field and the feminization of education jobs kept teaching firmly viewed as a trade, rather than on par with other professions, particularly at the preK–12 levels (LeQuire, 2016). Even as male-dominated university systems appeared around the world, doubts about whether one could be taught to educate remained prevalent in elementary and secondary education, keeping education firmly entrenched as a trade (LeQuire, 2016). Education theoretically functions as a profession today, but this history means it generally still functions like a trade (such as the need for teachers' unions, which are usually found in trades but not professions). This history signals a lack of trust in educators as professionals, and our top-down approaches to educational policy still mirror that lack of trust.

The authors believe that the best decisions for students will always come from the educators who *know* them, who may or may not live in their neighborhoods but who are in the classroom with these young people every day. While we understand the argument for federal oversight and standardized objectives, we also recognize that federal oversight has more often ignored the needs of their less vocal or empowered constituencies, or even suggested such needs aren't valid, and that success lies in catching up with and doing school like everyone else. And that translates into educational mandates that actually *don't* produce the same desired outcomes for everyone, particularly for those who begin at a supposedly "disadvantaged" point as learners, no matter how much policymakers want to believe that standardization is helpful.

To confront such policy concerns, educators need to pose viable solutions for and new pathways toward what we believe will work best. As educators, we need to courageously redefine what we think a successful education could look like, and we need to create space for experimentation and creativity in the classroom, to bring out the best in our teachers as much as our students. We also need to encourage our former and current students to go into policy work, particularly those who come from marginalized communities or identities. And most importantly, we need to make visible and amplify all that schools are doing well in spite of the restrictions and demands, particularly when they do so through a less standardized and more localized, personalized model like the landscape.

Schools can do this through strategic partnerships with the press, as well as with universities, nonprofit organizations, companies, and even local government. Partnerships with the press have their risks, and Jennifer remembers many news articles about the Open School which didn't capture the ethos of the school accurately. But carefully selected community partnerships can help a school demonstrate its success, particularly with local policymakers of all kinds. Whether students are presenting a solution to reduce water waste to their local city government, offering solutions to homelessness in their community, or leveraging their networks to create broader changes in policy, every time someone in power sees your students problem solve and advocate for themselves, you won't just be elevating student agency and achievement. You'll be demonstrating that more localized educational policy has the potential to ensure a more relevant, successful education inside each school, particularly when it comes to ensuring inclusive prosperity.

The following sections address two aspects we find of critical consideration when contemplating the future of education policy: (1) a return to Indigenous ways and (2) technology assisting education. These two seemingly disparate topics highlight that the future of education policy must look back at the same time as it looks forward.

Back to Indigenous Ways

Indigenous knowledge has often been marginalized and overlooked in education. Moving forward into the future of education, specifically in an era of climate change and unrest, rooted in modern Western imperialism, demands looking back. Thomas (2022) clearly highlights that while social-emotional learning may be a new fad in education, Indigenous learning has been grounded in well-being of individuals and communities for millennia. And while a whole-child approach is resurging after a little over a hundred years of dormancy, Indigenous communities have perpetually grounded learning in whole-child outcomes. Herb Lee of the Pacific American Foundation has long proposed that a move back to Indigenous values, and a re-grounding in Indigenous knowledge benefits all students, no matter their race, ethnicity, or location (personal communication, January 23, 2020). The landscape is an ecosystem. It's not a model of individuals in a sterile environment. The model embraces a social-constructivist approach to learning, meaning that other individuals on the landscape play a key role in one's learning (T. O'Neill, personal communication, November 20, 2021). The educator is part of that ecosystem. As in O'Neill's students' advocacy project described earlier, so are community partners, historic sites, and people in and out of the context of the school. In this way, Indigenous knowledge, community-based leaders, and informal educators take back the importance that they had once—and that they should have today.

One way some communities are doing this is to reimagine the future of education in ancient terms. Indigenous communities across the globe are exploring how their ancestral ways of teaching and learning may be more successful at preparing students for the future than what their colonizing governments have been able to provide.

The World Indigenous Nations Higher Education Consortium (WINHEC; n.d.a) was dreamed up by Indigenous elders from across the globe during the World Indigenous Peoples Conference in Machu Picchu, Peru. One evening, while discussing Indigenous self-determination, this group of elders came on a truth. For Indigenous people to be politically self-determined, they need to be in positions of decision making within the current system. To do so means attaining higher education degrees. Yet as each elder spoke, it became clear that the process of attaining these degrees was itself a colonization of the mind. Students would enter into higher-education programs seeking to decolonize their communities, but would emerge from those programs with a certain degree of intellectual colonization, as the process of earning a higher degree has been created by and for a Eurocentric-way of thinking. Written sources receive credence over oral sources, even if those written sources have been proven one-sided, biased, or even xenophobic (Chilisa, 2012). Knowledge passed down from generation to generation through story is undervalued in higher education, and in most cases, is completely inadmissible in academia (Chilisa, 2012). To further highlight this point, even this section on Indigenous knowledge is cited using Western academic conventions in order to meet the prescribed standards of academia as they currently exist.

The elders gathered that day concluded that to earn a postgraduate degree that best supported the self-determination of their people meant that degree programs themselves needed self-determination. The programs and those who designed them needed to be freed from colonized requirements and models. Therefore, the accrediting bodies themselves must be freed of colonial baggage and "owned" by the Indigenous people themselves. This orientation echoes Paulo Freire's (2000) claim that "No pedagogy which is truly liberating can remain distant from the oppressed . . . by presenting for their emulation models from among the oppressors. The oppressed must be their own example in the struggle for their redemption" (p. 36).

WINHEC (n.d.b) was founded as an Indigenous accrediting body. While Western accrediting bodies provide both domains of quality and the descriptors of what that quality should look like (for example, the domain of good governance should look like an elected board made up of diverse constituencies), WINHEC works with Indigenous-serving institutions to determine what quality looks like in each Indigenous context. Might good governance look like an elected board at one school, yet be a tribal council of elders at another? Yes! WINHEC (n.d.b) found the root of educational change—the system that determines outcomes and gives credence to a degree—and has disrupted the system at its primal level.

Similarly, the Kaiapuni school system was created in the state of Hawai'i to provide a bilingual and bicultural educational experience for kindergarten through twelfth-grade students (Hawaii Public Schools, 2015). The program is not limited to students of Native Hawaiian ancestry but is guided by standards and outcomes that are grounded in Hawaiian epistemology (a Hawaiian way of thinking). The program's bilingual and bicultural design acknowledges that for Native Hawaiian students, success in the world means reconnecting to cultural and linguistic roots that have been severed for generations, as well as gaining the skills to be able to navigate a Western, colonized world.

Many pedagogies echo this navigation of two spaces, including research by Māori scholars in Aotearoa (New Zealand; Macfarlane et al., 2012). Māori researchers call out the concept of *culturally safe* schools, where students have the freedom to be who they are as individuals and as members of a community (Macfarlane et al., 2012). Most importantly, the Māori movement points out the tangible benefit for students when they associate positively with their home culture.

These systems are clearly designed to benefit Indigenous communities. Yet the lessons learned about navigating multiple worlds, multiple languages, and feeling positively toward your cultural heritage, are applicable to all learners. Sometimes to move forward, we must look back. Lessons from Indigenous cultures around the globe illustrate the power of engaging the full community in the process of education. Surrounding learning in the context of culture, and embracing the power of place, are strategies that are reemerging in modern education, all of which have all been proven effective for centuries.

Technology Assisting Education

We have been fairly light leaning on technology as a tool for educational change in this book. This is not because technology isn't powerful. But technology is a *tool*, not an *outcome*. Learning is the goal, and technology can quickly supplant that goal, taking energy and focus from students and educators, and placing those resources on the technology itself.

This doesn't mean technology should play no role in the future of education. In fact, it would be naïve to say so. Beyond the obvious uses of educational technology to support skill building, technology has proven itself in taking up the work on lower levels of learning. As described in chapter 5 (page 145), there are different levels of educational outcomes, from the simplest to the most complex: content, skills, concepts, and traits of learning. Technology, specifically artificial intelligence (AI), is more efficient and effective than humans in delivering content, and is now helping students develop discipline-specific skills.

Cutting-edge programs such as Century Tech use AI to understand not just if a student got an answer right or wrong, but *why*, and then prescribe the right learning nuggets to address that issue (CENTURY, n.d.). Why is this more efficient and effective than having an educator do this? Well, if we go back to the need to acknowledge that school is also babysitting, then we need to acknowledge that great teaching asks our educators to know what each student can do, where they are struggling, and help them grow into their next stage of understanding. This is possible if you are teaching a single discipline to eighteen students, but with elementary teachers responsible for multiple disciplines and twenty-five to thirty students, and with secondary teachers often seeing student loads upward of 150 or more students per semester, how can we expect any teacher to know where each student is in their understanding of each discipline? Imagine the challenges for any specials teacher, such as those teaching world languages, who literally teaches three hundred or more students in a week. Technology allows personalization to happen more cheaply than if it were the role of a quality educator, freeing up the educator's time to focus on students.

Does that mean we should sit students in front of computers all day? Certainly not! Technology has only been truly successful at these lowest levels of outcomes, like addressing content-based learning and helping to support simple discipline-specific skill growth (Kelly, 2020; National Public Radio, 2014). Certainly, educators were forced to employ technology constantly during the COVID-19 pandemic, and educators did what we had to, to make sure learning continued in spite of lockdowns. But that doesn't mean technology is the whole future of education. As we see on a global level with drops in educational achievement during the pandemic (UNICEF, 2020), technology does not serve all students all the time and has its limitations when it comes to higher-level skill building and content learning (Kelly, 2020; National Public Radio, 2014). However, if educators can spend less time on these lower levels of learning, that means they can spend more time facilitating students' more significant learning and growth on the landscape. Educators can use teacher time to facilitate projects that address big important concepts, and grow the traits of learners, such as critical thinking and creativity.

One example of this approach done successfully is the mathematics hub at the International Community School in Addis Ababa, Ethiopia (ICS Addis, 2019). The International Community School has done away with secondary mathematics courses. Instead, students use technology to support a personalized learning path (ICS Addis, 2019). Students have access to one-to-one tutoring to help them where they may get stuck, and teacher time is leveraged to help students *apply* mathematical thinking through the facilitation of project-based learning. These students now see mathematics as a language with which to understand and express the world, a tool that they don't just learn about but *use* through relevant hands-on projects. And students move forward at their own pace. Educators aren't wasting time teaching to the middle, leaving behind those who may need more scaffolded support or boring those who may have previously acquired the content being taught. By managing mathematics education this way, student behavior problems have decreased, and student appreciation of mathematics' importance has increased.

Technology is a necessary tool in the changing formula of education. The trick is that it must be part of the *input* side of the equation. Technology can and should support learning, but if left unchecked, it can easily become the outcome itself. The future holds huge changes, and technology will certainly play a bigger and bigger role each year. If we embrace technology as an accelerator, it has the potential to transform education for the benefit of students and educators.

PERSPECTIVES ON WORD CHOICE
Student Centered Versus Student Driven

The term *student centered* has long dominated progressive education, and the authors have chosen to use it throughout this book because, in most educational contexts, it's their necessary first step toward student protagonism. However, the term still has its limitations, and the authors had many discussions about whether it really captured what we wanted to convey with the landscape model. Student centered, though it focuses on the student as the center of learning, still suggests that this centering occurs because the *teacher* has designed learning experiences to make that happen. Perhaps the teacher-as-designer is a paradigm we need, given our long history of teacher-centered practices. And there's nothing wrong with teachers designing to place students as protagonists in their learning journey, but let's be realistic: the term suggests that the teacher still owns the power in the classroom, and that students are allowed to be in charge at the will of that teacher. Student-centered design is an important first step, but the authors do have a broader vision of what's possible, and it's not driven by teachers. It's driven by students and supported by teachers.

Student-driven learning suggests just that. The term *student driven* suggests that teachers are still learning designers, but that they establish structures, systems, and design *in collaboration with students*. It suggests that students drive their own experiences and directions on the pathway, with the support of adults, and that we recognize their inherent power over their own learning journey, not that educators allow them limited power occasionally. Perhaps this is the defining line *rightful presence* asks us to consider (Barton & Tan, 2020), which we introduced at the beginning of this book. Do we assume adults always hold the power to include or not, to center learning on students or not, or do we actually believe students have an essential *right* to their own educational protagonism?

Jennifer backed off from the term *student driven* years ago, when an adolescent psychologist working with a high-pressure private school told her the term put undue pressure on students—and in that environment, perhaps it did represent additional stress for students, particularly if educators were pushing students to drive their own learning. For many schools, shifting to student-driven learning might feel like too much too fast, and that's why we've used the term *student centered* with the landscape model. It may be that educators are better served to work their way toward student-driven learning by engaging in student-centered practices initially, as it may feel more manageable to assume a bit more control over students' choices. Student-driven learning certainly requires more scaffolding from educators, to build the levels of autonomy and self-management necessary, and to support students as they learn, fail, and grow along the journey. But the authors want to recognize that student-driven learning is, for us, the best horizon to strive for, the highest peak or *kulia i ka nu'u* we would love to see education reach. The One Stone school, described in the next section, is a remarkable example of just how far student-driven learning might be taken, and while it will look different in preschool than it does in high school, we believe their model can teach educators a great deal about what it really means to put students in the driver's seat.

What Education Could Be

As we consider the future of education, the authors want to push the boundaries of our readers' thinking a touch more. As we worked on this book, we found ourselves so tied to the way things *are* that we sometimes held back on the way they *could be*. We both believe in a sort of education that puts the landscape model into its most innovative, even radical form. And we are not alone.

Educational thought leader, professor, and author Yong Zhao (2021) believes that modern education shouldn't be focused on creating a workforce, but on educating human beings. Criticizing the concept of college and career readiness, Zhao (2021) asserts, "You can't get people ready for all the colleges. You can't get them ready for careers that have not been invented. It is your job to help children to become who they *are*." He espouses an education focused on debate and dialogue, on the use of evidence and critical thinking about its quality, and on the ability to work with and solve authentic challenges. These areas, he feels, are essential steps toward building students' skills as future citizens, far more important than most of the standards we teach and test. While Zhao (2021) recognizes that the concept of *citizenship* varies from country to country, he believes education should help form good people who know themselves, who understand their civic responsibilities and help to maintain a civil system, even in times of division. Recognizing that no one is good at everything—and that the adult world doesn't even ask us to be good at everything, allowing us to outsource and collaborate across skill sets—Zhao (2021) asks the most important questions for the future of education: Why are we so convinced that all students must learn and be good at the exact same things to be successful? And why are policymakers the ones deciding what other people's children need to be good at?

Sir Ken Robinson believed that systems built by humans could be rebuilt by humans, however daunting that might seem (as cited in Robinson, 2021). The key, he believed, was to focus our energy on the people who are moveable, and not spend so much time arguing with those who aren't willing to change their thinking about education. Quoting her father in an event for What School Could Be, daughter Kate Robinson (2021) told viewers that education can and should be "a provocation more than a prescription," and that even small changes enacted by an individual teacher can make a monumental difference for the students in that classroom. So what might it look like to build an entire school with such moveable educators, in collaboration with the students they serve?

One of the most hope-inspiring models we've seen is One Stone, an independent school in Boise, Idaho, which is rewriting what student driven might mean and entail (C. Carlson, personal communication, December 8, 2021). Adopting student driven rather than student centered very intentionally, as students truly drive their own learning experiences, One Stone's model for student protagonism offers a glimpse of what might be possible for the future of education. When Chad Carlson, director of research and design, first got involved in One Stone, early in the ideation process before the doors even opened, he knew the heart of their work needed to start with students. "It just seemed so simple, you know? Start with the human being. Start with the person that you're working with. And everything else is secondary" (personal communication, December 8, 2021). With a deep focus on developing relationships between students and educators, called *coaches* instead of teachers, One Stone strives for students to work shoulder to shoulder with adults on real challenges, both inside and beyond their local community, and to build the mindsets, creativity, skills, and knowledge to be successful adults.

The commitment to student-driven learning is evident across the design of their programming, all of which was co-constructed with students and continues to evolve as students' needs demand. Two-thirds of the board of directors is made up of students, and the board chair is always a student. Students participate in running the school on all levels, from maintenance and infrastructure to preparing the organization's taxes with the financial director. They empower students to help design courses, create the daily schedule, run school events, manage messaging with the broader community, and more. Students are the center of their own assessment as well, and their reflections and evidence provide the core for charting their growth in the thirty-two skills and competencies that make up the school's homegrown portrait of a graduate, the bold learning objectives, known at One Stone as *the BLOB*. In fact, students participate in determining the components of the BLOB and are involved in reiteration work as the need arises. A wide array of learning experiences allows students to grow those skills and competencies, and the *One Stone Growth Transcript* creates a visual representation of their progress, much like the progress-based approaches explored in chapter 5 (page 117).

The learning experience at One Stone comprises three primary components.

1. **Design Lab**, where students use the design-thinking process to solve a community-based problem, in collaboration with real community partners, including organizations, companies, civic leaders, and other individuals

2. **Experiences**, which are interdisciplinary project-based endeavors that bring together various disciplines and include community partners and use of the community as a learning lab (Students participate in two or three of these varied-length projects, codesigning them with the coaches.)

3. **Living in Beta**, which Carlson describes as a *way-finding program* designed to help students find and explore their purpose and start to understand how they can actualize that purpose beyond high school (personal communication, December 8, 2021)

In addition, students have opportunities to take disciplinary-focused workshops, to participate in experiential service, to serve as interns, to design for real businesses and organizations, and much more. Students work closely with coaches to determine the kinds of learning experiences they need to grow their competencies over the four years of high school. Behind all this, a credit system is at work, to ensure that students graduate with all areas mastered, as well as a digital tool that aggregates the information that ultimately becomes the growth transcript sent to universities.

One Stone does significant outreach to colleges and universities, to make sure they understand the sorts of learners they'll get from this particular school. So far, they've found universities very receptive to this gradeless, progress-based way of articulating student learning, and they've had very few issues that might be described as impeding students' ability to attend university where they wish. Says Carlson, "The broad range of schools accepting the growth transcript is very inspiring; it gives me a lot of hope about the direction of higher education, what they're willing to take and what they're looking for" (personal communication, December 8, 2021).

People often ask Carlson how he knows kids are learning, especially given that students help establish their own goals and manage their own self-evaluation. His reply? "That's a great question, but how do you know *anyone's* ever learning? When you look into the window of a more traditional school where students are sitting in rows and the teacher is talking at the front, there's an assumption that learning is happening. But most of it is daydreaming" (C. Carlson, personal communication, December 8, 2021). At One Stone, evidence of learning comes from the students themselves, and while there is certainly a learning curve and scaffolding to do to get a fourteen-year-old ready to be accountable and responsible for their own highest levels of growth and autonomy possible, students eventually realize that this is all about *them,* not the external expectations of a teacher or parent, and they become self-motivated learners.

Carlson believes there are many reasons they've been able to make this model work as well as it does (personal communication, December 8, 2021). Their hiring process is extensive, including multiple interviews with different groups, including students, so One Stone has a chance to get to know the mindset of applicants and can hire those who demonstrate a deep belief in teenagers. They run a weeklong retreat with adults before each school year, to build community and culture intentionally. They make sure coaches get feedback, just like students do, and they have a strong mentoring program to complement professional development workshops. But more important is their inherent belief, as a community, in young people. Because they stay focused on what is in the best interest of students, and believe in them, One Stone's community is able to embrace ambiguity, be adaptable, and build an educational model that mirrors life beyond the schoolhouse.

And that, Carlson believes, may be the most important priority for the future of education: to build educational systems that are actually relevant for students, and that prepare them for lives of purpose (personal communication, December 8, 2021). Instead of relying on compliance models that discipline students for any lack of motivation, relevant education that mirrors the world beyond school creates waves of student ownership and empowerment. And the more students enjoy their education, the more their engagement increases. Carlson says:

> For me, success is students doing things that make the world a better place, students doing things because they are purposeful and mindful and *excited* about what they're doing. That is the greatest indicator of success that students can go and live a fulfilled life, and that we've given them the tools to figure out what they want to do and go pursue it—and then when that's not working to be able to iterate on the challenges and pivot. To me, *that* is success. (personal communication, December 8, 2021)

The authors hope that One Stone serves as a model and inspiration to those educators and families seeking something different. Like the Open School, Wai'alae Elementary Public Charter School, the High School for the Recording Arts, Hanahau'oli School, LearnLife, and The School in Rose Valley, among others, One Stone demonstrates that what we believe could happen is in fact possible, and not just in after-school programs or alternative schools. And all our best examples have one thing in common: these schools were using elements of the landscape model long before the authors came up with the metaphor. They are schools where educators know their students, fully and deeply, and understand the communities and cultures they come from (ecosystem). They are schools that honor, celebrate, and challenge every student in ways that leverage the strengths they bring into the schoolhouse with them, allowing every student to define his, her, or their own learning goals (horizon). And they are schools that find ways to individualize the learning itself, that have created systems and schedules and options that ensure every child can reach those goals (pathway).

Perhaps it really is time to burn the forest down. At the very least, it's time to change the systems that aren't working anymore; they were built by humans, and that means they can be rebuilt by humans as well. The authors hope the landscape model helps educators to do so.

Reflective Questions

Respond to the following questions alone or with your school team.

- To what degree has your educational community found ways to honor and include a more local vision of what is possible in education? How have you confronted disconnects between educational policy and local culture in your community?
- When you think of the future of education without limitations, what do you want to imagine that future holds?

- Which people in your educational community share your vision? How might you bring colleagues on board and build momentum around an increasingly shared vision?

- If you asked the young people that you educate or work with how they want to make the world a better place, what might they say? How might you amplify their constructive ideas and help catalyze them into action?

Takeaways

The following summarizes key ideas from the chapter.

- The future requires radical shifts in thinking about the purpose and form of education.

- The future of education should mirror the evolution of humans and adapt to the needs of the times.

- Educational policy needs to trust local educators and ancient ways of educating to meet the needs of students in any given community.

- We (the authors) and you (the reader) are not alone in our desire to build better educational systems for our young people.

Synthesis Tool, Part 3

This worksheet is designed to help readers capture core insights and help with planning toward implementation. Please explore the following questions as you read, ideally in small leadershipteams, faculty teams, or both.

- How well are your current evaluation and grading systems aligned with the goals of personalized learning and student protagonism?

- Where are opportunities for improvement in your current evaluation and grading systems?

- What might be the challenges of adapting your evaluation and grading systems?

- How might you best address those challenges?

- What are the next steps needed?

- How well does the landscape model align with your school's mission, vision, and values right now? Which elements of your aspirations might need to be revisited?

- How well do you believe your current faculty will adapt to the landscape model? What will be your recruitment priorities for future hiring?

- Which challenges are most likely to come up in your community, and which solutions might you use to address them?

- Who are your internal allies for this work, and how might you best leverage them?

- Who are your most important external partners for this work, and how might you best leverage their support?

- Which elements of your current curriculum might you need adjust, and in what ways?

- Which professional development topics are most urgent for your faculty to succeed?

- How inclusive is your current school culture, and what needs to shift in order to ensure inclusive prosperity for every student?

- How might local educational policy complicate your efforts on the landscape? How might you confront those challenges?

- How might local educational policy support your efforts on the landscape? How might you leverage those opportunities?

- How might you leverage ancient (Indigenous) ideas about learning and life in order to increase the relevance and sustainability of your school's choices?

- How might your school use technology to advance these initiatives?

- How do you hope your students might go on to change the world?

- What are the next steps needed?

EPILOGUE

Why This Work Matters

*I created many drops in the cloud, and I created every drop
in its own form so that there are no
two drops with the same form, since if two drops had the
same form they would blur the earth
and it would not bear fruits.*

—Otherness *from Talmud Bavli, Bava Batra 15a*

The future of schooling is exciting and terrifying all at once. It is clear that schools must evolve, and COVID-19 has already forced significant, rapid changes in many educational contexts. Some of that change has been positive, with educators and parents around the world learning to leverage educational technology—and more importantly, recognizing that learning can and does occur outside the schoolhouse. But in some cases, the pandemic has also taken us back to a more industrial, standardized model, both online and in person, with increased fears of *missing content* and *learning loss* dominating debate among policymakers, rather than embracing the opportunity to transcend content. Most dire, issues of equitable access to quality education have exploded in underserved regions that lack technology, undermining decades of progress toward equal access to good education around the world (UNICEF, 2020). What education looks like thirty years from now must include a discussion of what it means to be educated, and must address the kinds of resources we are willing to put toward education.

Ultimately, the future of education will require a deeper understanding of the *why* behind what we do in school, and each community's why may be different. While we have spent over a century trying to standardize education across the world, comparing our outcomes across countries and competing for rankings on measures like PISA, the reality is that every community context will aspire to something deeply *theirs* if we don't allow the colonization of education to continue. Every community has its values, leaders, challenges, aspirations, and solutions for the future of its region. Each community has different ideas about what it means to be educated, too; in one community, the ability to grow a productive garden to feed one's family may be far more important than one's knowledge of advanced calculus. Assuming the two communities should have the same educational system and outcomes devalues what makes each community unique. Ultimately, this race to the "best" education possible, standardized and compared globally, has caused more disenfranchisement than inclusion, and has likely contributed to many cultures' struggles with *brain drain*—the loss of their best and brightest to other parts of the world. Why have we convinced ourselves that education must look the same everywhere when our communities are so wonderfully rich with diversity and difference? Wouldn't it be smarter to leverage that diversity than to quash it?

What the authors find most compelling is the opportunity for education to foster the change makers each community needs, young people who know how to identify problems, build and leverage networks, and rewrite the rules of their societies for the better. We believe that education's goal should be to foster such change makers, young people who know how to work from their strengths to contribute something meaningful and useful, perhaps even innovative, to their communities—and without damaging what makes each community unique. Every school is filled with potential change makers, students who can become humble enough to listen to and learn from their elders, young people who, once aware of the challenges of their community and practiced in the art of solution building, will be able to contribute in meaningful and constructive ways. Every culture contains its own kind of brilliance, as does every individual, if only we as educators create the conditions to let that brilliance develop and flourish.

But do schools create space for young people to find their *ikigai*, that intersection of what they love, what they're good at, what they can be paid for, and what the world needs (Hasegawa, Fujiwara, Hoshi, & Shinkai, 2003)? And do we value all the possible *ikigais* they might pursue, or do we judge some students' purpose as somehow less than what traditional education calls success? Do we create opportunities for students to sit with the elders and understand why their community's values matter, and to discuss and practice solution building with their peers and experts around the world, or do we standardize their education to make sure they get the highest scores possible on national, state, and provincial exams? The future of education requires that we shift our thinking—away from conformity and standardization, and toward a deep and powerful recognition of the uniquely and beautifully human found everywhere.

Anthropologist, ethnobotanist, author, and photographer Wade Davis (2009) frames this idea more clearly than anyone we've read:

> We share a sacred endowment, a common history written in our bones. It follows . . . that the myriad of cultures of the world are not failed attempts at modernity, let alone failed attempts to be us. They are unique expressions of the human imagination and heart, unique answers to a fundamental question: What does it mean to be human and alive? (Kindle location 232–236)

As Davis's (2009) work suggests consistently, our very survival on the planet requires that we foster that diversity of culture, that diversity of knowledge, experiences, and practices, and learn from it to build a more sustainable, peaceful world.

An ecosystem in nature relies on every member of the system, differences included; an ecosystem cannot survive without that diversity. The more limited the gene pool of a given species, the less likely it will survive, much less thrive. Diversity ensures survival, whether we're talking about human genetics or the natural world around us. Similarly, the ecosystem of any given society (or, in miniature, any given organization) relies on diversity to thrive, as it ensures we have a constant flow of new ideas, solutions, and even dissent from different kinds of thinkers. Only in schools and factories do we still insist on a race toward identical outcomes.

Just as diversity is valuable in the ecosystems of nature and society, it is valuable in the schoolhouse. The future of education depends on this recognition, on seeing the diversity of identities, talents, passions, and needs not a nuisance we have to put up with to get every child to the same point, but as a powerful gift we can leverage to build a better future beyond the schoolhouse, as well as inside its walls.

Appendix

Table A.1 (page 262) lists all the strategies from each chapter in part 2, indicating for which age group or groups each works, and who the intended user is. Please note that most strategies listed here are appropriate for students and educators to use.

Table A.1: Implementing the Landscape Model—Strategies Referenced in Part 2

	Page Number	PreK and Early Learners	Primary Years	Middle Years	High School	Support or Training Needed	Teacher Activity	Student Activity
The Ecosystem								
Journaling			*	*	*		*	*
Iceberg of Culture			*	*	*		*	*
Cross the Line				*	*	*	*	*
Affinity Groups			*	*	*	*	*	*
Brave Space				*	*	*	*	*
Empathy Interviews		*	*	*	*		*	
Place-Based Learning—Concentric Circles		*	*	*	*		*	*
Virtual or In-Peson Home Visits		*	*	*	*		*	
KWL and RAN Charts		*	*	*	*			*
Question Formulation Technique			*	*	*		*	*
Socratic Seminars			*	*	*		*	*
The Horizon								
A Letter to Myself		*	*	*	*		*	*
The Headline of My Year		*	*	*	*		*	*
Storyboards and Vision Boards		*	*	*	*		*	*
WOOP		*	*	*	*		*	*

	Page Number	PreK and Early Learners	Primary Years	Middle Years	High School	Support or Training Needed	Teacher Activity	Student Activity
SMART Goals			*	*	*		*	*
ANCHOR			*	*	*		*	*
Student-Led Conferences		*	*	*	*	*	*	*
Portrait of a Graduate		*	*	*	*		*	
SOAR Model Analysis		*	*	*	*		*	*
Capstone Projects			*	*	*			*
The Pathway								
Passion Projects			*	*	*			*
Affinity Mapping		*	*	*	*			*
Design Thinking as a PBL Structure		*	*	*	*	*	*	*
Portfolios		*	*	*	*		*	*
Workshop Model for Skill-Based Disciplines		*	*	*	*	*		*
Student Shadowing		*	*	*	*		*	
Student-Centered Iterative Unit Planning		*	*	*	*		*	
Zone of Proximal Development		*	*	*	*		*	
Collaborative Protocol for Defining Outcomes		*	*	*	*		*	
Wise Criticism		*	*	*	*		*	

References and Resources

10 ways journaling benefits students [Blog post]. (2020, December 30). University of St. Augustine for Health Sciences. Accessed at www.usa.edu/blog/ways-journaling-benefits-students on March 22, 2022.

20Time.org. (n.d.). *Students will be future ready if you give them time.* Accessed at www.20time.org on December 11, 2021.

3M. (n.d.). *Life with 3M.* Accessed at www.3m.com/3M/en_US/careers-us/working-at-3m/life-with-3m on December 11, 2021.

Adler, M. J. (1984). *The Paideia program: An educational syllabus.* New York: Touchstone.

Aksakalli, A. (2018). The effects of science teaching based on critical pedagogy principles on the classroom climate. *Science Education International, 29*(4), 250–260. https://doi.org/10.33828/sei.v29.i4.7

Alessandra, T., & O'Connor, M. J. (1996). *The platinum rule: Discover the four basic business personalities and how they can lead you to success.* New York: Grand Central.

Aljazeera, & Reuters. (2021). *'No room for debate': Hong Kong outlines security law for schools.* Accessed at www.aljazeera.com/news/2021/2/5/hong-kong-unveils-security-law-teaching-for-six-year-olds on March 28, 2022.

Anderson, J. (2009). *Dean Theodore Sizer, 1932–2009.* Accessed at www.gse.harvard.edu/news/09/10/dean-theodore-sizer-1932-2009 on May 3, 2022.

Anderson, M. D. (2015). *Why* schools *need more teachers of color—for White students.* Accessed at www.theatlantic.com/education/archive/2015/08/teachers-of-color-white-students/400553 on December 13, 2021.

Anti-Defamation League. (n.d.). *Moving from safe classrooms to brave classrooms.* Accessed at www.adl.org/education/resources/tools-and-strategies/moving-from-safe-classrooms-to-brave-classrooms on April 27, 2022.

Appel, M., & Kronberger, N. (2012, December). Stereotypes and the achievement gap: Stereotype threat prior to test taking. *Educational Psychology Review, 24*(4), 609–635.

Auernhammer, J., & Roth, B. (2021). *The origin and evolution of Stanford University's design thinking: From product design to design thinking in innovation management.* Accessed at https://doi.org/10.1111/jpim.12594 on March 28, 2022.

AVID. (n.d.). *The history of AVID.* Accessed at www.avid.org/our-history on December 20, 2021.

Barro, C. (2018, March 31). *The 'experimental' concept of grouping students by ability instead of age divides experts.* Accessed at https://thenewdaily.com.au/life/2018/03/31/age-based-vs-stage-based-classes on January 26, 2022.

Barshay, J. (2018, May 21). *Two studies point to the power of teacher-student relationships to boost learning.* Accessed at https://hechingerreport.org/two-studies-point-to-the-power-of-teacher-student-relationships-to-boost-learning on March 22, 2022.

Barton, A. C., & Tan, E. (2020). *Beyond equity as inclusion: A framework of "rightful presence" for guiding justice-oriented studies in teaching and learning.* Accessed at https://journals.sagepub.com/doi/pdf/10.3102/0013189X20927363 on January 6, 2022.

Battelle for Kids. (2019). *Framework for 21st century learning.* Accessed at http://static.battelleforkids.org/documents/p21/P21_Framework_Brief.pdf on December 11, 2021.

Bauer-Wolf, J. (2019, January 17). *Survey: Employers want "soft skills" from graduates.* Accessed at www.insidehighered.com/quicktakes/2019/01/17/survey-employers-want-soft-skills-graduates on February 10, 2022.

Belet, M. (2017). The importance of relevance to student lives: The impact of content and media in introduction to sociology. *Teaching Sociology, 46*(3), 208–224.

Bell, M. K. (2015). *Making space.* Accessed at www.learningforjustice.org/magazine/summer-2015/making-space on December 9, 2021.

Berger, R. (2014, March 1). *When students lead their learning.* Accessed at www.ascd.org/publications/educational-leadership/mar14/vol71/num06/When-Students-Lead-Their-Learning.aspx on October 15, 2021.

Bishop, R. S. (1990). *Mirrors, windows, and sliding glass doors.* Accessed at https://scenicregional.org/wp-content/uploads/2017/08/Mirrors-Windows-and-Sliding-Glass-Doors.pdf on December 4, 2021.

Blackburn, B. (2018). *Productive struggle is a learner's sweet spot.* Accessed at www.ascd.org/el/articles/productive-struggle-is-a-learners-sweet-spot on December 21, 2021.

Bloom, B. (Ed.). (1956). *Taxonomy of educational objectives: The classification of educational goals; Handbook I: Cognitive domain.* New York: Longman.

Bonior, A. (2018, December 12). *7 ways to build in a relationship* [Blog post]. Accessed at www.psychologytoday.com/us/blog/friendship-20/201812/7-ways-build-trust-in-relationship on March 22, 2022.

Breda, T., & Napp, C. (2019). *Girls' comparative advantage in reading can largely explain the gender gap in math-related fields.* Accessed at www.pnas.org/content/116/31/15435 on October 18, 2021.

Budhia, S. (2017, December 27). *Racial prejudice in the American education system: Effects of racism on Black students' lives and academic success.* Accessed at https://openamericas.org/2017/12/27/racial-prejudice-in-the-american-education-system-effects-of-racism-on-black-students-lives-and-academic-success on February 10, 2022.

Burges, P. (2017, January). *Culturally responsive evaluation and assessment.* Proceedings from CREA Hawaii meeting, Hawaii.

Calkins, L. (2001). *The art of teaching reading.* Harlow, England: Longman.

Calkins, L., & Hartman, A. (2013). *Launching the writing workshop.* Portsmouth, NH: Heinemann.

Centers for Disease Control and Prevention. (n.d.). *Lesbian, gay, bisexual, and transgender health: LGBT youth.* Accessed at www.cdc.gov/lgbthealth/youth.htm on January 7, 2022.

CENTURY. (n.d.). *Home page.* Accessed at https://app.century.tech on January 23, 2022.

Changing the Face of Medicine. (n.d.). *Dr. Mae C. Jemison.* Accessed at https://cfmedicine.nlm.nih.gov/physicians/biography_168.html on December 6, 2021.

Chemaly, S. (2015, February 12). *All teachers should be trained to overcome their hidden biases.* Accessed at https://time.com/3705454/teachers-biases-girls-education on October 18, 2021.

Cherry, K. (2019). *What is the negativity bias?* Accessed at www.verywellmind.com/negative-bias-4589618#:~:text=Verywell%20/%20Brianna%20Gilmartin-,What%20Is%20the%20Negativity%20Bias?,feel%20the%20joy%20of%20praise on January 30, 2022.

Chilisa, B. (2012). *Indigenous research methodologies.* Thousand Oaks, CA: SAGE.

Ciotti, K. (2012). *Student-led conferencing.* Honolulu, HI: Maryknoll School.

Ciotti, K. (2020, August). *Student-centered unit planning.* AISE Professional Development Day.

City, E. A., Elmore, R. F., Fiarman, S. E., Teitel, L., & Lachman, A. (2018). *Instructional rounds in education: A network approach to improving teaching and learning.* Boston: Harvard Education Press.

Claxton, G. (2017). *The learning power approach.* Accessed at https://docplayer.net/221402170-The-learning-power-approach-professor-guy-claxton.html on March 22, 2022.

Cohn-Vargas, B., & Steele, D. M. (2015, October 21). *Creating an identity-safe classroom* [Blog post]. Accessed at www.edutopia.org/blog/creating-an-identity-safe-classroom-becki-cohn-vargas-dorothy-steele on March 28, 2022.

Colorado State University Extension. (n.d.). *Program planning: A guidebook for Colorado State University Extension.* Accessed at https://extension.colostate.edu/docs/staffres/program/Program-Planning-Guidebook.pdf on October 29, 2021.

Columbia Social Work Review. (2020). *Educational affinity groups: The why and how.* Accessed at https://journals.library.columbia.edu/index.php/cswr/announcement/view/275 on March 22, 2022.

Concept to Classroom. (2019). *Constructivism as a paradigm for teaching and learning.* Accessed at www.thirteen.org/edonline/concept2class/constructivism on March 22, 2022.

Conzemius, A. E., & O'Neill, J. (2014). *The handbook for SMART school teams: Revitalizing best practices for collaboration* (2nd ed.). Bloomington, IN: Solution Tree Press.

Cordray, D., Pion, G., Brandt, C., Molefe, A., & Toby, M. (2012). *The impact of the Measures of Academic Progress (MAP).* Accessed at https://files.eric.ed.gov/fulltext/ED537982.pdf on March 22, 2022.

Cronin, A. (2016, July 8). *Student-led conferences: Resources for educators* [Blog post]. Accessed at www.edutopia.org/blog/student-led-conferences-resources-ashley-cronin on January 19, 2022.

d'Erizans, R. (2018, July 27). *Welcome to the 2018–19 school year!—Inclusive prosperity* [Blog post]. Accessed at https://robertoderizans.wordpress.com/2018/07/27/welcome-to-the-2018-19-school-year-inclusive-prosperity on October 18, 2021.

Dance, A. (2021, July 15). Has the pandemic put an end to the SAT and ACT? *Smithsonian Magazine.* Accessed at www.smithsonianmag.com/innovation/has-pandemic-put-end-to-sat-act-180978167 on January 21, 2022.

Davis, W. (2009). *The wayfinders: Why ancient wisdom matters in the modern world* [Kindle version]. Accessed at Amazon.com.

DeDonno, M., & Fagan, J. (2013). The influence of family attributes on college students' academic self-concept. *North American Journal of Psychology, 15*(1), 49–62.

d'Erizans, R. (2018, July 27). *Welcome to the 2018—19 school year!—Inclusive prosperity* [Blog post]. Accessed at https://robertoderizans.wordpress.com/2018/07/27/welcome-to-the-2018-19-school-year-inclusive-prosperity on October 18, 2021.

Dewey, J. (1938). *Experience and education.* New York: Free Press.

Dintersmith, T. (Producer), & Whiteley, G. (Director). (2018). *Most likely to succeed* [Motion picture]. United States: Edu21c Foundation.

Driessen, E. (2016). Do portfolios have a future? *Advances in Health Sciences Education, 22*(1), 221–228.

Duncan-Andrade, J. M. R., & Morrell, E. (2008). *The art of critical pedagogy: Possibilities for moving from theory to practice in urban schools.* New York: Lang.

Duncan, J., Zawistowski, C., & Luibrand, S. (2020). *50 states, 50 different ways of teaching America's past.* Accessed at www.cbsnews.com/news/us-history-how-teaching-americas-past-varies-across-the-country on December 13, 2021.

EdLeader21. (n.d.). *Do you have a 21st century, deeper learning vision for every student?* Accessed at www.battelleforkids.org/how-we-help/portrait-of-a-graduate on December 11, 2021.

EL Education. (n.d.). *The who, what, and why of portfolios and passage presentations.* Accessed at https://eleducation.org/resources/the-who-what-and-why-of-portfolios-and-passage-presentations on January 30, 2022.

EL Education. (2016, October 4). *Austin's butterfly: Models, critique, and descriptive feedback* [Video file]. Accessed at https://youtu.be/E_6PskE3zfQ on January 21, 2022.

Fischer, C., Malycha, C. P., & Schafmann, E. (2019). *The influence of intrinsic motivation and synergistic extrinsic motivators on creativity and innovation.* Accessed at https://doi.org/10.3389/fpsyg.2019.00137 on March 28, 2022.

Fisher, C. (1973). *Behaviorism and behavioralism.* Accessed at https://psycnet.apa.org/record/1975-24411-001

Fountas, I. C., & Pinnell, G. C. (2017). *The Fountas & Pinnell literacy continuum: A tool for assessment, planning, and teaching.* Portsmouth, NH: Heinemann.

Freire, P. (2000). *Pedagogy of the oppressed* (M. B. Ramos, Trans.). New York: Continuum. (Original work published 1968)

Frey, N., & Fisher, D. (2013). *Gradual release of responsibility instructional framework.* Accessed at https://pdo.ascd.org/lmscourses/pd130c005/media/formativeassessmentandccswithelaliteracymod_3-reading3.pdf on December 9, 2021.

Fritson, K. K. (2008). *Impact of journaling on students' self-efficacy and locus of control.* Accessed at https://doi.org/10.46504/03200809fr on March 28, 2022.

Fuller, J. (2020, September 27). *Our systems of learning will evolve when we lead with empathy* [Blog post]. Accessed at http://dkfoundation.org/working-on/jessica-fuller/our-systems-of-learning-will-evolve-when-we-lead-with-empathy on October 18, 2021.

Gallup. (n.d.). *Learn how the CliftonStrengths assessment works.* Accessed at www.gallup.com/cliftonstrengths/en/253676/how-cliftonstrengths-works.aspx on December 9, 2021.

Gardner, S., & Albee, D. (2015). *Study focuses on strategies for achieving goals, resolutions.* Accessed at https://scholar.dominican.edu/cgi/viewcontent.cgi?article=1265&context=news-releases on February 10, 2022.

Garza, K. (2017). *The closer you get.* Accessed at www.battelleforkids.org/learning-hub/learning-hub-item/the-closer-you-get on October 28, 2021.

Gay, G. (2018). *Culturally responsive teaching: Theory, research, and practice* (3rd ed.). New York: Teachers College Press.

Gershenson, S., Hart, C. M., D., Hyman, J., Lindsay, C., & Papageorge, N. W. (2018). *The long-run impacts of same-race teachers* [Working paper]. Accessed at https://nicholaswpapageorge.files.wordpress.com/2018/11/w25254.pdf on March 28, 2022.

Getting Smart, eduInnovation, & Teton Science School. (2017). *What is place-based education and why does it matter?* Accessed at www.gettingsmart.com/wp-content/uploads/2017/02/What-is-Place-Based-Education-and-Why-Does-it-Matter-3.pdf on February 16, 2022.

Gibb, S. (2013). Soft skills assessment: Theory development and the research agenda. *International Journal of Lifelong Education, 33*(4), 455–471.

Gibson, V. (2018). *Arts education squeezed out across Ontario schools, new report says.* Accessed at www.thestar.com/news/gta/2018/04/03/arts-education-squeezed-out-across-ontario-schools-new-report-says.html on December 13, 2021.

Godsil, R. D., Tropp, L. R., Goff, P. A., Powell, J. A., & MacFarlane, J. (2017). *The science of equality in education: The impact of implicit bias, racial anxiety, and stereotype threat on student outcomes.* Accessed at https://perception.org/wp-content/uploads/2017/05/Science-of-Equality-Education.pdf on October 18, 2021.

Google. (n.d.) *Genius hour—Engineering solutions.* Accessed at https://sites.google.com/a/sduhsd.net/genius-hour/what-is-genius-hour on December 11, 2021.

Graybill, O. (2019, September 24). *Four ways to create equitable discussion using Socratic seminar.* Accessed at https://www.teachingchannel.com/blog/four-ways-to-create-equitable-discussion-using-socratic-seminar on February 10, 2022.

Ha, S. S. (2017). *The value and impact of capstone projects.* Accessed at https://doi.org/10.1145/3127942.3127952 on March 28, 2022.

Hall, E. T. (1976). *Beyond culture.* Garden City, NY: Anchor Press.

Hanahau'oli School. (n.d.). *Hanahau'oli School.* Accessed at www.hanahauoli.org on January 23, 2022.

Harland, T. (2003). Vygotsky's Zone of Proximal Development and problem-based learning: Linking a theoretical concept with practice through action research. *Teaching in Higher Education, 8*(2), 263–272.

Hasegawa, A., Fujiwara, Y., Hoshi, T., & Shinkai, S. (2003). Regional differences in ikigai in elderly people: Relationship between ikigai and family structure, physiological situation and functional capacity. *Nihon Ronen Igakkai Zasshi, 40*(4), 390–396.

Hasso Plattner Institute of Design at Stanford University. (n.d.). *An introduction to design thinking: Process guide.* Accessed at https://web.stanford.edu/~mshanks/MichaelShanks/files/509554.pdf on December 8, 2021.

Hattie, J. (2012). *Visible learning for teachers: Maximizing impact on learning.* Abingdon-on-Thames, England: Routledge.

Hattie, J., Masters, D., & Birch, K. (2016). *Visible learning into action: International case studies of impact.* Abingdon-on-Thames, England: Routledge.

Hawaii Public Schools. (2015). *The foundational and administrative framework for Kaiapuni Education Hawaiian Language Immersion Program.* Accessed at www.hawaiipublicschools.org/DOE%20Forms/KaiapuniFrameworkFinal.pdf on March 22, 2022.

Herold, B. (2016). *1-to-1 laptop initiatives boost student scores, study finds.* Accessed at www.edweek.org/technology/1-to-1-laptop-initiatives-boost-student-scores-study-finds/2016/05 on December 20, 2021.

Hidalgo, N. M. (1993). Multicultural teacher introspection. In T. Perry & J. Fraser (Eds.) *Freedom's plow: Teaching in the multicultural classroom* (pp. 99–106). New York: Routledge.

Holub, J., & Kruse, J. (2020, February). *Inquiry and design: Using science and engineering to understand particle motion and thermal energy.* Accessed at www.nsta.org/science-scope/science-scope-february-2020/inquiry-and-design on February 16, 2022.

hooks, b. (1994). *Teaching to transgress: Education as the practice of freedom.* New York: Routledge.

Hyatt, K. (2019). *The "1 in 60 rule" explained!* Accessed at https://aopa.com.au/the-1-in-60-rule-simply-explained on December 10, 2021.

Ibe, N. A., Howsmon, R., Penney, L., Granor, N., DeLyser, L. A., & Wang, K. (2018). Reflections of a diversity, equity, and inclusion working group based on data from a national CS education program. *Proceedings of the 49th ACM Technical Symposium on Computer Science Education,* 711–716.

ICS Addis. (2019, October 17). *The HS Math Hub* [Video file]. Accessed at www.youtube.com/watch?v=5NmSuAZuLJM on March 22, 2022.

Islam, M. R., & Khan, Z. N. (2017). *Impact of socio-economics status on academic achievement of secondary school students.* Accessed at http://ndpublisher.in/admin/issues/EQv8n34.pdf on March 28, 2022.

Iwase, J. (2019). *Leading with aloha: From the pineapple fields to the principal's office.* Honolulu, HI: Legacy Isle.

Iwase, J. (2021). *Educating with aloha: Reflections from the heart on teaching and learning.* Honolulu, HI: Legacy Isle.

Jakes, T. D. [@BishopJakes]. (2017, January 18). *If you can't figure out your purpose, figure out your passion. For your passion will lead you right into your purpose. #WednesdayWisdom* [Tweet]. Twitter. Accessed at https://twitter.com/bishopjakes/status/821688845972414464 on December 10, 2021.

Jefferson County Open School. (n.d.). *Mission, goals, and philosophy.* Accessed https://jcos.jeffcopublicschools.org/about_us/mission_goals_philosophy on January 23, 2022.

Johnson, L. (2006). *"Making her community a better place to live": Culturally responsive urban school leadership in historical context.* Accessed at https://doi.org/10.1080/15700760500484019 on March 28, 2022.

Jones, J. (2020, March 9). *The Summerhill School, the radical educational experiment that let students learn what, when and how they want (1966).* Accessed at www.openculture.com/2020/03/summerhill-school.html on February 2, 2022.

Kauflin, J. (2017). *America's top 50 companies 1917–2017.* Accessed at www.forbes.com/sites/jeffkauflin/2017/09/19/americas-top-50-companies-1917-2017/?sh=38e9338d1629 on October 18, 2021.

Keirsey (n. d.). *What is Keirsey?* Accessed at www.keirsey.com on January 31, 2022.

Kelly, H. (2020). *Kids used to love screen time. Then schools made Zoom mandatory all day long.* Accessed at www.washingtonpost.com/technology/2020/09/04/screentime-school-distance on February 16, 2022.

Kent, R. (2016). *Affinity diagram.* Accessed at www.sciencedirect.com. www.sciencedirect.com/topics/engineering/affinity-diagram on February 16, 2022.

Kitchens, K., & Brodnax, N. (2021). *Race, school discipline, and magnet schools.* Accessed at https://journals.sagepub.com/doi/10.1177/23328584211033878 on February 16, 2022.

Kivel, P. (2002). *Examining class and race.* Accessed at https://paulkivel.com/resource/examining-class-and-race on January 23, 2022.

Klein, J. D. (n.d.). *Creating space for self-management in PBL: When teachers step back, students step up* [Blog post]. Accessed at https://my.pblworks.org/resource/blog/creating_space_for_self_management_in_pbl_when_teachers_step_back_students on January 23, 2022.

Klein, J. D. (2016, September 11). Language matters in education: Putting vigor over rigor. *The Shared World*. Accessed at www.principledlearning.org/post/language-matters-in-education-putting-vigor-over-rigor on January 18, 2022.

Klein, J. D. (2017). *The global education guidebook: Humanizing K–12 classrooms worldwide through equitable partnerships*. Bloomington, IN: Solution Tree Press.

Klein, J. D. (2018). *Falsos paradigmas: Una Buena educación sí puede ser divertida*. El Tiempo. August 13, 2018. Accessed at www.eltiempo.com/vida/educacion/la-educacion-si-puede-ser-divertida-columna-de-jennifer-d-klein-255432 on January 18, 2022.

Klein, J. D. (2020). Bringing innovative practices to traditional contexts: Navigating the challenges of change. In J. W. Richardson (Ed.), *Bringing innovative practices to your school: Lessons from international schools* (pp. 98–109). New York: Routledge.

Klein, J. D. (2022a, January 17). *Education for Global Citizenship and Intercultural Learning*. Colegio Gran Bretaña Profesional Development Conference.

Klein, J. D. (2022b, February 3). *Assessment as evaluation for growth: Best practices in student-centered, personal(ized) assessment*. Denver, CO: Tri-Association of Schools Professional Development Course.

Klososky, S. (2018). *Keynote address at ASB Unplugged*. American School of Bombay, India. February 23.

Koesel, B. (2020, August). *Balanced literacy* [Virtual presentation].

Kohn, A. (2011). *The case against grades*. Accessed at www.alfiekohn.org/article/case-grades on October 18, 2021.

Kohn, A. (2021, March 20). *What matters isn't how well a teacher holds students' attention; it's whether a teacher knows enough about how learning happens to stop being the center of attention* [Tweet]. Twitter. Accessed at https://mobile.twitter.com/alfiekohn/status/1373257627065585666 on February 10, 2022.

Kubik, T. (2018). *Unprepared for what we learned: Six action research exercises that challenge the ends we imagine for education*. New York: Lang.

Kurt, S. (2020, August 18). Vygotsky's Zone of Proximal Development and scaffolding. *Educational Technology*. Accessed at https://educationaltechnology.net/vygotskys-zone-of-proximal-development-and-scaffoldi on May 2, 2022.

Ladson-Billings, G. (1994). *The dreamkeepers: Successful teachers of African American children*. San Francisco: Jossey-Bass.

Ladson-Billings, G. (2014). *Culturally relevant pedagogy 2.0: A.k.a. the Remix*. Accessed at https://doi.org/10.17763/haer.84.1.p2rj131485484751 on March 28, 2022.

Ladson-Billings, G. (2021). *Culturally relevant pedagogy: Asking a different question*. New York: Teachers College Press.

Låg, T., & Sæle, R. G. (2019). *Does the flipped classroom improve student learning and satisfaction? A systematic review and meta-analysis*. Accessed at https://journals.sagepub.com/doi/full/10.1177/2332858419870489 on December 13, 2021.

Lagueux, R. C. (2014). *A spurious John Dewey quotation on reflection*. Boston: Academia. Accessed at www.academia.edu/17358587/A_Spurious_John_Dewey_Quotation_on_Reflection on January 13, 2022.

Langberg, A. (1993). Empowering students to shape their own learning. In G. A. Smith (Ed.), *Public schools that work: Creating community* (pp. 129–154). New York: Routledge.

Laur, D., & Ackers, J. (2017). *Developing natural curiosity through project-based learning: Five strategies for the preK–3 classroom*. New York: Routledge.

Learner Variability Project. (n.d.). *Encourage student self-advocacy*. Accessed at https://lvp.digitalpromiseglobal.org/content-area/math-pk-2/strategies/encourage-student-self-advocacy-math-pk-2/summary on January 23, 2022.

Lee, L. (2019). *For leaders, getting real buy-in for school initiatives*. Accessed at www.edutopia.org/article/leaders-getting-real-buy-school-initiatives on March 28, 2022.

LeQuire, S. (2016, May 4). The history of women as teachers. *The Western Carolina Journalist*. Accessed at https://thewesterncarolinajournalist.com/2016/05/04/the-history-of-women-as-teachers on May 2, 2022.

Lewis, S. (2014). *The rise: Creativity, the gift of failure, and the search for mastery*. New York: Simon & Schuster.

Li, Z., & Qiu, Z. (2018). *How does family background affect children's educational achievement? Evidence from contemporary China*. Accessed at https://doi.org/10.1186/s40711-018-0083-8 on March 28, 2022.

Lipset, M., & Simmons, T. (2021). The 10 equity commandments: Creating learning spaces that serve the needs of every learner. *Education Reimagined*. Accessed at https://education-reimagined.org/the-10-equity-commandments-creating-learning-spaces-that-serve-the-needs-of-every-learner/ on January 24, 2022.

Locke, J. (1997). *An essay concerning human understanding*. London: Penguin Books. (Original work published 1690)

Lucas, F. (2018, June 26). *Techniques for empathy interviews in design thinking*. Accessed at https://webdesign.tutsplus.com/articles/techniques-of-empathy-interviews-in-design-thinking--cms-31219 on February 10, 2022.

Lynch, M. (2016). *4 reasons why we need more minority instructors in schools and colleges*. Accessed at www.theedadvocate.org/4-reasons-why-we-need-more-minority-instructors-in-schools-and-colleges on March 22, 2022.

Macfarlane, A., Glynn, T., Cavanagh, T., & Bateman, S. (2007). Creating culturally-safe schools for Māori students. *Australian Journal of Indigenous Education*, *36*(1), 65–76.

Macfarlane, A., Macfarlane, S., Savage, C., & Glynn, T. (2012). *Inclusive education and Māori communities in Aotearoa New Zealand*. Accessed at www.researchgate.net/publication/330185643_Inclusive_education_and_Maori_communities_in_Aotearoa_New_Zealand on March 28, 2022.

MacKenzie, T. (2016). *Dive into inquiry: Amplify learning and empower student voice*. Del Mar, CA: Elevate Books Edu.

Mader, J. (2022). *A state funded pre-K program led to 'significantly negative effects' for kids in Tennessee*. Accessed at https://hechingerreport.org/a-state-funded-pre-k-program-led-to-significantly-negative-effects-for-kids-in-tennessee/ on January 26, 2022.

Mahr, L. (2020). *Education reform and the transition to standards-based grading education in the United States*. Accessed at https://nwcommons.nwciowa.edu/cgi/viewcontent.cgi?article=1262&context=education_masters on March 22, 2022.

Malouff, J. M., & Thorsteinsson, E. B. (2016). *Bias in grading: A meta-analysis of experimental research findings*. Accessed at https://doi.org/10.1177/0004944116664618 on October 18, 2021.

Marston, W. M. (2015). *Emotions of normal people*. Sacramento, CA: Creative Media Partners. (Original work published 1928)

Matus, D. (n.d.). *To what extent did the industrial revolution change American social, economic, and political life?* Accessed at https://education.seattlepi.com/extent-did-industrial-revolution-change-american-social-economic-political-life-6960.html on December 17, 2021.

Maxwell, J. C. (2000). *Failing forward: Turning mistakes into stepping stones for success.* Nashville, TN: Nelson.

Mayberry, K. (2016). *With mounting globalisation, and workers jumping from one country to the next, where do expat kids call home?* Accessed at www.bbc.com/worklife/article/20161117-third-culture-kids-citizens-of-everywhere-and-nowhere on December 13, 2021.

McChesney, C., Covey, S., & Huling, J. (2016). *The 4 disciplines of execution: Achieving your wildly important goals.* New York: Free Press.

McKenna, A., Jacobs, A., Desai,. N., Pope, S., Harman, M., Lemen, D., et al. (2019, March 29). *Students share thoughts on the power of passion projects.* Accessed at www.ednc.org/students-share-thoughts-on-the-power-of-passion-projects on March 28, 2022.

McTighe, J., & Wiggins, G. (2012). *Understanding by Design framework.* Accessed at https://files.ascd.org/staticfiles/ascd/pdf/siteASCD/publications/UbD_WhitePaper0312.pdf on December 12, 2021.

McTighe, J., & Wiggins, G. P. (2013). *Essential questions: Opening doors to student understanding.* Alexandria, VA: Association for Supervision and Curriculum Development.

Merrow, C. (2018, July 18). *Journaling as an SEL practice* [Blog post]. Accessed at https://empoweringeducation.org/blog/journaling-as-a-social-emotional-practice on March 28, 2022.

Meyer, H.-D., & Benavot, A. (2013). *PISA, power, and policy: The emergence of global educational governance.* Oxford, England: Symposium Books.

Michael, A. (2015). *Raising race questions: Whiteness and inquiry in education.* New York: Teachers College Press.

Mills College. (2020, November 3). *Confronting implicit bias: Promoting equity in education* [Blog post]. Accessed at https://online.mills.edu/blog/confronting-implicit-bias-in-education on January 7, 2022.

Moll, L. C., Amanti, C., Neff, D., & Gonzalez, N. (1992). Funds of knowledge for teaching: Using a qualitative approach to connect homes and classrooms. *Theory Into Practice, 31*(2), 132–141.

Moore, J. (2011). Behaviorism. *The Psychological Record, 61*(3), 449–464.

Morales, H. S., & Mena, R. G. (2017). *Student self-evaluation and autonomy development in EFL learning.* Accessed at https://revistas.ucr.ac.cr/index.php/rlm/article/view/27695 on March 28, 2022.

Morris, S. M. (2021, June 9). *When we talk about grades, we are talking about people* [Blog post]. Accessed at www.seanmichaelmorris.com/when-we-talk-about-grading-we-are-talking-about-people on October 18, 2021.

Muic, K. (2020). *Benefits of student-led conferences.* Accessed at www.teachhub.com/classroom-management/2020/10/benefits-of-student-led-conferences on December 10, 2021.

National Center on Safe Supportive Learning Environments. (2011). *Family-school-community partnerships.* Accessed at https://safesupportivelearning.ed.gov/training-technical-assistance/education-level/early-learning/family-school-community-partnerships on March 28, 2022.

National Governors Association Center for Best Practices & Council of Chief State School Officers. (n.d.a). *Common Core State Standards for English language arts and literacy in history/social studies, science, and technical subjects: Appendix B—Text exemplars and sample performance tasks*. Washington, DC: Authors. Accessed at www.corestandards.org/assets/Appendix_B.pdf on March 28, 2022.

National Governors Association Center for Best Practices & Council of Chief State School Officers. (n.d.b). *Common Core State Standards for English language arts and literacy in history/social studies, science, and technical subjects: Appendix C—Samples of student writing*. Washington, DC: Authors. Accessed at www.corestandards.org/assets/Appendix_C.pdf on March 28, 2022.

National Public Radio. (2012, July 9). *Joy Harjo's 'crazy brave' path to finding her voice*. Accessed at www.npr.org/transcripts/156501436?storyId=156501436 on October 18, 2021.

National Public Radio. (2014, October 6). *Even techies limit their children's screen time*. Accessed at www.npr.org/sections/alltechconsidered/2014/10/06/354102012/even-techies-limit-their-childs-screen-time on March 22, 2022.

Nauss, S. (2010). *Student led conferences: Students taking responsibility* [Master's thesis, Southern Wesleyan University]. Accessed at https://files.eric.ed.gov/fulltext/ED516784.pdf on February 10, 2022.

Nduagbo, K. C. N. (2020, July 23). *How gender disparities affect classroom learning*. Accessed at www.ascd.org/el/articles/how-gender-disparities-affect-classroom-learning

Nelsestuen, K., & Smith, J. (2020). *Empathy interviews*. Accessed at https://learningforward.org/wp-content/uploads/2020/10/tool-empathy-interviews.pdf on December 21, 2021.

Newman, T. (2021, May 11). *Sex and gender: Meanings, definition, identity, and expression*. Accessed at www.medicalnewstoday.com/articles/232363#gender on March 28, 2022.

Next Generation Science Standards. (n.d.). *5-LS2—1 ecosystems: Interactions, energy, and dynamics*. Accessed at www.nextgenscience.org/pe/5-ls2-1-ecosystems-interactions-energy-and-dynamics on October 18, 2021.

New York University Steinhardt. (2021). *An asset-based approach to education: What it is and why it matters*. Accessed at https://teachereducation.steinhardt.nyu.edu/an-asset-based-approach-to-education-what-it-is-and-why-it-matters on December 21, 2021.

Nhất Hạnh, T. (1994). *A joyful path: Community, transformation, and peace*. Berkeley, CA: Parallax Press.

NGSS Lead States. (2013). *Next Generation Science Standards: For states, by states*. Washington, DC: The National Academies Press.

Nichols, A., & Dynarski, M. (2017, July 13). *More findings about school vouchers and test scores, and they are still negative*. Accessed at www.brookings.edu/research/more-findings-about-school-vouchers-and-test-scores-and-they-are-still-negative on March 22, 2022.

Nieto, S. (1996). *Affirming diversity: The sociopolitical context of multicultural education*. London: Longman.

NMBL Strategies (2021). *Four alternatives to a SWOT analysis*. Accessed at https://quickbooks.intuit.com/ca/resources/business/why-soar-analysis-may-be-better-than-swot-analysis on January 26, 2022.

No Child Left Behind (NCLB) Act of 2001, Pub. L. No. 107-110, § 115, Stat. 1425 (2002).

Obear, K. (2013). Navigating triggering events: Critical competencies for social justice educators. In L. M. Landreman (Ed.), *The art of effective facilitation: Reflections from social justice educators* (pp. 151–172). Sterling, VA: Stylus Publishing.

Oddone, K. (2016). *Making the leap: Students as creators, not consumers* [Blog post]. Accessed at http://blog.scootle.edu.au/2016/11/02/making-the-leap-students-as-creators-not-consumers on January 6, 2021.

Oettingen, G., Kappes, H. B., Guttenberg, K. B., & Gollwitzer, P. M. (2015). Self-regulation of time management: Mental contrasting with implementation intentions. *European Journal of Social Psychology, 45*(2), 218–229.

Ogle, D. (1986). K-W-L: A teaching model that develops active reading of expository text. *The Reading Teacher, 39*(6), 564–570.

Olsen, K. (2020). *Effects of block scheduling vs traditional period scheduling on the academic achievement of middle school students* [Master's thesis, California State University, Monterey Bay]. Accessed at https://digitalcommons.csumb.edu/cgi/viewcontent.cgi?article=1895&context=caps_thes_all on March 22, 2022.

Ondrasek, N., & Flook, L. (2020). *How to help all students feel safe to be themselves.* Accessed at https://greatergood.berkeley.edu/article/item/how_to_help_all_students_feel_safe_to_be_themselves on March 22, 2022.

Ormond, C. G. A. (2013). *Place-based education in practice.* Accessed at https://doi.org/10.1007/978-94-6209-221-1_2 on March 28, 2022.

Otte, J. W. (2015). *Appreciative inquiry makes research future forming* [Doctoral dissertation, Tilburg, Netherlands: Tilburg University]. Accessed at https://pure.uvt.nl/ws/portalfiles/portal/8727348/Otte_Appreciative_09_11_2015.pdf on October 29, 2021.

Peregrine Global Services. (2020). *SOAR analysis guide and template.* Accessed at https://peregrineglobal.com/wp-content/uploads/SOAR-Template.pdf on October 29, 2021.

Perry, J., Lundie, D., & Golder, G. (2018). *Metacognition in schools: What does the literature suggest about the effectiveness of teaching metacognition in schools?* Accessed at https://doi.org/10.1080/00131911.2018.1441127 on March 28, 2022.

Phillips Exeter Academy. (n.d.). *Harkness.* Accessed at www.exeter.edu/excellence/how-youll-learn on December 9, 2021.

Posner, R. (2009). *Lives of passion, school of hope: How one public school ignites a lifelong love of learning.* Boulder, CO: Sentient.

Price, D., & Mangano, D. (2019, March 28). *Passion projects: Engaging students in their own learning.* Accessed at www.ednc.org/passion-projects-engaging-students-in-their-own-learning on January 23, 2022.

Quaglia Institute for School Voice and Aspirations. (2016). *School voice report 2016.* Accessed at https://quagliainstitute.org/dmsView/School_Voice_Report_2016 on March 22, 2022.

Rahman, I., & Gupta, R. (2021). *Hungarian anti-LGBTQ+ campaign: Restricting portrayals of homosexuality to minors.* Accessed at www.jurist.org/commentary/2021/11/rahman-gupta-hungarian-anti-lgbtq on December 13, 2021.

Ramel, D. (2021). *Is AI coming for your dev job or not? A tale of two surveys.* Accessed at https://visualstudiomagazine.com/articles/2021/08/18/robot-jobs.aspx on March 28, 2022.

Redd, G. (2021, August). *Distributive leadership* [Zoom]. Best Schools in the Middle East.

Ren-Etta Sullivan, D. (2016). *Cultivating the genius of black children: Strategies to close the achievement gap in the early years.* St. Paul, MN: Redleaf Press.

Rheinberg, F., & Engeser, S. (2018). Intrinsic motivation and flow. *Motivation and Action,* 579–622. https://doi.org/10.1007/978-3-319-65094-4_14

Richardson, W. (2012). *Why school? How education must change when learning and information are everywhere* [Kindle version]. New York: TED Conferences.

Right Question Institute. (n.d.). *What is the QFT?* Accessed at https://rightquestion.org/what-is-the-qft-2 on December 9, 2021.

Riopel, L. (2019, June 14). *The importance, benefits, and value of goal setting.* Accessed at https://positivepsychology.com/benefits-goal-setting on March 22, 2022.

Robinson, K. (2008). *Developing imagination in education* [Video file]. Accessed at www.youtube.com/watch?v=qYJhpvj23vk on December 7, 2021.

Robinson, K. (2016). *Creative schools: The grassroots revolution that's transforming education.* New York: Penguin.

Robinson, K. (2021, October 5). *Gamechanger series: A conversation with Kate Robinson and Anthony Dunn* [Video file]. Accessed online at https://vimeo.com/629410643/3081af2a3e on January 9, 2021.

Rose, J. (2012, May 9). How to break free of our 19th century factory-made education system. *The Atlantic.* Accessed at www.theatlantic.com/business/archive/2012/05/how-to-break-free-of-our-19th-century-factory-model-education-system/256881 on May 2, 2022.

Ross, D. (2019). *Place-based education anchors learning in the community.* Accessed at www.gettingsmart.com/2019/03/11/place-based-education-anchors-learning-in-the-community on March 28, 2022.

Rotzel, G. (1971). *The school in rose valley: A parent venture in education.* Baltimore, MD: Johns Hopkins Press.

Ryan, R. M., & Deci, E. L. (2018). *Self-determination theory: Basic psychological needs in motivation, development, and wellness.* New York: Guilford Press.

Sackett, P. R., Kuncel, N. R., Beatty, A. S., Rigdon, J. L., Shen, W., & Kiger, T. B. (2012). The role of socioeconomic status in SAT-grade relationships and in college admissions decisions. *Psychological Science, 23*(9), 1000–1007.

School Reform Initiative. (n.d.). *Affinity mapping.* Accessed at http://schoolreforminitiative.org/doc/affinity_mapping.pdf on February 10, 2022.

Schwartz, K. (2016, March 22). *Beyond data: Building empathy in adults through student shadow days.* Accessed at www.kqed.org/mindshift/44417/beyond-data-building-empathy-in-adults-with-student-shadow-days on February 14, 2022.

Seçgin, T., & Sungur, S. (2020). *Investigating the science attitudes of students from low socioeconomic status families: The impact of problem-based learning.* Accessed at https://iubmb.onlinelibrary.wiley.com/doi/10.1002/bmb.21447 on March 28, 2022.

Sengupta-Irving, T., & Agarwal, P. (2017). Conceptualizing perseverance in problem solving as collective enterprise. *Mathematical Thinking and Learning, 19*(2), 115–138. https://doi.org/10.1080/10986065.2017.1295417

Serin, H. (2017). *The role of passion in learning and teaching.* Accessed at https://ijsses.tiu.edu.iq/index.php/volume-4-issue-1-article-7 on March 28, 2022.

Silver, D., Berckemeyer, J. C., & Baenen, J. (2015). *Deliberate optimism: Reclaiming the joy in education.* Thousand Oaks, CA: Corwin.

Sinek, S. (2009). *Start with why: How great leaders inspire everyone to take action.* New York: Portfolio.

Sinek, S. (2018, October 3). *The golden circle: Presenter slides and notes.* Accessed at https://simonsinek.com/product/share-the-golden-circle-presenter-slides-and-notes on March 28, 2022.

Sinek, S. (2019, July 1). *Simon Sinek on education* [Video file]. Accessed at www.youtube.com/watch?v=LO4l5XpOc-s on January 21, 2022.

Singapore Math Inc. (n.d.). *What is Singapore math?* Accessed at www.singaporemath.com/what-is-singapore-math on December 20, 2021.

Singleton, G. E. (2015). *Courageous conversations about race: A field guide for achieving equity in schools* (2nd ed.). Thousand Oaks, CA: Corwin.

Sotiriou, S. A., Lazoudis, A., & Bogner, F. X. (2020). *Inquiry-based learning and e-learning: How to serve high and low achievers.* Accessed at https://doi.org/10.1186/s40561-020-00130-x on March 28, 2022.

Southard, J. (2017). *Colonial education* [Blog post]. Accessed at https://scholarblogs.emory.edu/postcolonialstudies/2014/06/20/colonial-education on January 7, 2022.

Sparks, S. D. (2019, March 12). *Why teacher-student relationships matter: New findings shed light on best approaches.* Accessed at www.edweek.org/teaching-learning/why-teacher-student-relationships-matter/2019/03 on October 18, 2021.

Specia, A., & Osman, A. (2015). *Education as a practice of freedom: Reflections on bell hooks.* Accessed at https://files.eric.ed.gov/fulltext/EJ1079754.pdf on February 10, 2022.

Squire, V., & Darling, J. (2013). The "minor" politics of rightful presence: Justice and relationality in city of sanctuary. *International Political Sociology, 7*(1), 59–74.

Stavros, J., & Cole, M. L. (2013). SOARing towards positive transformation and change. *Development Policy Review, 1*(1), 10–34.

Stavros, J., Cooperrider, D., & Kelley, D. L. (2003). *Strategic inquiry! Appreciative intent: Inspiration to SOAR—A new framework for strategic planning.* Accessed at www.academia.edu/19912532/Strategic_Inquiry_Appreciative_Intent_Inspiration_to_SOAR_A_New_Framework_for_Strategic_Planning on December 11, 2021.

Stead, T. (2014). Nurturing the inquiring mind through the nonfiction read-aloud. *The Reading Teacher, 67*(7), 488–495.

Steele, C. M., & Aronson, J. (1995). Stereotype threat and the intellectual test performance of African Americans. *Journal of Personality and Social Psychology, 69*(5), 797–811.

Sterling, L. (2016). *Coding in the curriculum: Fad or foundational?* Accessed at https://research.acer.edu.au/cgi/viewcontent.cgi?article=1297&context=research_conference on March 22, 2022.

Stiggins, R. J. (2005). From formative assessment to assessment FOR learning: A path to success in standards-based schools. *Phi Delta Kappan, 87*(4), 324–328.

Stommel, J. (2018, March 11). *How to ungrade* [Blog post]. Accessed at www.jessestommel.com/how-to-ungrade on October 18, 2021.

Strauss, V. (2020, June 21). *It looks like the beginning of the end of America's obsession with student standardized tests.* Accessed at www.washingtonpost.com/education/2020/06/21/it-looks-like-beginning-end-americas-obsession-with-student-standardized-tests on March 28, 2022.

Strive HI. (2021). *Inouye Elementary.* Accessed at www.hawaiipublicschools.org/Reports/StriveHIInouyeEl21.pdf on March 28, 2022.

Style, E. (1988). *Curriculum for as window and mirror. Listening for All Voices, Oak Knoll School monograph.* Summit, NJ. Accessed at https://nationalseedproject.org/Key-SEED-Texts/curriculum-as-window-and-mirror on April 11, 2022.

Taub, M., Sawyer, R., Smith, A., Rowe, J., Azevedo, R., & Lester, J. (2020). *The agency effect: The impact of student agency on learning, emotions, and problem-solving behaviors in a game-based learning environment.* Accessed at www.sciencedirect.com/science/article/abs/pii/S0360131519303318 on January 7, 2022.

Terada, Y. (2021, February 21). *New research makes a powerful case for PBL.* Accessed at www.edutopia.org/article/new-research-makes-powerful-case-pbl on October 18, 2021.

Theisen-Homer, V. M. (2018). *Teaching for human connection: Relationships, race, and the training of teachers* [Doctoral dissertation, Harvard Graduate School of Education].

Theisen-Homer, V. (2019, September 3). *How can we support more empowering teacher-student relationships?* [Blog post]. Accessed at www.edweek.org/teaching-learning/opinion-how-can-we-support-more-empowering-teacher-student-relationships/2018/09 on January 31, 2022.

Thomas, H. (2022, January 13). *Indigenous knowledge is overlooked in education. But it has a lot to teach us.* Accessed at www.edsurge.com/news/2022-01-13-indigenous-knowledge-is-often-overlooked-in-education-but-it-has-a-lot-to-teach-us on March 22, 2022.

Thornton, C. (2021, July 4). *'This could change their lives': Test-optional requirements helped first-generation applicants.* Accessed at www.usatoday.com/story/news/2021/07/04/shifting-test-optional-during-covid-led-more-college-applicants/7845411002 on February 1, 2022.

Timon, A. (2021). *Arts, humanities are first on the chopping block as US state governments face deficits.* Accessed at www.wsws.org/en/articles/2021/01/08/arts-j08.html on December 13, 2021.

Tolisano, S. R., & Hale, J. A. (2018). *A guide to documenting learning: Making thinking visible, meaningful, shareable, and amplified.* Thousand Oaks, CA: Corwin.

Tomlinson, C. A. (2017). *How to differentiate instruction in academically diverse classrooms* (3rd ed.). Alexandria, VA: Association for Supervision and Curriculum Development.

Tomlinson, C. A., & Strickland, C. A. (2008). *Differentiation in practice: A resource guide for differentiating curriculum, grades 9–12.* Hawker Brownlow Education.

Tough, P. (2014). *How children succeed: Confidence, curiosity and the hidden power of character.* Boston, MA: Houghton Mifflin Harcourt.

Turner, A. (2017). How does intrinsic and extrinsic motivation drive performance culture in organizations? *Cogent Education, 4*(1). https://doi.org/10.1080/2331186x.2017.1337543

UNESCO. (2022). *Education: From disruption to recovery.* Accessed at https://en.unesco.org/covid19/educationresponse on January 12, 2022.

UNICEF. (2020). *Education and COVID-19.* September. Accessed at https://data.unicef.org/topic/education/covid-19 on January 12, 2022.

United Kingdom. (1988). *Education Reform Act.* Accessed at https://www.legislation.gov.uk/ukpga/1988/40/contents on May 2, 2022.

United Nations. (2000). *Resolution adopted by the General Assembly.* Accessed at https://undocs.org/en/A/RES/55/2 on December 16, 2021.

United Nations. (2015a). *4. Goals: Ensure inclusive and equitable quality education and promote lifelong learning opportunities for all.* Accessed at https://sdgs.un.org/goals/goal4 on December 6, 2021.

United Nations. (2015b). *Resolution adopted by the General Assembly on 25 September 2015.* Accessed at https://undocs.org/A/RES/70/1 on December 16, 2021.

University of Hawai'i at Hilo. (n.d.). *UH Hilo stories.* Accessed at https://hilo.hawaii.edu/chancellor/stories on October 29, 2021.

University of Reading. (n.d.). *Why is feedback important?* Accessed at www.reading.ac.uk/internal/engageinfeedback/Whyisfeedbackimportant/efb-WhyIsFeedbackImportant.aspx on January 26, 2022.

U.S. Department of Education. (2009). *Race to the Top program: Executive summary.* Accessed at www2.ed.gov/programs/racetothetop/executive-summary.pdf on March 20, 2015.

Valli, L., Stefanski, A., & Jacobson, R. (2016). School-community partnership models: Implications for leadership. *International Journal of Leadership in Education, 21*(1), 31–49.

van Loon, M. H., de Bruin, A. B. H., van Gog, T., & van Merriënboer, J. J. G. (2013). Activation of inaccurate prior knowledge affects primary-school students' metacognitive judgments and calibration. *Learning and Instruction, 24,* 15–25.

Van Rossum, C. (2018, November 13). *Rosetta Lee transcript.* Accessed at http://mvmag.pub/2018/11/13/rosetta-lee-transcript on October 18, 2021.

Verhoeven, M., Poorthuis, A. M. G., & Volman, M. (2018). *The role of school in adolescents' identity development. A literature review.* Accessed at https://link.springer.com/article/10.1007/s10648-018-9457-3#Abs1 on January 26, 2022.

Vitaud, L. (2018, September 12). *Who: The A method for hiring by Geoff Smart and Randy Street.* Accessed at www.welcometothejungle.com/en/articles/who-the-a-method-for-hiring-by-geoff-smart-and-randy-street on February 16, 2022.

Vygotsky, L. S. (1978). *Mind and society: The development of higher psychological processes.* Cambridge, MA: Harvard University Press.

Vygotsky Learning Conference. (n.d.). *Zone of Proximal Development (ZPD).* Accessed at https://vygotskyetec512.weebly.com/zone-of-proximal-development.html on October 29, 2021.

Wagner, T. (2009). *Global achievement gap.* New York: Basic Books.

Wagner, T., & Dintersmith, T. (2016). *Most likely to succeed: Preparing our kids for the innovation era.* New York: Scribner.

Walsh, C. E. (1996). *Education reform and social change: Multicultural voices, struggles, and visions.* Mahwah, NJ: Erlbaum.

Wang, Z. (2013, December). *Effects of heterogeneous and homogeneous grouping on student learning* [Master's thesis, University of North Carolina]. Carolina Digital Repository. Accessed at https://cdr.lib.unc.edu/concern/dissertations/9z903079v on February 14, 2022.

Wass, R., & Golding, C. (2014). Sharpening a tool for teaching: The Zone of Proximal Development. *Teaching in Higher Education, 19*(6), 671–684.

Waterford.org. (2019). *Why strong teacher relationships lead to students engagement and a better school environment.* Accessed at www.waterford.org/education/teacher-student-relationships on December 21, 2021.

Westmont College. (n.d.). *Infusing cultural awareness in teaching. Adapted from the work of Paul Kivel and Martin Cano.* Accessed at www.westmont.edu/sites/default/files/InfusingCulturalAwarenessinTeaching.doc on January 18, 2022.

What School Could Be. (n.d.a). *Curiosity time.* Accessed at https://vimeo.com/328722320 on May 20, 2022.

What School Could Be. (n.d.b). *Essential skills and mindsets.* Accessed at https://whatschoolcouldbe.org/essential-skills-mindsets on April 13, 2022.

What School Could Be. (n.d.c). *Genius time.* Accessed at https://whatschoolcouldbe.org/genius-time on April 13, 2022.

What School Could Be. (n.d.d). *What school could be.* Accessed at https://community.whatschoolcouldbe.org/posts/mobilize-your-community-portrait-of-a-graduate on January 30, 2022.

Wheaton, A. G., Chapman, D. P., & Croft, J. B. (2016). School start times, sleep, behavioral health, and academic outcomes: A review of the literature. *Journal of School Health*, *86*(5), 363–381.

Wiggins, A. (2017). *The best class you never taught: How spider web discussion can turn students into learning leaders*. Alexandria, VA: Association for Supervision and Curriculum Development.

Williamson, R., & Blackburn, B. (2019). *How leaders develop stakeholder ownership*. Accessed at www.middleweb.com/40573/how-leaders-develop-stakeholder-ownership on January 23, 2022.

Wilson, C. E. (2020). *The effects of inquiry-based learning and student achievement in the science classroom*. Accessed at https://scholar.umw.edu/cgi/viewcontent.cgi?article=1391&context =student_research on February 16, 2022.

World Indigenous Nations Higher Education Consortium. (n.d.a). *About us*. Accessed at https://winhec.org/About-us on May 11, 2022.

World Indigenous Nations Higher Education Consortium. (n.d.b). *Accreditation*. Accessed at https://winhec.org/accreditation on December 21, 2021.

World Leadership School. (2020). *Group dynamics manual 2020–21*. Accessed at https://drive .google.com/file/d/1Mj2RaPapEN9MnaPpD9NQrm21MwKczJib/view?usp=sharing on February 1, 2022.

Wright, K., Shields, S., Black, K., & Waxman, H. (2018). *The effects of teacher home visits on student behavior, student academic achievement, and parent involvement*. Accessed at www.adi .org/journal/2018ss/WrightEtAlSpring2018.pdf on February 10, 2022.

Yauch, J. (2015, April 22). *The power of student-led conferences [Blog post]*. Accessed at www.leaderinme.org/blog/the-power-of-student-led-conferences on February 10, 2022.

Yoon, H. J., Hyoyeon I., Niles, S. G., Amundson, N. E., Smith, B. A., & Mills, L. (2015). The effects of hope on student engagement, academic performance, and vocational identity. *The Canadian Journal of Career Development*, *14*(1), 34–45.

York, B. (2014). *Know the child: The importance of teacher knowledge of individual students' skills (KISS)*. Accessed at http://cepa.stanford.edu/content/know-child-importance-teacher -knowledge-individual-students-skills-kiss on February 16, 2022.

Youth.gov (n.d.). *Sexual orientation and gender identity*. Accessed at https://youth.gov/youth -topics/lgbt on January 13, 2022.

YWCA Minneapolis. (2021). *Anti-bias curriculum for the preschool classroom*. St. Paul, MN: Redleaf Press.

Zhao, Y. (2012). *World class learners: Educating creative and entrepreneurial students*. Thousand Oaks, CA: Corwin.

Zhao, Y. (2021). *Gamechanger series: A conversation with Yong Zhao*. Accessed at https://community.whatschoolcouldbe.org/posts/18164893?utm_source=manual on January 9, 2022.

Zmuda, A. (2016). *Developing empathy for students through shadowing*. Accessed at www.learningpersonalized.com/developing-empathy-students-shadowing on February 14, 2022.

Index

A

a'ole pau ka 'ike i ka halau ho'okahi, 239–240
academic excellence
 capstone projects, 114–115
 defining the horizon for, 109–111
 portrait of the graduate, 109, 111–112
 SOAR model analysis, 112–114
access, 1–2
accountability
 challenges, 182–184
achievement
 defining, 13–14
Ackers, J., 166
Ackers-Clayton, J., 7–8, 39, 53, 79, 204–207, 235
Adler, M. J., 90
Advancement Via Individual Determination (AVID), 7
adventure/survival skills. *See* survival skills
advising, 221
affinity groups, 17, 78–79, 262
 identity development, 78–79
affinity mapping, 17, 122, 124–126, 173, 263
after-school programming, 186
Agarwal, P., 54
agency, 8
 charting the pathway, 37–39
 defined, 37–38
 student protagonism, 10–11
Albee, D., 95
Amanti, C, 70
American International School (Cairo, Egypt), 27–28, 82
ANCHOR, 17, 100, 103–104, 263
Anderson, A., 8, 191
Apni Shala Foundation (India), 39, 57–58, 95, 196
Appel, M., 34
appreciative inquiry, 204–205
arc of professional learning, 211–212
 eight topics to include, 212
artificial intelligence, 244–245
aspirational values, 203–204
aspirations, 205
assessments, 16
 authentic, 15
 based on deficits, 48
 co-constructed rubrics, 172–175
 designing, 141
 feedback-revision circles, 165–172
 formative evaluation, 165–172
 growth on the landscape, 155–156
 problems with traditional grading, 156–164
 progress-based, 143–145, 227–228
 reflective questions, 175–176
 student protagonism, 164–165
 takeaways, 176
asset mapping
 external, 207
 internal, 206–207
 tapping into the community, 206–209
asset orientations, 212
asset-based mindsets, 118–121
asset-based teaching and learning, 6
asset-based thinking, 48–50
assets
 leveraging, 121–130
assuming the best intentions, 180
authentic assessment. *See* assessment
Avante Global School (Cartagena, Colombia)
 Parent Pavilion, 189

B

Baenen, J., 57
Bard College, 186–187, 237
Barton, A. C., 12–14
Battelle for Kids, 105
becoming comfortable with the uncomfortable, 208–209
beginning from questions, 180
behaviorism, 140–141
being open to learning, 180
being present, 180
believing in every student, 46, 57–59, 149, 165–166, 172
 educator profiles, 196–197
Berckemeyer, J. C., 57
Berger, R., xvii, 15, 104–105, 166
Bishop, R. S., 199

Blackburn, B., 183
blank slate. *See* empty vessel myth
Bloom's taxonomy, 11, 14
Bold Learning Objectives (BLOB), 249
brainstorming, 123–124, 172
brave spaces, 6, 17, 180, 212–213, 228, 262
  identity development, 76–78
building relationships. *See* relationship building
Burges, P., 108
buy-in challenges, 182–184

C

Calkins, L., 132
Caobos, 189
capstone projects, 17, 114–115, 263
career exploration, 123
Carlson, C., 248, 250–251
Century Tech, 244
chalk talks, 125
challenges
  buy-in and accountability, 182–184
  educational management technologies, 181–182
  implementation, 177
  in international school settings, 187–188
  in private and public school settings, 177–179
  in traditional and progressive contexts, 184–187
  parents and other caregivers, 188–190
  policies and politics, 190–193
  reflective questions, 193
  takeaways, 193–194
  tolerance for, 5–6
  understanding and discussing identity, 179–181
Chapman, S., 68–70
Chemaly, S., 163
"choose your own pathway" course, 185
Ciotti, K., 38, 42, 76, 81, 108, 110, 159, 187, 200, 209
  kulia i ka nu'u, 34–35
City, E. A., 214
classroom norms, 179–180
Claxton, G., 159
clear expectations, 71–72

CliftonStrengths, 67
Clinton, W. J., 146
coaching teams, 6
co-constructed rubrics, 172–175
coding, 238
Cohn–Vargas, B., 34
collaboration, 105
collaborative protocol for defining outcomes, 17, 147–148, 216, 263
collective responsibility, 12–13
College Board, 55
colonialism, 3
commandments, 202
Common Core State Standards, 43, 217
communication, 105
  with parents/caregivers, 188–190
community norms, 202–203
community-based learning, 209–210
competition, 158–160
complex transdisciplinary skills, 145–146
concentric circles
  for educators, 209–210
  integrating students' contexts into the classroom, 81–84
  sample, 83
concepts, 145–146, 244
conferring, 133–134
conscientização, 52
constructivism, 140–141
content, 145–146, 244
Conzemius, E. A., 101
Cooperrider, D., 112
Covey, S., 223–224
COVID-19 pandemic, 2–3
  celebrations of learning, 230
  elimination of SATs, 18
  forced rapid changes, 257
  grouping students, 218–219
  reshaped educational thinking, 18–19
  school is also childcare, 236
  shifting assessment practices, 158
  virtual home visits, 84
creativity, 105, 123–124
critical pedagogy, 13
  challenging the dominant theory, 45, 51–53

critical thinking skills, 105
Cronin, A., 105
"cross the line" activity, 17, 46, 262
  identity development, 74–76
cultural intelligence, 70
culturally-mediated instruction, 29
culturally-responsive recruiting, 198
culturally-responsive teaching, 42–43, 212, 228
  defined, 28
  educator profiles, 196–197
culture, 27
  identity development, 73–74
  perspectives on defining the horizon, 68–70
  perspectives on, 27–28
  school, 221–225
  visible vs. deep, 73
curiosity, 161
curriculum adjustment, 215–218
Cushman-Patz, B., 214

D

d'Erizans, R., 12, 58, 94, 142, 197
Daniel K. Inouye Elementary School (Wahiawa, Hawaii), 95
Davis, W., 259
deeper learning, 15
deficit-based assumptions, 48, 119
Denver Center for International Studies, 208
design labs, 249
design thinking, 42, 51, 212–228
  as a PBL structure, 17, 122, 126–129, 263
  cycle, 128
  Ivy League schools using, 18
  shift toward at Ivy League schools, 178
  student protagonism, 10–11
Dewey, J., 2, 71, 237
differentiation, 39–40, 117
Dintersmith, T., 159
DiSC, 67
discipline-specific skills, 145–146
  supporting student growth in, 130–136
diversity
  too simplistic, 11–12

documentation
  of, for, and *as* learning, 169
  student-led, 167–172
dominant theory
  challenging, 51–53
drill and kill, 54
drive-by PD, 211
Drucker, P., 237

E

ecosystem, 3–4, 16–17, 65–67
  culture, 27–28
  defined, 9
  holding space for identity development, 67–79
  inclusive values, 26–27
  integrating students' contexts, 79–85
  laying the groundwork for change, 226–227
  myth of the empty vessel, 24–25
  perspective on what students bring, 95–97
  questions about, 229
  reflective questions, 92
  sex and gender, 29–31
  socioeconomic status, 28–29
  strategies, 17
  synthesis tool, 151
  systems approach, 183–184
  takeaways, 92
  "third culture kids," 187–188
  understanding the broader context, 25–27
  understanding where students are, 85–92
EdLeader21, 111
Educating with Aloha (Iwase), 95
education
  back to indigenous ways, 242–244
  evolution to follow human development, 236–238
  next frontier, 239–242
  technology assisted, 244–247
  what it could be, 247–250
Education Reform Act (U.K.), 7
Education Reimagined (Lipset & Simmons), 202
educational management technologies (LMS)
  challenges of, 181–182
educational outcomes, 117–118

collaborative protocol for defining, 17, 147–148
culturally responsive teaching, 42–43
defined, 9
leveraging asset-based mindsets and communication, 118–121
leveraging assets, 121–130
myth of standardization, 35–37
personalized learning, 39–42
planning units, 136–142
progress-based assessment, 143–145
  redefining, 145–146
  reexamining, 142–143
  sample continuum, 144
strategies, 17
student agency, 37–39
supporting student growth, 130–136
synthesis tool, 152
using wise criticism, 148–149
what it means to chart, 37
educator portfolios, 196–197, 214–215
  sketch, 215
educator recruitment, 196–200
Edutopia (Cronin), 105
efficiency vs. efficacy, 159–160
EL Education, 130
electives, 185
empathy, 161
empathy interviews, 17, 262
  integrating students' contexts into the classroom, 80–81
empty vessel myth, 24–25, 91
engaged pedagogy, 52–53, 211–212
equity, 206
essential skills, 55–56
Evergreen State College, 187, 237
experiences, 249
explicit biases, 4–5
external asset mapping, 207
extrinsic motivation, 160–162

F

Facebook, 237–238
factory model, 3–5
  challenges of implementation, 184–187
  grading, 155–156
  evolution of, 236–238
  vs. landscape model, 6–10

fail up and forward, 180–181
feedback-revision circles, 165–167
  student-led documentation of growth, 167–172
Fielding International, 7
15 percent culture, 123
flex blocks, 185
formative evaluation, 165–167
  student-led documentation of growth, 167–172
Fountas, I. C., 144
four Cs (Battelle for Kids), 105
Freire, P., 2, 13, 52, 243
from open schooling to the ivory tower, 173–175
Fryberg, S., 110–111
funding, 192
Funds of Knowledges (Moll et al.), 70

G

Gallup, 67
Gardner, S., 95
Gay, G., 28
gender bias, 5
genius time, 124
Gimnasio Los Caobos (Bogotá, Colombia), 26–27, 38, 107, 184, 222–223
global awareness, 123
global competencies, 212
The Global Education Handbook (Klein), 48, 53
GLSEN, 68
goal setting
  ANCHOR, 100, 103–104
  headline of my year, 99
  letter to myself, 97–99
  SMART goals, 100–102
  storyboards and vision boards, 99–100
  student-led conferences, 100, 104–107
  to support defining the horizon, 95–97
  WOOP, 100–101
Godsil, R., 148
"golden circle" analogy, 55
Golding, C., 142
Gonzalez, N., 70
grades as currency, 158–160
  danger of, 173–175
grading
  extrinsic motivation, 160–162

factory model, 155–156
funding tied to, 179
implicit bias, 162–164
problems with, 156–160
vs. evaluation, 158–159
grading orientation vs. learning orientation, 161
Great Books program, 90
group contacts, 168
guided groups, 134–135
guiding principles, 45–46
  believing in every student, 46, 57–59
  critical pedagogy, 45, 51–53
  inclusive prosperity, 45, 48–50
  personalized learning, 46, 56–57
  purposeful and vigorous learning, 45, 53–56
  reflective questions, 59–60
  student-centered educational practices, 45, 50–51
  students vary in gifts and needs, 45–47
  takeaways, 60
  zone of proximal development, 45, 47–48

H

Hale, J. A., 169
Hall, E. T., 73
Hampshire College, 237
Hanahau'oli School (Honolulu, Hawaii), 138, 144, 187, 251
Hanh, T. N., 52
Harkness method discussions (Phillips Exeter Academy), 91
Harvard University, 18
  Instructional Rounds protocol, 214
  shift toward design thinking and PBL, 178
Hattie, J., 165
having fun, 180
headline of my year, 17, 97–99, 262
HiFusionEd, 42
High School for the Recording Arts (St. Paul, Minn.), 183–184, 197, 202–203, 219–221, 251
  Don't sleep on nothin', 203
High Tech High (San Diego, Calif.), 159
home visits, 66
  virtual, 84–85
honoring students, 108, 110–111
hooks, b., 52–53, 59, 211–212
hope, 57–59
horizon, 4, 6, 9, 16–17, 93–95
  defining for academic excellence, 109–115
  goal setting, 95–97, 100–108
  identifying aspirations, 97–100
  individual and peaks, 34–35
  myth of the well-rounded student, 31–33
  perspectives on defining, 68–70
  questions about, 229
  reflection questions, 115–116
  shifting, 227
  strategies, 17
  synthesis tool, 151
  systems approach, 183–184
  takeaways, 116
  "third culture kids," 187–188
  what it means to define, 33–34
how do we know we are succeeding? 205
Huling, J., 223–224
human development
  education evolution to follow, 236–238

I

"I do, you do, we do" model, 213
iceberg of culture, 17, 73–74, 262
identity
  challenges of understanding and discussing, 179–181
identity development, 67–70
  affinity groups, 78–79
  brave space, 76–78
  cross the line, 74–76
  holding space for, 70
  iceberg of culture, 73–74
  journaling, 71–73
ikigai, 258
immeasurables, 161–162
impact evaluation, 228–230
implementation, 195–196
  curriculum adjustment, 215–218
  educator profiles and recruitment, 196–200
  impact evaluation, 228–230
  professional learning, 211–215
  reflective questions, 230
  shared vision, 201–205
student and course reorganization, 218–221
student protagonism, 221–225
takeaways, 231
tapping into the community, 206–210
three-year development plan, 225–228
implicit biases, 4–5, 175, 196–197
  deconstructing, 212, 225–226
  impact of, 162–164
inclusion
  too simplistic, 11–13
inclusive prosperity, 12, 206
  defined, 11–13
  ensuring, 46
  shift to asset-based thinking and relationships, 45, 48–50
inclusive values
  perspective, 26–27
Indigenous immersion experiences, 228
Indigenous place-based learning, 7, 242–244
industrial model. *See* factory model
inquiry learning
  student protagonism, 10–11
inquiry strategies, 85–86
institutionally-centered schools, 8
Instructional Rounds protocol, 214
instrumentally focused relationships, 50
intercultural competencies, 212–213, 228
interdependence, 6, 41, 208
internal asset mapping, 206–207
internal curriculum audit, 215–218
International Community School (Addis Ababa, Ethiopia), 245–246
International School of Brussels, 121–122, 168, 223
international school settings
  challenges, 187–188
Iwase, J., 95–97

J

jagged profile (Zhao), 32, 206
Jakes, T. D., 122
Jemison, M., 5

Johnson, S., 40
journaling, 17, 164, 262
  identity development, 70–73
  student growth assessment, 170–172
"just in time" feedback, 166

K

Kaiapuni school system (Hawai'i), 243–244
Kelley, D. L., 112
key performance indicators (KPIs), 2223–224, 29
Kiersey Temperament Sorter, 67
Kivel, P., 46, 74
Klein, J. D., 10–11, 38, 48, 53, 66, 76, 119, 125–126, 158–159, 170–175, 180, 184, 186–187, 189, 192, 198, 212–214, 220, 222–224, 240
  individual horizons and peaks, 34–35
  perspective on word choice, 59
  perspectives on inclusive values, 26–27
Klososky, S., 238
knowledge economy, 237
know-wonder-learn (KWL) charts (Ogle), 17, 140, 168
  understanding where students are in the ecosystem, 87–88
Kohn, A., 41, 160–161
KPIs. *See* key performance indicators
Kronberger, N., 34
Kubik, T., 40
kulia I ka nu'u, 34–35, 115
Kumar, R., 39, 57–58, 95, 196, 198–199, 224, 238
KWL and RAN charting, 17, 87–88, 262

L

Ladson-Billings, G., 27–28
landscape model, 3, 5–6, 16
  believing in every student, 46, 57–59
  challenges of implementation, 177–194
  core challenges, 16
  critical pedagogy, 45, 51–53
  ecosystem, 3–4, 9, 24–31, 65–92
  eight principles, 16
  guiding principles, 45–46
  horizon, 4, 9, 31–35, 93–116
  impact evaluation, 228–230
  implementation, 63, 195–231
  implications, 16
  inclusive prosperity, 12–13, 45, 48–50
  leading, 153
  opportunities for the future, 235–252
  pathway, 4, 9, 35–43, 117–150
  personalized learning, 46, 56–57
  purposeful and vigorous learning, 45, 53–56
  reflective questions, 43–44, 59–60
  rightful presence, 10, 13–15
  student-centered educational practices, 45, 50–51
  student growth assessment, 155–176
  student protagonism, 10–11
  students vary in gifts and needs, 45–47
  takeaways, 43–44, 60
  three elements, 23–24
  understanding, 21
  visual, 25
  vs. traditional teaching, 6–10
  zone of proximal development, 45, 47–48
Langberg, A., 49, 174, 187
Laur, D., 166
Leading with Aloha (Iwase), 95
leaning into discomfort, 180–181, 208
learning for mastery, 15
"learning loss," 18, 247
learning traits, 145–146
learning–centered schools, 8
learnish, 172
LearnLife (Barcelona, Spain), 251
Lee, H., 30, 242
Lee, R. E. R., 118–119
letter to myself, 7, 97–99, 262
leveraging asset-based mindsets and communication, 118–121
leveraging assets, 121–122
  affinity mapping, 124–126
  design thinking, 126–129
  design-thinking circle, 128
  passion projects, 122–124
  student portfolios, 129–130

Lewis, S., 33
LGBTQ+ students, 3–31
  censorship of teaching about, 191
  creating safe space, 68
  critical pedagogy through the lens of, 58
  perspectives on defining the horizon, 68–70
Lime Design, 42
Lipset, M., 202–203
Living in Beta, 249
LMS. *See* educational management systems
Local Initiatives Support Corporation, 209
Local Leaders Creating Placemaking Toolkit (Local Initiatives Support Corporation), 209
Locker, F., 189
logical inquiry, 123

M

Ma ka hana ka 'ike, 136
MacKenzie, T., 85–86
makawalu, 26
malama 'aina, 97
Malouff, J. M., 162–163
Mangano, D.,1 23
Mann, H., 7, 246–237
Māori movement, 244
Marston, W. M., 67
Massachusetts Institute of Technology (MIT), 18
  shift toward design thinking and PBL, 178
Mastery Transcript Consortium, 178
McChesney, C., 223–224
McTight, J., 137
Measures of Academic Progress (MAP) Growth Test (NWEA), 187
metacognitions, 112–114
Michael, A., 70
MidPacific Institute (Honolulu, Hawaii), 112
milestones, 168
Millennium School (San Francisco, Cal.), 12
Mills College, 5
mirrors, 199
mission statements, 201–202

modeling as professional development, 213–215
Moll, L. C., 70
Montessori education, 11
Moodle, 182
Morris, S. M., 175
Most Likely to Succeed (Dintersmith & Whiteley), 159
motivation
  extrinsic, 160–162
multiple lenses, 27–28, 51–53
myths
  empty vessel, 24–25
  standardization, 35–37
  well-rounded student, 31–33

N

narrative responses, 229
National School Reform Faculty, 125
native capacities, 49
Neff, D., 70
Nieto, S., 42–43
No Child Left Behind Act (U.S., 2002), 7, 35, 146
Northwest Evaluation Association (NWEA)
  MAP Growth Test, 187

O

O'Neill, J., 101
O'Neill, T., 27, 239–240, 242
Obear, K., 76
Oettingen, G., 100
Ogle, D., 87
One Stone (Boise, Idaho), 248–250
  BLOB, 249
Open School (Lakewood, Colo.), 158–159, 173–175, 187, 192, 219–221, 240, 251
  opportunities, 204–205
  opportunities for the future, 235–236
    education evolution, 236–238
    next frontier in education, 239–247
    reflective questions, 251–252
    takeaways, 252
    what education could be, 247–251
  opportunity gaps, 46
optimism, 57–59
ouch, 180
outcomes. *See* educational outcomes

P

parents/caregivers
  challenges of implementation, 188–190
passage experiences, 219–220
Passages (Open School, Colorado), 123
passion, 162
passion projects, 17, 122–124, 263
pathway, 4, 16–17, 35, 117–118
  assessing progress, 227–228
  culturally responsive teaching, 42–43
  defined, 9
  leveraging asset-based mindsets and communication, 118–121
  leveraging assets, 121–130
  myth of standardization, 35–37
  personalized learning, 39–42
  planning units, 136–142
  questions about, 229
  reexamining what the outcomes should be, 142–143
  strategies, 17
  student agency, 37–39
  supporting student growth, 130–136
  sustaining the journey, 227–228
  synthesis tool, 152
  systems approach, 183–184
  "third culture kids," 187–188
  what it means to chart, 37
PBL. *See* project-based learning
Pedagogy of the Oppressed (Freire), 52
peer evaluation, 165–166
Pelletier, K., 121–122, 167, 182, 223
personal learning, 117
personalized learning, 15, 39–42, 46, 56–57, 117
perspectives
  culture, 27–28
  danger of grades, 173–175
  defining the horizon, 68–70
  honoring students, 108
  honoring students' horizons, 110–111
  inclusive values, 26–27
  what students bring to the learning ecosystem, 95–97
  word choice, 54–55, 59, 158–159, 246–247
Peters, R. G., 138
Phillips Exeter Academy, 91
Pinnell, G. S., 144
PISA, 258
place-based learning
  concentric circles, 17, 81–84, 262
  indigenous, 7, 242–244
planning units, 136
  planning cycle, 138
  student-centered iterative unit planning, 137–141
  zone of proximal development, 141–142
platinum rule, 26–27
policies and politics
  challenges of implementation, 190–193
policy-makers
  challenges of implementation, 178–179
Poorthuis, A. M. G., 171
portrait of the graduate, 17, 109, 111–112, 226
Posner, R., 220
practical skills, 123
prior knowledge and experiences, 8
private schools
  challenges of implementing the landscape model, 177–179
privilege. *See* "cross the line" activity
problem–based learning
  student protagonism, 10–11
productive struggle, 54
professional development, 17, 211
  arc of, 211–212
  modeling as, 213–215
  priorities, 226–228
  self-reflection and self-discovery, 211–213
profiles. *See* educator profiles
Programme for International Student Assessment (PISA), 36, 55
progress-based assessment, 143–145
progressive contexts

challenges of implementation, 184–187
project-based learning (PBL), 6, 15, 212
  AP courses, 50
  curriculum adjustment, 217–218
  design thinking as, 17, 122, 126–129
  expanding the concept, 79
  journaling, 71–73
  shift toward at Ivy League schools, 178
  student protagonism, 10–11
  success of, 49
project blocks, 185
protagonism. *See* student protagonism
protocols, 180
  asset mapping, 209
  concentric circles, 209–210
  Instructional Rounds, 214
public schools
  challenges of implementation, 177–179
Punahou School (Honolulu, Hawaii), 187
purposeful and vigorous learning, 45, 53–56

Q

Quaglia Institute for School Voice and Aspirations, 229
question formulation technique (QFT; Right Question Institute), 17, 86, 262
  understanding where students are in the ecosystem, 88–90
questions
  about the ecosystem, 228–229
  about the horizon, 229
  about the pathways, 229
  beginning from, 180
  concentric circles, 210
  creating, 124
  "cross the line" activity, 75–76
  grounded in concept, 72–73
  student-generated, 86–87
  virtual home visits, 85

R

Race to the Top (U.S., 2009), 7, 35–36
racism
  censorship of teaching about, 191
  higher suspension rates for minorities, 5
  implicit biases, 162–164
  perspectives on defining the horizon, 68–70
RAN charts (Stead), 17, 140, 168
  sample, 89
  understanding where students are in the ecosystem, 86–88
reciprocally focused relationships, 50
recruitment. *See* educator recruitment
redefining educational outcomes, 145–146
Reed College, 237
reflection, 124
  concentric circles, 210
  professional learning, 211–213
reflection and discussion tool for teachers on the landscape, 225, 232–234
reflective questions
  challenges of implementation, 193
  ecosystem, 92
  growth assessment, 175–176
  guiding principles, 59–60
  horizon, 115–116
  implementation, 230
  introduction, 19
  landscape model elements, 43–44
  opportunities for the future, 251–252
  pathway, 149
Regan, P., 29–31, 58, 68
Reggio Emilia education, 11
relationship building, 48–50, 248
  among peers, 78–79
  challenges, 179–181
RESCHOOL Colorado, 8, 136, 186, 190–193, 198
  REVOLVE, 126
research, 124
resilience, 162
respecting confidentiality, 180
responsive recruiting, 198
restorative practices, 180
results, 205
Richardson, W., 161–162
Right Question Institute, 88–90
rightful presence, 10
  defined, 13–15
risk-taking, 181
Robinson, Kate, 193, 248
Robinson, Ken, 2–3, 7, 23, 36, 193, 248
role organization, 206–209
Rotzel, G., 48–49, 157–158, 192
rubrics. *See* co-constructed rubrics

S

Salazar, A., 189
sample scorecard for school leaders, 200
scaffolding, 250
  self- and peer evaluation, 165–167
  student and course reorganization, 221
  student-led documentation, 167–172
school culture
  student protagonism, 221–225
School for Examining Essential Questions of Sustainability (Honolulu, Hawaii), 214
The School in Rose Valley (Rose Valley, Penn.), 48, 157, 174, 194, 251
School Reform Initiative, 125
School Voice Report 2016 (Quaglia Institute for School Voice and Aspirations), 228–229
Seçgin, T., 29
selected courses, 185–186
self-discovery, 211–213
self-evaluation, 165–167, 250
self-reflection. *See* reflection
Sengupta-Irving, T., 54
sex and gender, 29–31 (*see also* LGBTQ+ students)
sharing the well, 180
Silver, D., 57
Simmons, T., 202–203
Sinek, S., 55, 158
Singleton, G. E., 203, 211
Sizer, T., 237
skills, 244
SMART goals, 17, 100–102, 199, 263
Smart, G., 199

SOAR model analysis (Stavros et al.), 17, 112–114, 204–205
inquiry, 201
socioeconomic status, 28–29
   giveaways, 65–66
   SAT scores and, 29
   stereotypes, 48–50
Socrates, 7
Socratic seminars, 17, 86, 140, 159, 262
   understanding where students are in the ecosystem, 90–92
soft skills, 55, 162
solutions-oriented mindset, 5–6
spider-web discussions (Wiggins), 91
spray-and-pray method, 211
standardization, 4–5
   international schools, 187–188
   myth of, 35–37
   problems with, 7–8
Standardized Achievement Tests (SATs), 18
Stanford University, 18
   Hasso Plattner Institute, 80
   School of Engineering, 42
   shift toward design thinking and PBL, 178
Stavros, J., 112
Stead, T., 88
Steele, D. M., 34
stereotype threat, 30
stereotypes, 5
   Asian Americans, 5
   Black children, 5
   deficit, 48–49
Stommel, J., 160
storyboards and vision boards, 17, 99–100, 262
strategies
   affinity groups, 17, 78–79, 262
   affinity mapping, 17, 124–126, 263
   ANCHOR, 17, 103–104, 263
   brave space, 17, 76–78, 262
   capstone projects, 17, 114–115, 263
   collaborative protocol for defining outcomes, 17, 147–148, 263
   cross the line, 17, 74–76, 262
   defining the horizon for academic excellences, 111–115
   design thinking as a PBL structure, 17, 126–129, 263
   empathy interviews, 17, 80–82, 262
   goal setting to support defining the horizon, 100–107
   headline of my year, 17, 99, 262
   iceberg of culture, 17, 73–74, 262
   identifying aspirations to support defining the horizon, 97–100
   identity development, 70–79
   integrating students' contexts into the classroom, 80–85
   journaling, 17, 70–73, 262
   KWL and RAN charting, 17, 87–88, 262
   letter to myself, 17, 97–99, 262
   leveraging assets, 122–130
   passion projects, 17, 122–124, 263
   place-based learning— concentric circles, 17, 82–84, 262
   planning units, 136–142
   portrait of a graduate, 17, 111–112
   question formulation technique, 17, 88–90, 262
   shifting educational outcomes, 146–149
   SMART goals, 17, 101–102, 263
   SOAR model analysis, 17, 112–114
   Socratic seminars, 17, 90–92, 262
   storyboards and vision boards, 17, 99–100, 262
   student portfolios, 17, 129–130, 263
   student shadowing, 17, 135–136, 263
   student-centered iterative unit planning, 17, 137–141, 263
   student-led conferences, 17, 104–107, 263
   supporting student growth–132–136
   tapping into the community, 206–210
   understanding where students are in the ecosystem, 86–92
   virtual home visits, 17, 84–85, 262
   wise criticism, 17, 148–149, 263
   WOOP, 17, 100–101, 263
   workshop model for skill-based discipline, 17, 132–135, 263
   zone of proximal development, 17, 141–142, 263
strategy groups, 134
strengths, 204
strengths-based teaching and learning, 6, 212
student agency. *See* agency
student and course reorganization, 218–221
student choice
   defined, 37
student contexts
   concentric circles, 81–84
   empathy interviews, 80–81
   integrating into the classroom, 79
   virtual home visits, 84–85
student growth assessment, 155–156
   co-constructed rubrics, 172–175
   feedback-revision circles, 165–172
   formative evaluation, 165–172
   problems with traditional grading, 156–164
   reflective questions, 175–176
   student protagonism, 164–165
   takeaways, 176
student portfolios, 17, 122, 129–130, 263
student protagonism, 41–42
   building school culture, 221–225
   co-constructed rubrics, 172–175
   defined, 10–11
   in evaluation on the landscape, 164–165
   problem solving, 230
student shadowing, 17, 135–136, 263
student-centered educational practices, 15–16, 45, 50–51
student-centered iterative unit planning, 17, 137–139, 263

how do students learn best? 140–141
planning cycle, 138
what are students interested in/curious about? 140
what have students learned? 141
student-centered vs. student-driven education, 246–247
student-generated questions, 86–87
student-led conferences, 17, 104–107, 263
students
  context, 25–27
  culture, 27–28
  familial influence, 69
  grouping, 218–221
  honoring, 108
  jagged profiles, 32
  LGBTQ+, 3–31, 58, 68–70
  nonfamilial influence, 69
  sex and gender, 29–31
  socioeconomic status, 28–29
  vary in gifts and needs, 45–47
success, 1, 3
  defining, 205
  implementation for, 195–231
Sullivan, D. R.–E., 70
Summerhill School (Leiston, England), 192
Sungur, S., 29
supporting student growth, 130–132
  student shadowing, 135–136
  workshop model for skill–based disciplines, 132–135
survival skills, 56, 123
SWOT planning, 205
synthesis tools, 61, 151–152, 253–255
systems priorities, 227–228

T

Tabula rasa. See empty vessel myth
takeaways
  challenges of implementation, 193–194
  ecosystem, 92
  growth assessment, 176
  guiding principles, 60
  horizon, 116
  implementation, 231
  introduction, 20
  landscape model elements, 44

opportunities for the future, 252
pathway, 150
Tan, E., 12–14
tapping into the community, 206
  asset mapping and role organization, 206–209
  community-based learning, 209–210
task logs, 168
teacher vs. educator, 59
technology, 237–238
technology assisted education, 244–246
10 Ways Journaling Benefits Students, 71
Terada, Y., 50
terminology (*see also* word choice), 10–15
Theisen-Homer, V., 50
"third culture kids," 187–188
Thomas, H., 242
Thorsteinsson, E. B., 162–163
Three-year development plan, 196, 225–226
  laying the groundwork for change, 226–227
  shifting the horizon, 227
  sustaining the journey and assessing progress, 227–228
Tolisano, S. R., 169
Tomlinson, C. A., 39
toolkit for brave conversations, 225–226
Tough, P., 29
traditional grading
  competition and grades as currency, 158–160
  extrinsic motivation, 160–162
  grading orientation vs. learning orientation, 161
  impact of implicit biases, 162–164
  problems with, 156–157
traditional model. *See* factory model
traits of learning, 244
trust, 5–6
  culture of, 170
  establishing, 81, 221
  student-led documentation of growth, 167–172
20Time, 124

U

U. K. Education Reform Act, 35
Understanding by Design (UbD; McTighe & Wiggins), 137
Understanding where students are in the ecosystem, 85–86
  KWL and RAN charts, 87–88
  question formulation technique, 88–90
  Socratic seminars, 90–92
UNESCO, 2–3
United Nations
  Millennium Development Goals, 1
  Sustainable Development Goals, 1–2

V

values
  aspirational, 203–204
  inclusive, 26–27
  statements, 201–202
van Loon, M. H., 41
Verhoeven, M., 171
vigor vs. rigor, 54–55
virtual home visits, 17, 84–85, 262
vision
  appreciative inquiry, 204–205
  aspirational values, 203–204
  community norms, 202–203
  defined, 37
  mission, vision, and values statements, 201–202
  shared, 201
vision boards, 17, 99–100
Volman, M., 171
Vygotsky, L. S., 47

W

Wai'alae Public Charter School (Honolulu, Hawaii), 251
Waldorf education, 11
Wass, R., 142
well-rounded student myth, 31–33
Western imperialism, 242–244
what are out stakeholders asking for? 204–205
what can we build on? 204
what do we care deeply about? 205
What School Could Be, 112, 123, 124, 248

Innovation Playlist, 112
Whiteley, G., 159
Who Interview, 200
Wiggins, G., 91, 147
Williamson, R., 183
windows, 199
wise criticism, 17, 148–149, 263
WOOP, 17, 100–101, 263
word choice
   grading vs. evaluation, 158–159
   student centered vs. student driven, 246–247
   teacher vs. educator, 59
   vigor vs. rigor, 54–55
workshop model for skill-based disciplines, 17, 132–133, 263
   conferring, 133–134
   guided groups, 134–135
   strategy groups, 134
World Class Learners (Zhao), 239
World Indigenous Higher Education Consortium (WINHEC), 242–243
World Indigenous Peoples Conference (WINHEC), 242–243
World Leadership School, 103

Y
Y charts, 224–225

Z
Zhao, Y., 2, 32, 40, 48, 206, 239, 247–248
zone of proximal development, 17, 148, 164, 219, 263
   as a dynamic model, 141–142
   guided groups, 134–135
   honoring, 117
   planning units, 136
   serves all students, 45, 47–48

Global Education Guidebook
Jennifer D. Klein

Educators worldwide are striving to connect students to classrooms and experts, to humanize the world while preparing them to thrive in the 21st century. This practical guide shares steps and strategies to set up equitable global partnerships that benefit all learners.

BKF763

Equitable Instruction, Empowered Students
Carissa R. McCray

Learn practical strategies for ensuring each of your students feels valued, welcomed, and empowered. Author Carissa R. McCray provides the tools to combat biases inherent in education with pedagogy that encourages students to dismantle the injustices surrounding them.

BKG036

Finding Your Blind Spots
Hedreich Nichols

Author Hedreich Nichols infuses this book with a direct yet conversational style to help you identify biases that adversely affect your practice and learn how to move beyond those biases to ensure a more equitable, inclusive campus culture.

BKG022

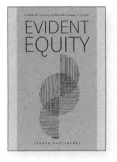

Evident Equity
Lauryn Mascareñaz

Make equity the norm in your school or district. *Evident Equity* provides a comprehensive method that leaders can use to integrate equitable practices into every facet of their school communities and offers real-life examples at the elementary, middle, and high school levels.

BKG032

Visit SolutionTree.com or call 800.733.6786 to order.

Wait! Your professional development journey doesn't have to end with the last pages of this book.

We realize improving student learning doesn't happen overnight. And your school or district shouldn't be left to puzzle out all the details of this process alone.

No matter where you are on the journey, we're committed to helping you get to the next stage.

Take advantage of everything from **custom workshops** to **keynote presentations** and **interactive web and video conferencing**. We can even help you develop an action plan tailored to fit your specific needs.

Let's get the conversation started.

Call 888.763.9045 today.

SolutionTree.com